Making Cent$ of Investment Planning

A GUIDE TO INVESTMENTS AND RETIREMENT

Also by James McSweeney

I $ee The Benefit
An HR Treasure Chest

Making Cent$ of Retirement Plans
An Employers Guide

Making Cent$ of Investing

A GUIDE TO INVESTMENTS AND RETIREMENT

By

James J. McSweeney

Comprehensive Benefit Services, Inc.

USA

Making Cent$ of
Investment Planning

Copyright © 2016

by James J. McSweeney

This book may be ordered through booksellers everywhere, or by
contacting:

Comprehensive Benefit Services, Inc.

www.askcip.com   admin@askcip.com

ISBN – 13: 978-0-9848683-4-6 (pbk)

ISBN – 13: 978-0-9848683-5-3 (ebk)

Printed in the United States of America

I would like to dedicate this book to my children—Shannon, Bobby and Olivia. You make me proud.

Author's Note:

Care has been taken to present this complicated information in a manner that is easy to understand.

Some of the material is repeated. Some of it is presented in different ways.

This book makes use of charts and graphs. Pictures help us understand things. Wherever possible, graphics were placed beside the most concise explanation possible. This creates some white space in this book. White space is good. It helps keep things simple.

There are a number of hyperlinks highlighted in this text. If you are reading a paper copy, you can enter this hyperlink information into your Internet browser and it will take you to Web pages that will help you learn more.

If you are reading this as an ebook, these links should be live. You may activate them from your reading device.

When you understand the concepts in this book, you should be able to make a good approximation of the assets you will need for retirement. You should also be able to build a strategy to get you there.

Good luck. You can do it.

CONTENTS

CHAPTERS

CHAPTERS

CHAPTERS

PAGE

FOREWORD

It is no secret that everyone needs to save for retirement. Without adequate savings, retirees must rely upon the government, their families and charities for support.

Americans are not saving enough. We invest poorly.

Most retirees depend upon Social Security for over half of their retirement income. Over one third of "retirement" income comes from working wages.

The government is deeply in debt. Social Security is highly flawed. The traditional nuclear family is vanishing like smoke. Supportive charities are struggling for donations.

The retirees of tomorrow must be able to support themselves. Everyone knows this. Wealth accumulation is high on everybody's "to do" list. So, why can't people save and invest effectively? There are many hidden reasons. Most of them can be fixed.

Perhaps you are someone who can't save enough, despite your intentions. Perhaps you save, but don't know how to invest properly.

This book introduces effective strategies that can help anyone increase their retirement saving and wealth accumulation.

This book will show you what to do. If you follow this book's advice, you can change your life forever.

repetitio est mater studiorum
Repetition is the mother of studies.

One reason that so many people don't save and invest effectively is that we don't *hear* the information. We are preoccupied with the moment. Investment information bounces off our brains like rain on a car windshield.

Therefore, this book repeats the same information in different ways. Each time, a little bit more will seep into your neurons and take root. In time, your understanding...and your investment behavior will change, if you let it. Make sense?

SEEING IS BELIEVING

More than a hundred pages of this book contain charts, tables and graphs. Some of these graphics took days to complete and years to evolve. But they are simple. These images are derived from many places—from basic investment theory to sophisticated, controlled human studies. They are important. Refer to them often.

Numbers were crunched from many sources. They are illustrated to impart important information *and* arouse your emotions. If you become angry, scared or confused as you read this, you are learning. If you develop a feeling of hopelessness...if you grow depressed over your finances...do *not* stop reading. This book has answers. You can do it.

repetitio est mater studiorum

REPETITION

Important information is repeated in this book. Sometimes the repetition is separated by a page or two. Other information is repeated after new portions of the book have been presented. This is necessary. Many important concepts can't be learned without sufficient head knocking. Get a helmet.

Building a proper financial knowledge base is like painting a wooden wall. It takes work and patience. The wood must be sanded. You might apply a coating of Bins to protect against sap seeping through the paint. You layer on filler to smooth out cracks, chips and dents in the wood. You sand again. You brush on primer. Maybe sand again. Finally, you add a coat of paint. Then another to finish the job. Building wealth is a similar, pragmatic process. It takes care and time.

PRACTICE

Think of elite professional athletes. Athletes at the top of their sport train hard each day—arriving at the stadium, track or gym long before others, and staying hours after their teammates have gone home. They practice, and then practice more.

Investing for long-term financial security requires understanding. It demands practice and perseverance. Good habits must be formed, and then reinforced—over and over again. Like a mantra. *I can do this.* Say it to yourself. *I can do this.* Then make it real.

TAKE POSITIVE ACTION

You need to take proactive steps to save and invest for your future. Employers might help. But it is up to you to take advantage of your opportunities.

This book provides education that can change your investment behavior, if you need it. Most people do.

LIFE IS COMPLICATED

People are complicated. We are ruled by habits and emotions that we don't understand and rarely control.

Research studies show that proper investment education can affect behavior in a positive way—especially when it comes to saving for retirement. Dramatic improvement is possible.

YOUR HIGHLY TRAINED CONSULTANT

Many of us don't have a financial advisor. Even some who have an advisor fall short of accomplishing their financial goals.

This book will teach you how to make informed retirement decisions, and stick to your plan.

INVESTMENT EDUCATION

Do we really need another book on investment education? Investment education is everywhere. We view it on television. We get it in the mail. We see it on store bookshelves and checkout aisles. We get advice from employers, financial advisors, friends and family members. Everybody has an opinion. The problem is: It doesn't work—at least for most of us. No one has tied all of the information together, and then presented the material in a simple way that can be easily understood and followed.

People ignore professional advice. We don't save enough. We invest poorly. This sets us up for a painful realization when it is far too late. For most of us, financial tragedy *can* be avoided.

THIS BOOK'S APPROACH

It is not enough to teach the facts. Effective education must also *motivate*. This is easy to say. It is challenging to implement. Remember the rain on the windshield? We must penetrate barriers that nature puts in the way of knowledge and action.

Changes in behavior must come from *within*. Internal change comes from new knowledge, combined with personal determination.

THE HUMAN CONDITION

Why don't people plan for retirement? Why does investment advice refuse to take root?

When the onion gets peeled to its core, the answer is simple - Human Nature. Our bodies are hard-wired to make decisions emotionally, not logically. We back emotional decisions with logic, but the decisions themselves are driven by feelings.

We do things that make us feel good. We avoid things that make us uncomfortable. We make "gut" reactions that run counter to our intellectual logic. Neuroscience now demonstrates that our gut actually *does* influence decisions. So do other things that we cannot see.

PHYSIOLOGY

Emotions are where investing begins. Our central nervous system sends signals to the rest of our bodies. Hormones and neurotransmitters are released. Feedback is received and adjustments are made—all without thinking. Every second of every day, we send and receive millions of messages that raise and lower blood pressure, adjust the heart rate, pupil dilation and the constriction of blood vessels. We feel relaxed...we feel stressed...we feel anger and pain...often without conscious thought.

It is hard to invest when it causes stress. Therefore, retirement education must adapt to human physiology before it can help us achieve our long-term financial goals. Retirement education must *increase* the stress of the status quo, and *reduce* the stress of change and making current sacrifice.

STRESS

When the stress of *not* saving becomes greater than the stress of saving and *taking risk*...When the stress caused by *not* saving overpowers today's desire for a latte or extra fast food, positive action will *reduce* stress.

Physical changes in investment behavior happen only with the *right* type of education.

INFORMED EDUCATION

This book transforms complex financial matters into simple concepts—one's that make sense. Once internalized, these concepts can change your physiological response to investing, and how you plan your financial future.

This may seem like a strange way to approach retirement planning, but it produces positive results.

Once physiology aligns with intellect, great things happen. We form an internal investment partnership that builds financial security and wealth.

Think of Ebenezer Scrooge in *The Christmas Carol*. As the story begins, Scrooge pinches pennies, to the point of his own discomfort. He takes financial security to the extreme. With the help of three ghosts, Scrooge is able to view what could have been, what is and what will be in his life—if he continues his present behaviors.

With new information, delivered to Scrooge in a way that he understands and feels, on a *visceral* level, Scrooge changes. Happily. He adjusts his life, because he understands that *today's actions have future consequences*. Scrooge changes his behavior and it brings him joy. He has *visualized* what *his* life will become—if he doesn't change. And what it can become if he does.

Imagine if you could take a trip thirty years into the future and see your two outcomes. One outcome shows you in a vacation home, playing golf or sitting on the lanai in a sunny warm climate. The other shows your present destination, huddled against the cold, living in subsidized housing or your child's basement. Which scene sounds better to you?

Could self-visualization convince you to forgo wasteful spending for a little more saving today? It can. When you learn why you must accumulate...When you viscerally internalize the concepts of inflation and purchasing power...When you comprehend the power of compound growth and Modern Portfolio Theory...you will feel compelled to act. And it will bring you comfort.

NUMBERS

This book presents numerical facts. Numbers make sense. Numbers matter. Numbers don't lie, although they do shade the truth if presented improperly or incompletely.

This book presents critical numbers without bias. It explains the ones that matter when it comes to saving and investing for retirement. It makes them personal.

An understanding of the numerical facts of your life will alter your perception of reality, in a way that may change your investment behavior forever.

FACTS

Understanding real facts can reduce fear. Facts can create new motivations, ones focused less on today's wasteful habits, and more on behaviors that create financial security for tomorrow.

ACTION

Nothing happens without positive action. Saving can't happen without the conscious decision to save. Meaningful investing can't happen without the decision to undertake risk. Once present and future needs have been quantified...Once the methodology and the risks are fully understood...you can develop a saving and investment plan that meets *your* financial goals, without causing too much stress.

GOALS

Science shows that we are more productive when we have specific, tangible goals. When long-term goals are set, and then broken into achievable, stair-step actions, even big goals become manageable. Short-term sacrifice becomes acceptable when it is part of a greater plan.

This book will help you set financial goals, and then direct your behavior to achieve them.

THE NUMBER

The NUMBER is a long-term, personal financial goal that can be broken down into manageable steps. Your number is a specific, tangible target for your savings and investments. This is the amount of money you will need in retirement to live the lifestyle you want.

FINANCIAL GPS

The NUMBER becomes the destination, your financial GPS. The number represents financial independence, as *you* define it.

If you deviate from your initial route, if inflation, income, expenses, or investment returns don't meet your initial calculations, your system must recalibrate. It determines a new route. This may represent more or less saving. It might cause a change in investment strategy. It could mean working another year or two, even getting a second job or working overtime. This will be *your* choice. You are in control of your own financial future.

The steps to achieving your number can start today. Achieving it will be an ongoing process that requires focused attention. It all starts with a plan—your retirement plan. Begin it now.

A PLAN FOR THE UNPREDICTABLE

Nobody can predict the stock market, global economic events or tax rates. No one can guarantee the future of Social Security and Medicare. It is impossible to accurately predict future income, health, job security, or the amount that might be needed for education or unexpected expenses. But everyone can plan. Planning is critical. This book makes it simple and understandable.

SUMMARY

Most people don't engage in the behavior needed to achieve financial independence. We lack the education, the motivation, and the strategies to overcome human nature—which stops us every chance it gets.

THIS BOOK'S STRATEGY

This book presents investment education with images and words. Important information is repeated, usually in different ways.

Once you understand your true financial picture...Once you understand the emotions that prevent you from taking those steps...

Once you develop the proper behaviors...you can take meaningful actions to accomplish your financial goals.

This book will teach you how to achieve financial independence, and motivate you to achieve it.

Let's begin.

S&C

Chapter One

_____R_____

Poor Financial Education

In 2014, The American College Of Financial Services commissioned a survey of 1,019 Americans with at least $100,000 in household assets. Participants were asked a series of basic financial planning questions in the form of a quiz. Only 19% received a passing grade. The average percentage of correct scores was 42%. No one scored an A.

Portions of this study have been published in USA Today: http://ow.ly/Jp6CN, AARP: http://ow.ly/Jp6Fw, and the Washington Post: http://ow.ly/Jp6Jf. Each of these news organizations presented stories with titles such as "America Fails Retirement Income Quiz."

Here are a few things that the study revealed:

- Only 31% of people know that 4% is the most they can afford to "safely" withdraw from their assets in retirement.

- Only 35% know that maintaining a portfolio of 50-60% in equities is more likely to maintain a sustainable income in retirement than a portfolio with 90-100% stocks or 20-30% stocks.

- Most people underestimate male life expectancy.

- Only 37% of people know that they can receive higher Social Security Benefits if they wait two years longer to retire.

- Only 39% understand that when interest rates rise, the value of existing bonds goes down.

- Less than 10% of people understand that small company stocks have produced a higher long-term return than big company stocks.

What does this study show?

- Americans need better financial education. Education bounces off our brains—naturally. We are programmed to avoid the investment noise. When we hear it, we find ways to forget it.

- Employers don't know how to overcome normal, human nature in their 401(k) plans. This leads to lower participation.

Financially, most people are lost. It's no wonder that most Americans must rely on Social Security for more than half of their retirement income. Let's get to work.

Chapter Two

_____R_____

Social Security & Retirement

- According to the Social Security Administration, more than 52% of retirees have income below $30,000 per year.

    o This includes Social Security *and* Continued Employment.

- Social Security Alone Is Keeping Nearly Half Of Retirees Out Of Poverty.

Source: Fast Facts & Figures About Social Security, 2014

Who Wants To Rely On Social Security For Their Retirement Income?

Why Does This Happen? Let's Figure It Out And Fix The Problem.

ABOUT SOCIAL SECURITY

When planning for retirement, it is important to understand the impact of Social Security. Social Security was created to *supplement* the income of retirees, not become its only source.

Social Security's founding concept was that workers would pay into a trust fund during their careers. Employers would match contributions into the fund for employees. This money would be held and distributed by a new organization called the Social Security Administration. At retirement, each worker would be paid a monthly income, based upon their age and the amount they had contributed to the program.

The deposits made by each *working* individual (and their employers) provide the benefits to retirees and beneficiaries. This is important to understand. Social Security *does not* work like a 401(k), defined contribution pension plan or a profit sharing plan.

There is no sum of money that is invested and held for each individual like a retirement plan. Money goes in one day. It is spent by the government by the next day. The Social Security trust fund holds a $2.8 trillion IOU issued by the U.S. government. Social Security makes the promise to pay retirement income in the future. But it has no actual cash to back up its promises.

The rules of Social Security can be modified by Congress at any time. They have been changed substantially over the years, and will be changed again in the future. There was no Social Security cost-of-living increase in 2015, despite very mild inflation.

When Social Security was created, the average life expectancy of retirees was age 66. Standard Social Security benefits began at age 65. The expected benefit period was *one year*.

From its start, Social Security was intended to provide just a small part of retirement income. It was designed as a hedge against people living too long. As Social Security evolved, it became the principal source of retirement income for most Americans. Social

Security *alone* is keeping one in four retirees out of poverty.

As the U.S. population ages, experts predict that Social Security will change dramatically by the time many of us retire.

As you plan for retirement, you must ask yourself this question: Can you rely on Social Security benefits for your retirement income? Or, will Social Security become another broken government promise?

Note: Social Security does not provide benefits for employees of many government organizations. Most government employees are covered by pensions instead. This is not a focus of this book. Check with your employer to and see if your earnings are credited for Social Security benefits, or if you earn pension credits instead. Then adjust accordingly.

Source: Social Security Administration

SOCIAL SECURITY FACTS

The Social Security Administration (SSA) conducts several in-depth financial studies each year. One study analyzes the state of current and future retirees. Some of the facts are startling. According to the Social Security Administration:

- 63.2 million people received benefits from programs administered by the Social Security Administration (SSA) in 2013. This is approximately *one fifth* of the nation's population.

- 5.5 million people were newly awarded Social Security benefits in 2013.

- 65% of aged beneficiaries received at least *half* of their income from Social Security in 2012.

- 55% of adult Social Security beneficiaries in 2013 were women.

Source: SSA Publication No. 13-11785 Released: September 2014

Many such facts are printed in Social Security publications every year. Some of the figures are updated annually. Others are compiled less often, such as when a new national census is prepared. The numbers are disturbing. Americans are *not* preparing properly for retirement. The goal of this book is to help change that.

Social Security Credits

Because Social Security can be a large part of retirement income, every eligible person should understand how the benefits are earned.

In order to receive full Social Security benefits, employees must obtain sufficient "credits." An individual earns a credit for every three months that they work and pay taxes into the Social Security system. A full-time employee earns four credits per year. Forty credits are currently required to receive full benefits. This equates to ten years of paying into the Social Security system.

Note: Prior to 1978, working in any part of a year earned four full credits.

One's monthly retirement benefit is determined by the amount paid into the system. At present, employees pay taxes of 6.2% upon annual earnings up to $118,500. Employers are taxed the same. Benefits are paid on a sliding scale. The higher your income average (for the minimum crediting period) the greater your benefit.

Self-employed individuals are taxed at a rate of 12.4%, on profits up to $118,500.

Each employee pays a maximum of $7,347. Self-employed individuals pay double that amount.

The more an individual pays into the Social Security system, the more benefit they will receive at retirement.

TIME IS MONEY

The longer you wait to receive Social Security, the greater your benefit. If you begin taking Social Security at age 70, you will receive substantially more than if you begin receiving benefits at age 65.

Retirement benefits are determined by two factors:

● Payment is based upon the income earned during the highest credit years. If income is below the maximum, the SSA credit lower earnings to the benefit account.

● Payment is based upon the age when income is first taken. If a worker delays retirement beyond "normal" retirement age, payments are increased.

Of 100 People Who Began At 25
And Are Turning 65 Today…

- **15 Are Dead**
- **29.7% have incomes under $20,000**
- **39.7% have incomes between $20,000 and $60,000**
- **30.6% have incomes over $60,000**

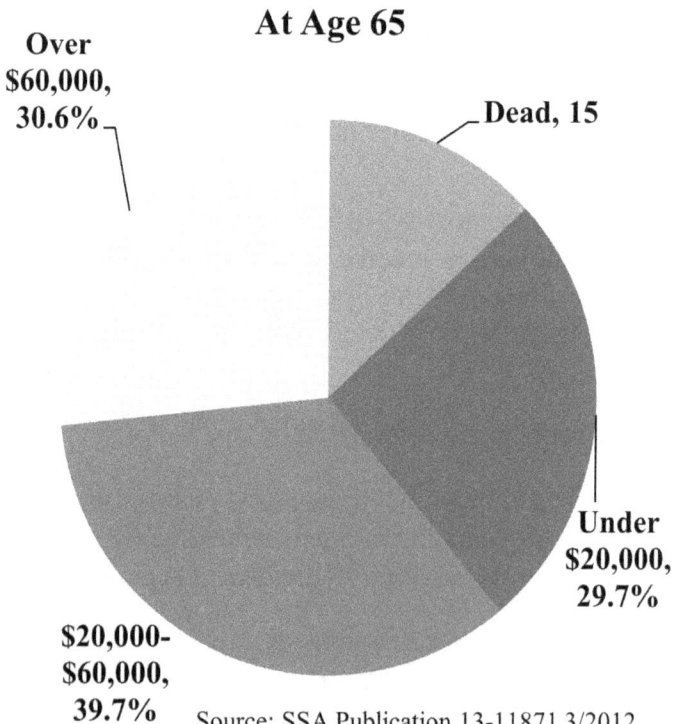

At Age 65

Over
$60,000,
30.6%

Dead, 15

Under
$20,000,
29.7%

$20,000-
$60,000,
39.7%

Source: SSA Publication 13-11871 3/2012

The preceding chart illustrates important figures that everyone should understand. Of people born 65 years ago, 15 did not live long enough to retire at 65. Of people born today, the Social Security Administration estimates that 13 will not live to age 65.

Retirement income:

- 29.7% of retirees have incomes below $20,000.

- 39.7% have incomes between $20,000 and $60,000.

- 30.6% have incomes above $60,000.

These figures *include work earnings* after age 65. Work earnings represent a significant portion of "retirement" income.

The following charts further explain the amount and distribution of income for retirees.

Sources Of Income At Retirement In 1999

Source: Social Security Administration: 2000

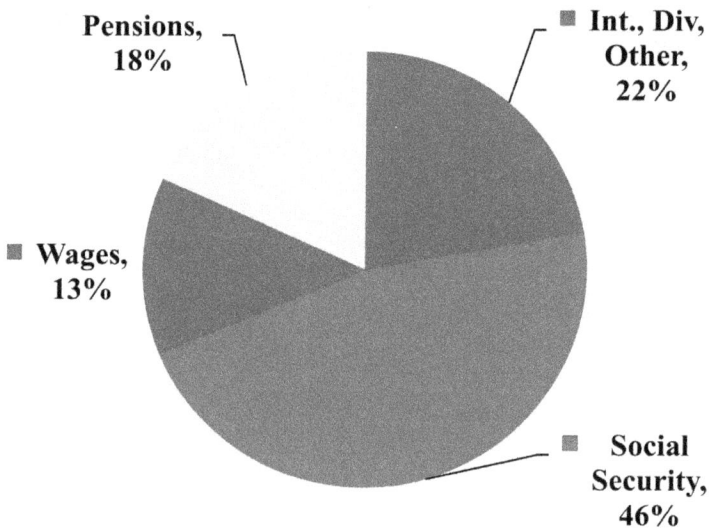

Pensions, 18%

Int., Div, Other, 22%

Wages, 13%

Social Security, 46%

The sources of income in retirement change over time. In 1999, Social Security provided 46% of retirement income for those age 65. Continued employment provided 13% of income.

Sources of Income In Retirement In 2014

Source: Social Security Administration Fast Facts & Figures 2014

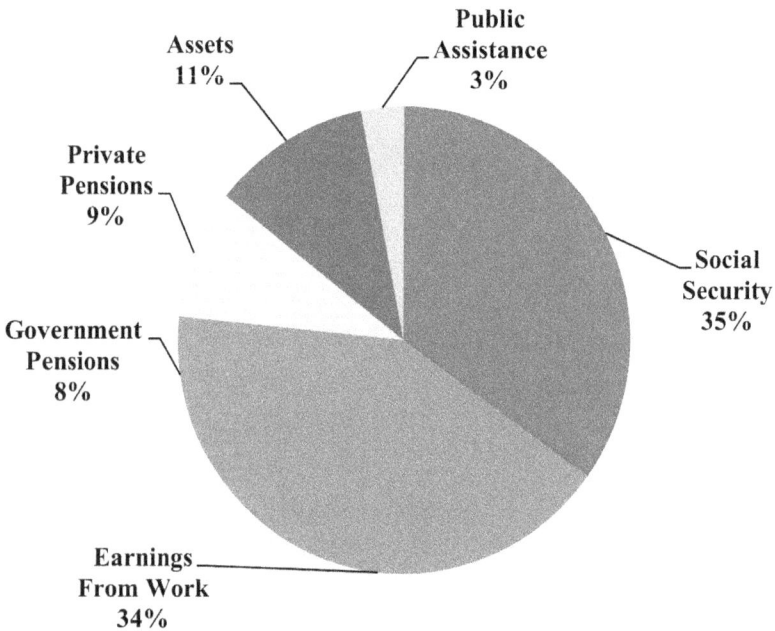

Public Assistance 3%

Assets 11%

Private Pensions 9%

Social Security 35%

Government Pensions 8%

Earnings From Work 34%

Note: Over 69% of "Retirement Income" comes from wages and Social Security

By 2014, the percentage of income provided by Social Security had fallen to 35%. This is a significant drop from 46% in 1999. The percentage of income from *current earnings,* at age 65, grew from 13% to 34%.

Some "retirees" are working longer because they *want* to. Many are working because they *have* to.

Over 69% of income beyond the age of 65 comes from just two sources: Social Security and Work (current earnings).

You must ask yourself these three questions:

- Do I want to work in retirement?
- Will I be able to work, or be able to find a job, after age 65?
- Will I be prepared financially for retirement?

If you don't have a plan, one will be provided for you. It won't be a plan you will like.

Everyone must create their own retirement strategy.

Regrettably, there is a design flaw in Social Security. Social Security was not designed to accumulate funds to provide income for retirement. Yes, there is a theoretical. $2.8 trillion "trust fund" for retirees. It consists solely of a government IOU.

In 2014, Social Security revenues were $884 billion. Expenditures were $859 billion. Over 97% of current Social Security revenues are being spent on *current* beneficiaries each year. They are *not* being accumulated for those who currently pay into the system. Soon, the government will be withdrawing from its IOU. By 2030, even this IOU will be depleted. Source: 2014 OASDI Trustees Report

If you are working, 97% of your Social Security taxes provide income for someone who is receiving benefits today. Any surplus Social Security revenues are used by the government to fund U.S. budget deficits. The money goes in one day and out the next. Hence, the IOU.

THE NUMBERS WON'T WORK

When Social Security first began, there were over 44 workers for each person receiving benefits. By 1970, there were less than four people working for each person receiving Social Security income. Presently, there are 2.3 workers for each person receiving benefits.

According to the Social Security Administration, by 2030, there will be just 1.7 people working for each person receiving Social Security income. The math is not favorable. Many experts, including the U.S. government, warn that there may be even fewer workers, as robots replace the workers of tomorrow.

Social Security...
Fewer Workers To Support Retirees

Workers Per Beneficiary

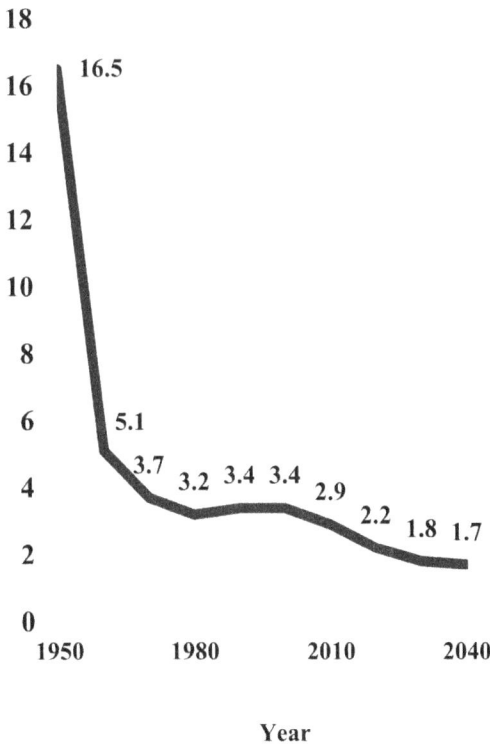

When Social Security began, many people working supported each Social Security recipient.

Currently, there are 2.8 people working for each person receiving Social Security Benefits.

In 2045, there will be 1.7 persons working for each person receiving Social Security benefits.

18

16 — 16.5

14

12

10

8

6 — 5.1

4 — 3.7   3.2 3.4 3.4   2.9

2 — 2.2 1.8 1.7

0

1950   1980   2010   2040

Year

Source: Social Security Administration

Income Spread In Retirement

**The median income of units age 65 or older is $28,056.
But there is a wide distribution of retirement incomes.**

Income Of Retirees

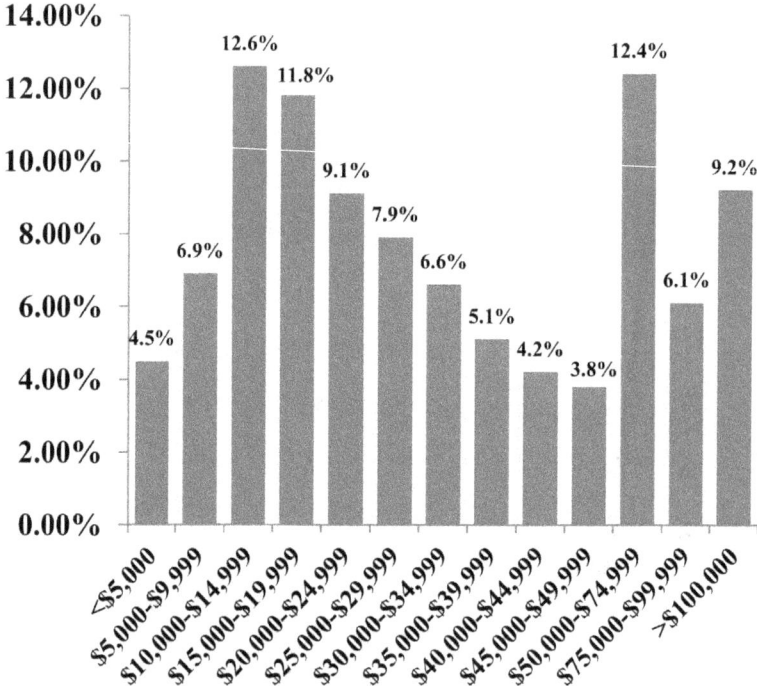

Source: Social Security Income of the Aged
Chartbook, 2012

This chart illustrates the distribution of income for those in retirement today. Where do you think your retirement income will be along this scale? If you don't know, this book will teach you how to figure it out.

You must determine of where you stand on this graph with your current plan. Then, decide what changes you want to create for *your* financial future.

Fact: More than 50% of Americans are retiring with incomes below $3,000 per month. Is that your current plan? If so, make a new one.

SOCIAL SECURITY BEWARE

A story in US News & World Report (August 18, 2014) predicted that as many as 47% of current jobs are at risk in the next twenty years.

http://www.usnews.com/news/blogs/data-mine/2014/08/18/robots-may-disrupt-half-of-all-us-jobs

Many workers are being replaced by machines. Do you want to rely on machines to pay for your retirement income?

In the future, employers who replace workers with machines may be forced to pay Social Security taxes for the ones they "employ." This may be the only way to preserve Social Security as it is promised.

If you have years until retirement, do not bank on Social Security for a major portion of your retirement income. The trends and the facts are not in your favor. Save for yourself.

$&C

Chapter Three

_____R_____

The Government Can't Help You

The US National Debt

According to the United States Treasury, the total United States debt on January 26, 2016 was as follows:

- $13,618,136,618,476.23   Debt Held by the Public
- $5,343,501,354,590.19   Intragovernmental Holdings
- $18,961,637,973,066.42   Total Public Debt Outstanding

Here is the U.S. website: http://www.treasurydirect.gov/NP/debt/current

Every year, the United States spends more money than it receives in taxes. It has been doing so for decades. According to the U.S. Treasury and the Federal Reserve, as of this writing, the U.S. national debt was nearly $19 trillion. This represents a debt of more than $158,000 per taxpayer.

The United States has made promises to most citizens, with Medicare & Medicaid, Social Security and Veterans' benefits.

When the "present value" of all U.S. promises, our "unfunded liabilities," is added to the U.S. national debt, the total debt balloons to more than $100 trillion. This represents a national debt of more than $800,000 per taxpayer.

Imagine adding an additional $800,000 in loans to your current financial picture. With a payment of 5% per year, this would add $40,000 to your yearly budget. This is our true national debt. And it keeps on growing...

The younger you are, the more important these liabilities will become. The U.S. government is growing deeper in debt. Meeting *your* retirement needs with Social Security will be weighed against all of the other promises made to U.S. residents.

It doesn't take a math genius to know that 1.7 people can't properly support each person receiving retirement benefits. At some point, the government will need to step in to make up the difference. With so many other budget requirements (and people) clamoring for money, maintaining the promises of Social Security seems unlikely.

Many experts predict that the lack of government funds will ultimately result in higher Social Security taxes. It may also lead to reduced and means-based benefits. For Example: In years past, Social Security payments to beneficiaries have increased to match inflation. In 2016, there was no Social Security increase, despite a slight increase in inflation.

If at all possible, don't rely on Social Security as you know it. Social Security will change in the upcoming years. Not for the better.

Note: U.S. debt figures, and more, are continually updated on a non-profit website at the following Web address:
www.usdebtclock.org.

National Debt Versus GDP In 2012

National Debt By Country

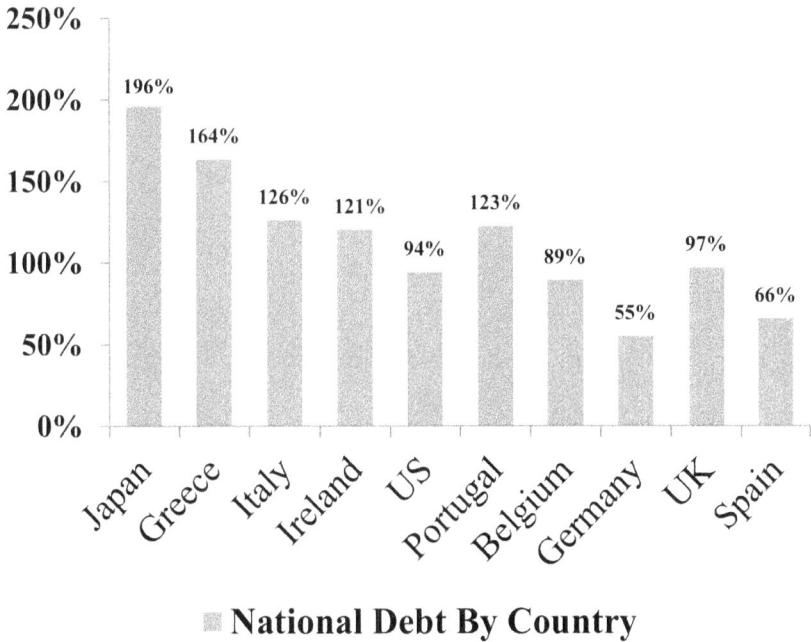

National Debt By Country

Source: World Bank
www.data.worldbank.org

The preceding chart compares the U.S. debt to that of other developed nations. U.S. liabilities are becoming similar to countries with distressed economies. Japan has been in virtual economic stagnation for thirty years. Spain, Portugal, Greece and Ireland have had some form of economic bailout during the past five years. There is no country, or group of nations, that can provide financial assistance to the United States if we fail.

The following illustration adds our unfunded liabilities to the U.S. debt. When U.S. debt is adjusted to include its unfunded promises, the ratio of debt to GDP skyrockets to more than 531%.

National Debt Including Unfunded Liabilities

National Debt By Country – US Adjusted To Include Unfunded Liabilities

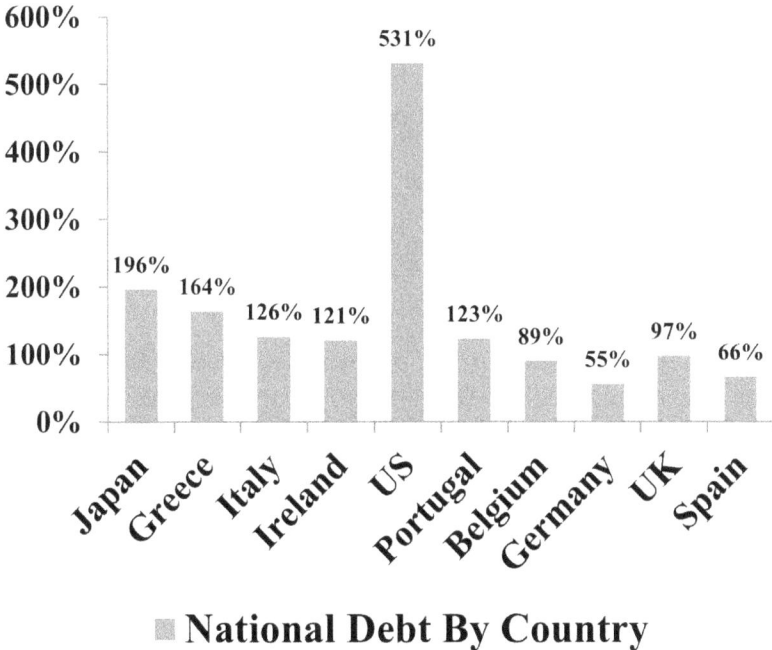

600%
500%
400%
300%
200%
100%
0%

531% US
196% Japan
164% Greece
126% Italy
121% Ireland
123% Portugal
89% Belgium
55% Germany
97% UK
66% Spain

Japan Greece Italy Ireland US Portugal Belgium Germany UK Spain

■ **National Debt By Country**

Source: World Bank, US Bureau of Economic Analysis, US Treasury

HOW BIG A PROBLEM?

Don't panic. The United States is not a third world country. However, after many years of making unfunded financial promises, something will need to give way. It already is.

The U.S. has extended the normal retirement age from 65 to 67, for those born after 1959. Inflation calculations are adjusted to reduce increases in Social Security benefits.

Veterans' hospitals are so underfunded that they make national headlines.

Government expenditures for health care have risen to 28% of total U.S. spending. That can't continue.

There has been a 22% increase in health care expenditures, over the past two years alone.

Source:https://www.whitehouse.gov/blog/2015/04/15/get-your-2014-federal-taxpayer-receipt

The U.S. has cut Medicare fee payments to doctors and hospitals. Hospitals are compelled (by law) to treat everyone, even those without insurance. Hospitals and doctors lose money with each Medicaid patient they treat. This is particularly challenging for hospitals and physicians in poor and urban areas. Medicaid payments are increasing rapidly, as more U.S. citizens, and new non-citizens are added to the Obamacare medical rolls.

According to USA Today (November, 2014 and the Sheps Center For Health Services Research), since 2010, more than 43 rural hospitals have had to close their doors. This trend appears to be growing worse, as costs increase and revenues fall. At some point, the government will need to support such hospitals. Otherwise, there will be no one left to care for the sick and injured in these critical demographic areas.

These medical problems are a just precursor of our country's future. Much of the nation's social infrastructure is dependent upon government spending. Our government is running short on money. Something will need to give.

If your plan is to rely on Social Security for your retirement, the math is not in your favor.

SMART THINKING

Smart thinking should lead you to rely on yourself, not Social Security. You should also plan for higher taxes in the future. Someone will need to pay for the government's past and future promises.

YOUR OWN PLAN

The good news is that you live in America. America is *still* the *land of opportunity*. You must seize control of your opportunity today. You can do this.

Total Debt During The Last Three Presidencies

- 1992 GDP – $6.54 Trillion

- Debt $4.17 Trillion – 1993 Clinton Takes Office

- 2000 GDP – $10.28 Trillion

- Debt $5.73 Trillion – 2001 Bush Takes Office

- 2008 GDP - $14.42

- Debt $10.61 Trillion – 2009 Obama Takes Office

- 2014 GDP – $17.42 Trillion

- Debt $18.14 Trillion – End of 2014

  Source: US Bureau of Economic Analysis

The preceding figures illustrate how our national debt has increased over the three most recent presidencies. As you can see, the political party of the president makes little difference with deficit growth.

Presidencies appear to be equal-opportunity spenders, with a big assist from Congress. Here are the figures in graphic form.

Trend of U.S. National Debt

Trillions

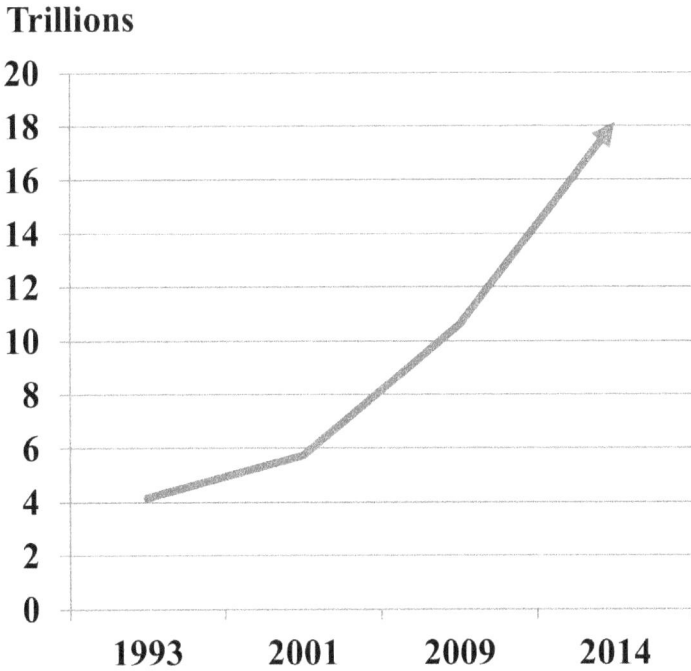

Growth of US Debt & GDP

Trillions

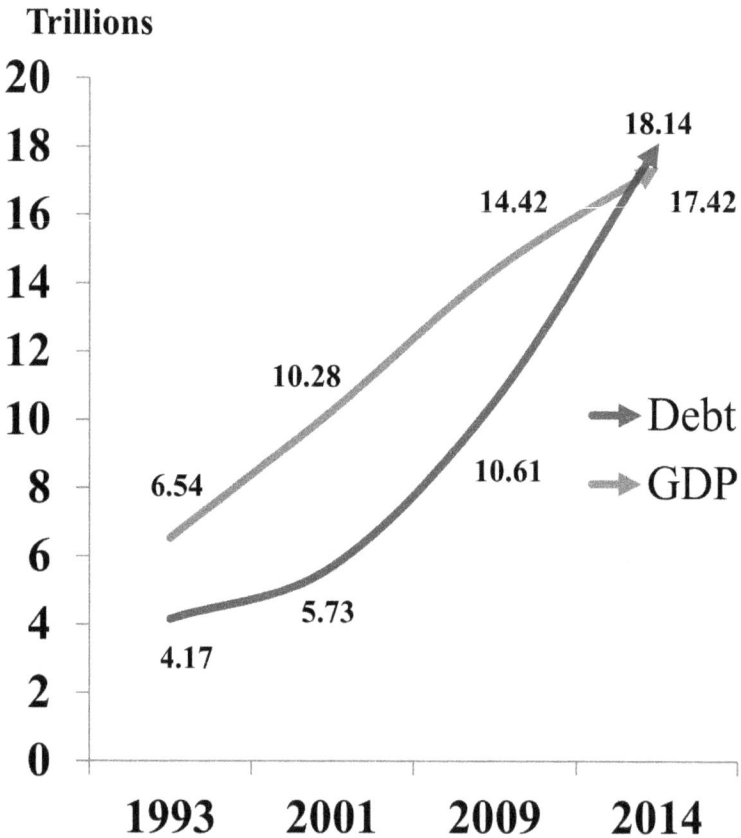

18.14
14.42
17.42
10.28
6.54
10.61
5.73
4.17

→ Debt
→ GDP

1993   2001   2009   2014

US Bureau of Economic Analysis

This graph shows our stated national debt (not including unfunded liabilities) as it relates to the economy, as measured by gross domestic product (GDP). GDP is the total value of all goods and services produced by U.S. business in a single year.

The numbers are trending in the wrong direction. The U.S. now owes more than everything it produces in any given year.

The following chart shows the trend of our national debt as a percentage of GDP. The math isn't trending well. Don't rely on the government. Plan for yourself if you can.

National Debt As % Of GDP

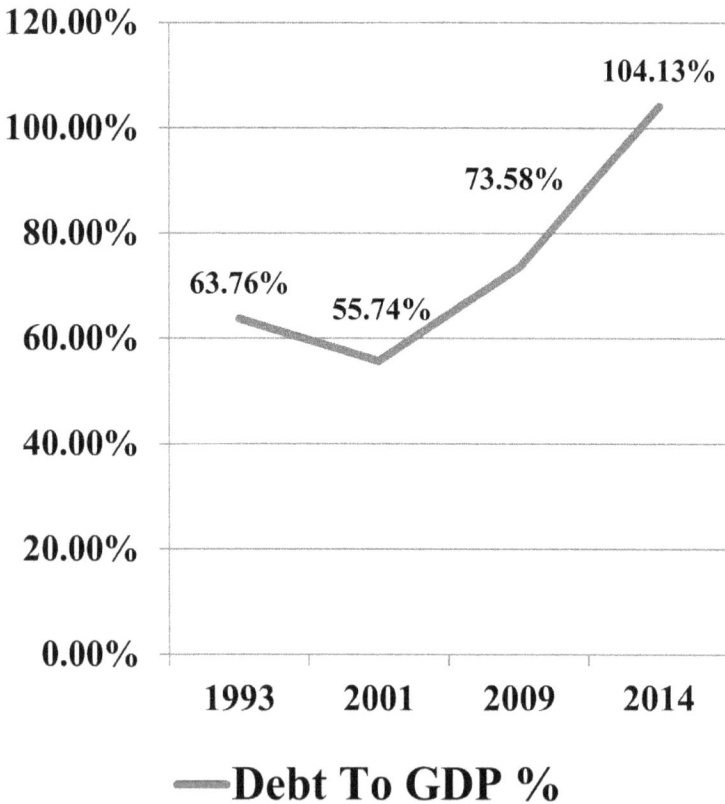

Debt To GDP %

GET THE PICTURE???   FEEL STRESSED???

No matter what your age, start saving now! Social Security Resources are dwindling. You will (probably) need more money in retirement than you think. The best plan is a self plan.

The following pages will help you decide how much you should save, and how to invest your money wisely.

$&¢

Chapter Four

R

Basic Facts Of Retirement

LIFE EXPECTANCY

When planning for retirement, you must understand life expectancy. Life expectancy determines how long you will need your money to last. In 2000, if a husband and wife retired together at age 65, on average, one of them would live to age 90. By 2014, life expectancy for the last survivor of a married couple (retiring together) had increased to 92. This trend is expanding. Some experts postulate that life expectancy will increase significantly with scientific and medical advancements.
Source:http://www.news.com.au/technology/science/researchers-believe-a-biological-revolution-enabling-humans-to-experience-everlasting-youthfulness-is-coming/story-fnpjxnqt-1227304902553

Life expectancy after retirement can be quite long. Scientists, at Google's medical research division (Google X) predict that today's young can live well beyond age 100, perhaps to 500 or more. This should be a good thing. It won't be if you run out of money.
Source:http://www.dailymail.co.uk/sciencetech/article-2986493/Google-says-s-possible-humans-live-500-YEARS-investing-firms-hoping-extend-lives-five-fold.html

This 2000 illustration shows life expectancy at various retirement ages. It shows life expectancy for men, women and a married couple. Women live longer than men. The life expectancy of the survivor is significantly longer than either alone.

The further you have until retirement, the longer you should plan to live. If you have 10 years or more until retirement, you should plan to live well into your 90s, like it or not!

Note: If you don't have enough money at the beginning of retirement, there is a good chance that you will run out while you still need it.

You should plan for a nice, long retirement. Start planning today.

How Long Will Retirement Last?

The following figures represent average life expectancies after retirement in 2000

Joint Age 55: 33 years

Joint Age 60: 30 years

Joint Age 65: 25 years

Joint Age 70: 21 years

Source: Life Expectancy
Table, Department of
Health & Human
Services (1990), IRS
Annuity Table VI

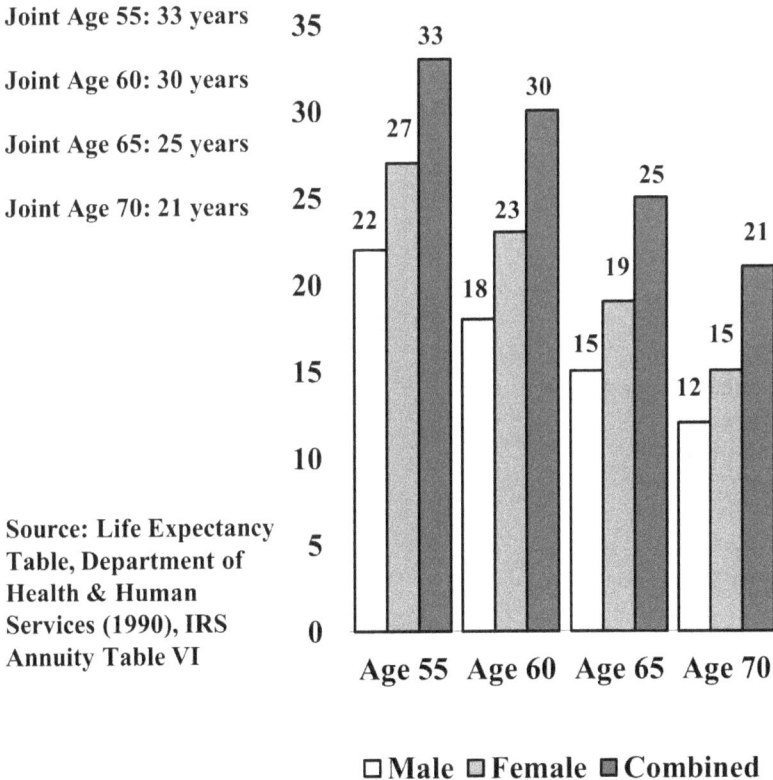

☐ Male ☐ Female ■ Combined

How Long Will Retirement Last?

2015: The following figures represent current average life expectancies after retirement. Notice how people are living longer. You must plan for a long retirement.

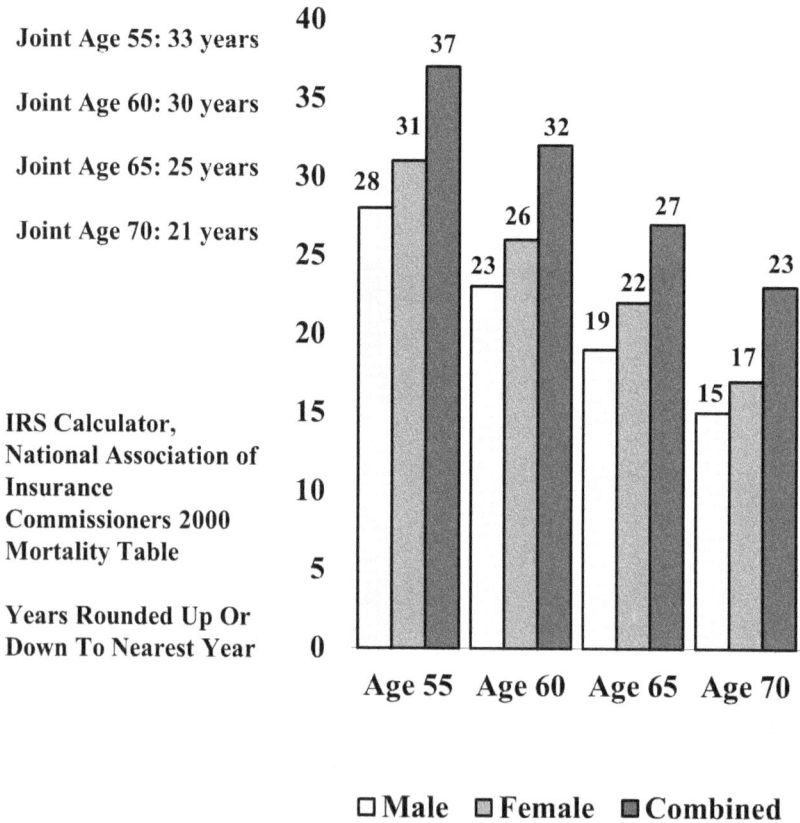

Joint Age 55: 33 years

Joint Age 60: 30 years

Joint Age 65: 25 years

Joint Age 70: 21 years

IRS Calculator,
National Association of
Insurance
Commissioners 2000
Mortality Table

Years Rounded Up Or
Down To Nearest Year

	Male	Female	Combined
Age 55	28	31	37
Age 60	23	26	32
Age 65	19	22	27
Age 70	15	17	23

□Male ▣Female ■Combined

This 2015 chart illustrates how life expectancy has grown since 2000. You should plan for many happy years in retirement.

How much money will you need? Probably more than you think.

You won't retire on today's income. You will retire on *tomorrow's income*. This means planning for inflation.

Do You Have A Plan To Increase Your Income During Retirement?

$5,000 Monthly Income With 3% Inflation

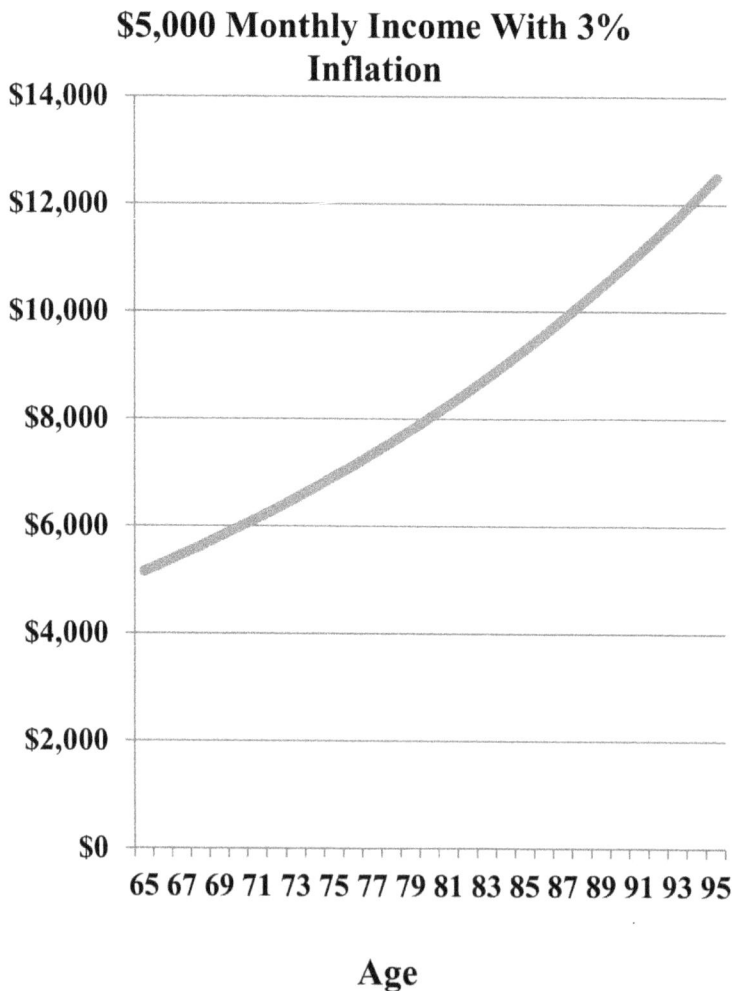

Age

INFLATION

Inflation plays a critical role in retirement planning. It is easy to underestimate the impact that inflation will have on your income needs.

Think back to when you were younger. Things cost less. Cars, fast food, housing, utilities...everything costs more today than it did thirty years ago.

If you begin retirement with a monthly income need of $5,000, by the time you reach age 95, it might take more than $12,000 per month to provide the *same* standard of living. This assumes an average price increase of 3%—which is the U.S. long-term inflation rate.

Things cost more money over time. You must plan for it.

The Financial Phases Of Life

Assets

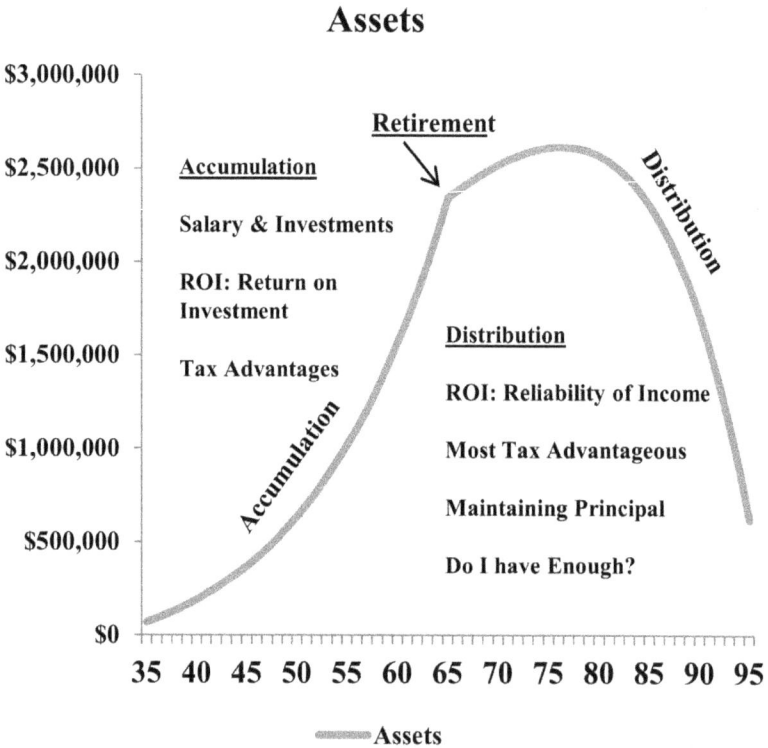

$3,000,000

$2,500,000 — **Accumulation**

Retirement

$2,000,000 — Salary & Investments

ROI: Return on Investment

$1,500,000 — Tax Advantages

Distribution

ROI: Reliability of Income

$1,000,000 — Most Tax Advantageous

Maintaining Principal

$500,000 — Do I have Enough?

$0

35 40 45 50 55 60 65 70 75 80 85 90 95

Accumulation

Distribution

Assets

FINANCIAL PHASES

When it comes to money, people experience two distinct financial phases during their lifetime.

ACCUMULATION

The first financial phase of life is accumulation. During the accumulation phase, we are most concerned with the long-term safety and the *return* on *our investments*. Let's call this ROI. ROI is the growth of our assets relative to inflation.

DISTRIBUTION

When we reach retirement, we begin a long distribution phase. This can last 30 years or more. In retirement, we become concerned with a different ROI, the *reliability of* our *income*.

We want to make sure that our money will be there for as long as we need it. We must invest tax-efficiently, with a portfolio that does not erode over time.

If we don't have an investment surplus, we must take more risk with our investments. Then, one bad year could upset a plan that took a lifetime to create.

Once we make it *through* retirement, we might be concerned with the distribution of our wealth. This is what we leave our heirs after we are gone.

Do You Want To Leave A Legacy?

Assets Over A Lifetime

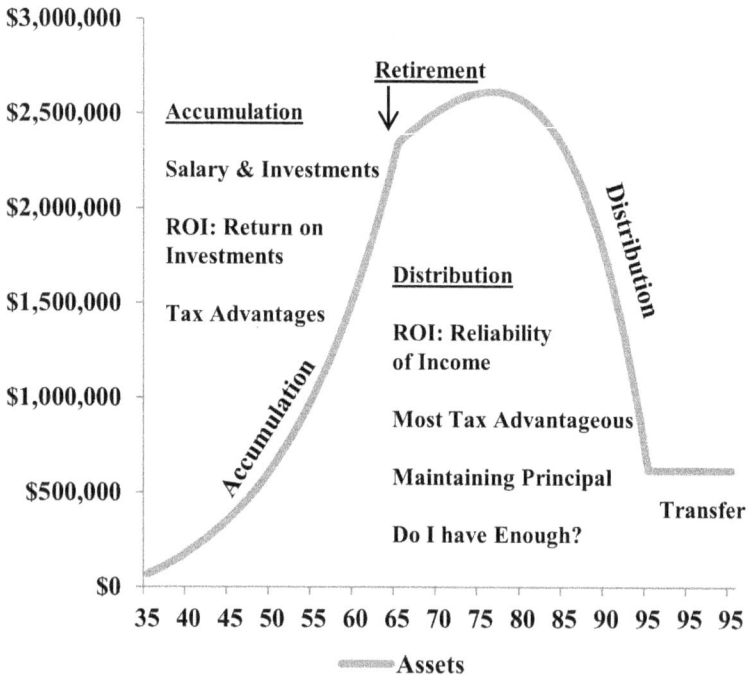

$3,000,000

$2,500,000 — **Accumulation**

Retirement
↓

Salary & Investments

$2,000,000 — **ROI: Return on Investments**

Distribution

$1,500,000 — **Tax Advantages**

ROI: Reliability of Income

$1,000,000 — *Accumulation*

Most Tax Advantageous

Distribution

$500,000 — **Maintaining Principal**

Transfer

Do I have Enough?

$0

35 40 45 50 55 60 65 70 75 80 85 90 95 95 95

━━━Assets

Many individuals want to leave a legacy for their children. A legacy won't be there if you run out of money. A legacy happens only if you plan accordingly. This means having enough assets to last a lifetime. If you want to leave something, you must invest and spend your money in a manner designed to keep it.

Chapter Five

_____**R**_____

Top Ten Money Mistakes

People make many mistakes with their money. Here are the top ten reasons that people don't achieve financial security.

People...

1. Procrastinate

2. Lack Specific Objectives

3. Don't Understand The Time Value of Money

4. Don't Plan For Inflation

5. Use Improper Tax Strategies

6. Make Poor Investment Choices

7. Have Inadequate Protection Against Unforeseen Losses

8. Spend Excessively (Then Save What's Not Left)

9. Have Unrealistic Expectations

10. Fail To Implement A Long-Term Plan

This book has illustrated how poorly most people plan for the future. Perhaps you are one of the few who saves aggressively and invests for retirement. If so, please accept the compliment you deserve. You will not regret any sacrifice you make today.

If you find it hard to save for retirement, there may be several reasons. Most of these roadblocks *can* be corrected, even if you think they can't. Little changes can send you on a path to financial security.

There are ten primary reasons why people do not achieve financial security. Let's discuss each one, and how they can affect your economic decisions.

1. Procrastination.

- There is an old saying that, "the road to failure is paved with good intentions." Few people plan to be poor. Everybody knows that they should save for retirement. It is just a matter of when to start. People wait too long, or never start at all. There is always an excuse not to save.

- Poverty in retirement is not the result of a low income during working years. Plenty of people with low incomes manage to save for retirement. Financial success is the result of focus and discipline. Retirement security begins with the decision to *be* financially independent. This decision must be turned into action—today.

- Procrastination can be overcome with education. It helps to have an easy way to save, like a 401(k). It also helps if your employer is willing to share some of the cost. Some employers can. Others can't.

- This book provides the education you need to overcome procrastination and begin planning today. It is up to you to take advantage of that knowledge.

Procrastination achieves nothing but disappointment. A successful financial future begins with **the decision to become financially secure**.

2. Lack Of Objectives

- If you turn on a GPS system, but don't enter a destination, will you get where you want to go? If you get into your car for a trip to an unfamiliar place, but have no directions, will you get there? While these questions seem absurd, they are not. We sit behind the wheel of the vehicle to our own economic security, but many of us never turn it on. Even if we start, we don't tell it where to go. We don't know how much we will need in retirement, how much money to save, and how to invest it.

- One of the most common, and easily corrected, obstacles to financial success is the lack of defined goals. Without goals, you have no destination. With no destination, you have nowhere to go.

- Creating a comfortable retirement should be started early. More time will give you a better chance of getting there.

- When you have finished reading this book, you should know how much you will need in retirement. You will know how much to save, and where to invest your savings.

Well-conceived and realistic goals are critical to achieving a comfortable retirement. You must set goals and then invest to achieve them.

3. Don't Understand The Time Value Money

- Most people, regardless of education, do not fully understand our financial system...or how money works.

- A concept that everyone must understand is the time value of money. A dollar invested today will become worth more than a dollar tomorrow. This is because we earn money on our savings, plus its earnings. If we save $1, and earn 10% per year (about the long term growth rate of the stock market), our savings will grow to $2 in 7.2 years. In 7.2 more years, our dollar doubles again, to $4. In 28.8 years, $1 grows to $16.

Money, when invested properly over time, should make more money. When we understand compounding, we will realize the importance of saving at the earliest possible time.

4. Inflation

- Historically, prices increase over time. As prices *increase*, the purchasing power of a dollar *decreases*.

- Just as $1 can increase over time with positive investment returns, the same dollar loses value if it sits doing nothing. Over the past century, inflation has averaged approximately 3% per year. If we hold a dollar, and don't invest it, in seven years (with 3% inflation) our dollar is worth just eighty-one cents. In fifteen years, the same dollar buys what sixty-four cents buys today.

Retirement goals cannot be based upon today's expenses. Accumulation objectives must be derived from values adjusted for future inflation.

Time Value Versus Inflation

- One dollar invested at 10% grows to four dollars in about fifteen years. With 3% inflation, $4 will buy what $2.65 buys today ($4 x .64). This a net gain in purchasing power. But we must *invest* to achieve it. We must take risk.

- If we don't invest to *outpace inflation*, our savings will be worth less in the future. The sooner we invest, the more we can buy tomorrow.

When investing for retirement, inflation *and* long-term investment accumulation must be coordinated into the plan.

5. Improper Tax Strategies

- Profits on personal investments are subject to current taxation. If we earn $100, this sum will be reduced by current taxes. If our tax bracket is 25%, $100 of profit becomes $75 after we pay Uncle Sam.

- The U.S. Government wants to encourage saving for retirement. Because of this, Congress voted to delay taxation on certain investments, such as those inside IRAs and qualified retirement plans. Tax deferral allows 100% of gains to be available for growth.

- Because of deferred taxation, people should take advantage of tax-favored retirement vehicles when they are available.

- Note: Congress sets limitations on how much any individual, or company, can place in most tax-favored vehicles.

Certain retirement vehicles offer tax advantages that help increase investment accumulation. Use them.

6. Making Poor Investment Choices

- The purpose of investing is to create wealth over time. Earnings become reinvested. Account balances compound.

- Poor investments work in reverse. Poor investments lower accumulation values, or significantly reduce their growth over time.

- You should avoid investments that promise extraordinary returns. Remember the saying, "If it sounds too good to be true, it probably is."

- Take the time to understand investments and how they work. Carefully research any individual company, or investment manager, with whom you invest.

- Don't chase the latest hot investment. Avoid "tips" you hear from your friends and neighbors. They lead to sleepless nights.

- Don't panic when the stock market falls, or get euphoric when it leaps upward. The stock market evens out. Over time, the market historically grows in the end.

- We fear things we don't understand. Make sure that you understand risk before you invest. Long-term investment gains demand short-term risk. Don't panic and sell when growth investments fall in value. They are behaving as they should.

Be Diversified

- We have all heard the saying, "Don't put all your eggs in one basket." This holds true with investing. History shows (as well as the math) that diversification is critical to safer, long-term investment growth. Sure, it is possible to pick the right stock or fund. It is more probable that you won't.

Diversification can reduce risk, without sacrificing potential investment returns. This book will soon show you how to invest like the pros.

7. Inadequate Protection Against Loss

- Most of us protect ourselves against certain potential losses. We insure our homes and our cars. We might buy life insurance, or insure our income with disability insurance.

- We should all consider *insuring our retirement*. This means planning for the unexpected. Save more than you think you will need. You can never have too much.

8. Excessive Spending

- Many of us could retire on what we spend at coffee houses and fast food restaurants. Small savings add up over time. The money saved by forgoing daily coffees, snacks, or a restaurant lunch, might be enough to provide a comfortable retirement. If you have the money for coffee and restaurants, you certainly have the money to plan for your retirement.

- According to CNN Money (6/24/2013), roughly 76% of the U.S. population lives paycheck to paycheck. 27% of Americans have no savings at all. Having money is a choice. It doesn't happen on its own. There was a popular country song by the Billy Hill Band that bemoans that there's "Too much month at the end of the money…" Don't make this your life's motto. Don't have too much month at the end of *your* money. *Save first*, and then spend.

- Don't borrow to buy unnecessary items, especially when your budget can't handle them.

- Long term borrowing for a home or investment property is financially responsible. Borrowing for a sports car in lieu of saving usually is not.

- Don't borrow money for the convenience. Credit cards are fine. Holding credit card debt is not. Credit card debt presents a huge financial cost over time.

Here is an example of making minimum payments on a credit card balance:

You owe $2,000.

Your interest rate is 18.5%.

You make minimum payments.

The minimum payment is 2.8% of your balance.

The payoff period is 11 years.

Interest costs over the loan payment period are $1,906. You have lost half your money.

- Ouch. This happens all the time.

This same $2,000 would make a nice retirement plan contribution.

If you can't keep yourself from holding credit card debt, then you need PLASTIC SURGERY. Cut your cards right now. Pay off your debt and never use them again.

TOO MANY PEOPLE SPEND FIRST AND SAVE WHAT IS (OR ISN'T) LEFT.

IF YOU SAVE FIRST, THEN SPEND THE REST, YOU CAN ENJOY A FINANCIALLY SUCCESSFUL RETIREMENT.

9. Unrealistic Expectations

Positive expectations are a good thing. Unrealistic expectations cause misery.

Unrealistic expectations come in MANY SHADES OF RED.

- People underestimate how much they will need in retirement.
- Investors have unrealistic return expectations *before* retirement.
- Investors think they will earn more *in* retirement, by working, and with their investments.
- People don't prepare for unexpected illness or accidents. People don't save enough for things that require significant funds (children, grandchildren, weddings, divorces, etc.).

This book explains effective planning for retirement, in ways that are simple to understand and easy to implement.

10. Failure To Implement A Long-term Plan

- Financial success cannot happen in a day, a year, or even a decade. Financial independence requires many years of attention and discipline.
- Most people do not understand the discipline and commitment required until it is too late.
- Don't let this happen to you.

Build a personal plan, and then set out to achieve it.

Chapter Six

R
_____

Retirement Methodology

GOALS IN RETIREMENT

Retirement means many things to many people. Once retired, some people don't work again. Others continue working in some capacity. Some need to work, but are unable to, because of poor health or the lack of jobs.

There are characteristics that most retirees do have in common. Most retirees want to:

- Increase Income.
- Invest With Lower Risk.
- Spend Less In Taxes.
- Preserve Their Money.
- Get A Senior Discount.

Unfortunately, these goals often run counter to reality. At retirement, most seniors experience the following:

- There Are Fewer Job Opportunities.
- Good Investment Returns Require Risking Principal.
- Income From Retirement Plans Is Taxed.
- Social Security Is Taxed If Earnings Are High.
- Principal Can Erode Rapidly.
- Senior Discounts Are Offered Everywhere If You Ask.

There is no substitute for having sufficient assets in retirement. It is hard to earn your way out of a shortfall, either by working or investing. Most people are forced to pare expenses more than they'd like. This means less entertainment, less travel, less money for family, less fun. Is this how you want to spend your retirement years?

METHODOLOGY FOR RETIREMENT PLANNING

- DETERMINE YOUR ASSETS
- PROJECT YOUR INCOME & ADDITIONS TO YOUR INVESTMENTS
- SET GOALS
- INVEST TOWARD YOUR GOALS
- COORDINATE YOUR INVESTMENTS WITH ALL OTHER FINANCIAL PLANNING

As you plan for retirement, you should understand what you are planning for. Your goal should be to accumulate enough money in retirement to provide the income and lifestyle that you desire. When you reach retirement, you will need to invest your money to provide the income you need, in a way to ensure that you don't spend it all before you die. The following pages illustrate the process you will need to follow.

PLANNING IN RETIREMENT

Asset Inventory

Proper planning *in* retirement should start with a complete inventory of what you own, especially your investment assets. When conducting your inventory, you may find that you have more or less money than you thought.

Sometimes, savings must be turned into investments to achieve greater returns. Sometimes assets are "found," such as old stock and bond certificates, heirlooms and other inherited assets.

Most states have a website where individuals can search for assets that have been lost along the way—uncashed paychecks or bank accounts, dormant investment accounts, even retirement plan accounts. About ten percent of us have an asset that has been forgotten or misplaced. It never hurts to see if you are one of the lucky recipients of some unexpected money.

Income Sources

Once you summarize your assets, you will need to determine your sources of income. An obvious income source is Social Security. If you don't have a detailed benefit statement, ask the Social Security Administration to send you one. Note the income you are entitled to today, and how that income will increase if you delay receiving it until a later date.

Check with old employers to see if you are entitled to retirement benefits. You may have been enrolled in a pension or profit sharing plan that you forgot, or didn't even know was in place. Some employees never roll 401(k) balances to a new employer or an IRA. Employers hold many billions of dollars in retirement plan assets for employees that no longer work for their companies.

Set A Goal

Once you know your assets and your income, you can begin to plan. Planning begins with setting a goal. Your retirement income goal will be derived from the income you need, what extras you would like, what you can afford, and the sacrifices you will make to achieve your objectives.

Create A Budget

Create a budget of your expenses. Include anything that you *must* pay in one column. Then make a list of non-necessities, like entertainment and travel. With these figures as a guide, set a monthly income goal for your retirement. You should then adjust this goal for future inflation. This book will show you how.

Rate Of Return

Once you understand your assets, income and goals, you can determine the rate of return you must earn on your investments to achieve them. We will discuss how to do this later in this book.

IF YOU HAVE A DEFICIT...WHAT TO DO

- SAVE MORE

- INVEST FOR HIGHER RETURNS

- REDUCE LIFESTYLE EXPENSES

- WORK LONGER

- TAP EQUITY IN YOUR HOME

- COMBINATION OF THE ABOVE

When you run your investment calculations, you will usually find one of two things:

- You Have More Than Enough Money
- You Face A Shortfall

If you have more than enough money, you should consider estate planning, and possibly gifting to your heirs. See a professional advisor before you do this.

If you face a shortfall, you have choices to make. If retirement is years away, you can begin saving and investing more.

Remember: If you *save first,* and then spend *the rest*, you will adjust your spending habits, and feel less sacrifice than you think.

Work Longer

If you are at retirement age and don't have the money to support your lifestyle goal, you might choose to work longer. By working, you may be able to delay taking Social Security or a pension until a later date. Delay will increase your income when you ultimately receive it.

Reduce Expenses

You can try to reduce expenses.

- You may need to negotiate reduced payoffs with your lenders, and absorb the hit to your credit score.
- You can cut spending on luxuries, even if they feel like necessities.
  - You may change your cable TV plan, make your cell phone your home phone, or dine at home rather than your favorite French restaurant.

Home Use

At retirement, many people have equity in their homes.

- You might sell your current home and buy a new home for less (Florida anyone?). You can use the net equity to invest in retirement.

- You may convert personal debt into a mortgage or a home equity line of credit. This can reduce monthly expenses significantly.

- If you watch television, you have probably seen advertisements for reverse home mortgages. With a reverse mortgage, you can elect to receive a monthly income that is secured by the equity in your home. You can also elect to take a lump sum, which you can then invest. Funds you receive from a reverse mortgage are not repaid until the mortgagor (you) dies or the home is sold. Please be aware that interest will accrue on any debt. When the home *is* sold, by you or your heirs, a significant debt may be owed on your property.

Summary: Rules For Successful Retirement Planning

There are a few simple rules that everyone should follow when planning for retirement. You should:

- Make a plan.
- Save first. Spend the rest.
- Plan for inflation.
- Use the tax code for your benefit.
- Make wise investment choices.

The following chapter illustrates how a real life couple adjusted their planning *in* retirement. Then this book will show you how to save and invest *for* retirement.

Chapter Seven

R
_____

Financial Planning

Most Americans have never worked with a professional financial advisor. If you are in this group, you should consider consulting one.

Mutual fund companies offer free education materials. This book shows how to use an online financial modeling tool that is available to all.

If you are enrolled in a 401(k), your employer can provide printed materials that can help you plan. The online tools with most 401(k)s are fairly robust.

Some companies make arrangements with financial advisors, who will meet with retirement plan participants in person, online or by phone.

Retirement planning can be complicated. But free options may be sufficient for you to plan. They do not work for everyone.

The following pages attempt to explain and simplify the financial planning process. Whatever your chosen method (financial planner, online or print tools, or a simple notepad), this book's graphics, combined with their explanations, should help you understand how to build and maintain your own basic financial plan.

The next two pages show the financial assets of John and Mary Smith as they plan to retire.

Here is a summary of what they own:

Asset	Value	Liability	Net Value
Real Estate			
Residence	$500,000	$115,000	$385,000
Liquid Assets			
Checking Accounts	$20,000		$20,000
Personal Assets			
Personal Property	$150,000		$150,000
Retirement Assets			
John's 401(k)	$950,000		$950,000
John's IRA	$30,000		$30,000
Mary's IRA	$15,000		$15,000
Mary's Pension	$20,000		$20,000
Total Investable Assets			**$1,050,000**

Income Sources:

John's Social Security:	$21,420/year
Mary's Social Security:	$10,924/year
Total Income Sources:	**$32,344/year**

Simplified Profile Sheet

Date:	October 1, 2015		Next Meeting:		October 1, 2015	

Client: John & Mary Smith
Address:

Phone: _____ Email: _____

Planners
Excellent Advisor

	R.B.	H.G.	S.N.	S.S.

PLANNED EXPENSES

1. $0   4.
2.   5.
3.

PLANNED EDUCATION EXPENSE: $0

FAMILY INFO

	Name	DOB	Age	SS#
Client:	John	10/01/1950	65	
Spouse:	Mary	10/01/1951	64	

	Name	DOB	Age	Occ.
Children:				

EARNED INCOME

Name	Source	Amount	401(k) Cont	Co. Match	OTHER INCOME	Amount
John	Lawyer	$100,000	$24,000	$0	Client Social Security:	$21,420
					Client Pension:	$0 60%
					Spouse Social Security:	$10,924
Other Annual Savings:			$10,000		Spouse Pension:	$0 50%
TOTAL ANNUAL SAVINGS:			$34,000		**RETIREMENT INCOME NEED:**	$75,000

Retirement Age: 65

Projected Inflation Rate: 3.00%

Projected SS Growth Rate: 1.00%

Projected Pension Growth Rate:

Other Documents:

Profile Sheet - Assets

LIQUID ASSETS	Owner	Value	PERSONAL USE ASSETS	Owner	Value	Liability
Checking	John	$10,000	Home	Joint	$500,000	$115,000
Checking	Joint	$10,000	Personal Property	John	$50,000	
			Personal Property	Joint	$50,000	
			Personal Property	Mary	$50,000	
ANTICIPATED ASSETS:						
Inheritance						
Stock Options						
Bonuses						
Other:						
			MORTGAGES & DEBT			

			Rate	Payment	Yrs. To Go	Extra $/mo

RETIREMENT ASSETS	Owner	Value	INVESTMENT ASSETS	Owner	Value
401(k)	John	$950,000			
IRA	John	$30,000			
IRA	Mary	$15,000			
County Retirement	Mary	$20,000			

NOTES

PERSONAL INFORMATION/FAMILY INFO

Every retirement plan involves life expectancy and marital status. If you are single and your health is poor, you may have a short retirement horizon. If you are married and healthy, your planning horizon will be far longer. Over thirty years.

EXAMPLE

This planning example illustrates John and Mary as they contemplate retirement. John is age 65. Mary will turn 65 in one year.

OBJECTIVES

Objectives are what you hope to accomplish financially. Our sample couple has chosen to develop an investment asset allocation for retirement.

Education

Paying for education expenses can be a big part of anyone's financial picture. This couple is not planning on tuition payments for children or grandchildren.

EARNED INCOME

Our example shows a current earned income of $100,000. Current annual retirement contributions are $24,000. This client hopes to retire today, but will continue to work, and save, if needed.

OTHER INCOME

Other income includes such sources as Social Security, annuities and pensions.

In our example, John has earned a larger Social Security benefit than Mary. Mary earned less during her "credit years" and will receive a smaller benefit. Note: In 40% of today's American households with children, the female is the major breadwinner.

http://www.pewsocialtrends.org/2013/05/29/breadwinner-moms/

A spouse can take their own Social Security benefit or 50% of the other spouse's benefit, whichever is higher. Social Security payments could be reduced by certain government pension benefits received, such as those for some teachers.

Mary has a small pension benefit from the local government. This will not be paid as a monthly income, but as a lump sum. This amount is included with the retirement plan portion of the profile, rather than as an income.

OBJECTIVES

In our example, John and Mary are hoping to draw a retirement income of $75,000 per year.

ASSUMPTIONS

Assumptions must be made in any planning.

- In this case, we plan on retirement today. John is age 65. Mary will be 65 in a year.

- The projected inflation rate is 3%. We will inflate the retirement income needed by 3% each year. If inflation is less than projected, John and Mary will need fewer investment assets. If inflation is higher, they will need more money to make up the shortfall.

- In theory, Social Security benefits will rise with the cost of living. The cost of living adjustments used by the government for determining Social Security growth are different than the actual increase in prices. Since the Social Security system has flaws in design, John and Mary make a conservative assumption. In their plan, Social Security payments are projected to grow at 1%. This is less than long-term inflation.

- Mary's pension is not an income stream. It is included in the retirement assets.

LIQUID ASSETS

Liquid assets are those you can sell at a moment's notice. Examples would be checking or savings accounts. Liquid assets usually don't earn very much. They are not an important part of "retirement accumulation assets," unless you convert them to a higher yielding form. If your total assets are substantial, liquid assets might be spent first, allowing your other assets to grow over time.

One popular retirement strategy involves maintaining enough in liquid assets to provide five years' worth of retirement income. This reduces the risk of withdrawing funds when the "markets" are down. Of course, this strategy reduces long-term returns.

PERSONAL ASSETS

Personal assets include such items as jewelry, art, furniture and cars. These are rarely part of investment calculations. There are exceptions to this rule. Collectibles, such as rare stamps and coins, may be liquidated over time to provide income. If so, these assets should be categorized as investment assets instead. Most financial planning software assumes that your home will not be used as an investment. If you plan to utilize equity from your home in retirement, an adjustment should be made.

MORTGAGES & DEBT

Mortgage and installment debt expenses will reduce your net income. These expenses must be amortized over time.

RETIREMENT ASSETS

Retirement assets are held inside tax-qualified retirement plans. They can also be owned in tax-favored investment vehicles, such as IRAs. Retirement assets escape current taxation, but will usually be taxed as ordinary income when withdrawn.

Some individuals own Roth IRAs. Roth IRAs grow without taxation. The money comes out tax free.

Retirement assets are typically invested for long-term growth. These investments tend to become less aggressive, as retirees approach retirement age.

ANNUITIES

Some assets may be held inside annuities. Annuities generally have two kinds of taxation. This depends upon whether the money placed inside the annuity was made with pre-tax or after-tax dollars. If the annuity consists of pre-tax dollars, such as an IRA rollover from a qualified plan, all money withdrawn will be taxed. If the initial source was made with after-tax dollars, withdrawals will be taxed until the annuity is depleted to its original basis. Then, withdrawals will be tax-free.

If annuitized, annuity payments will be partially taxed. The taxable amount will be based upon a percentage of gain divided by original principal. For example, if the gain represents 50% of the annuity value, only 50% of withdrawals will be taxed upon annuitization.

INVESTMENT ASSETS

Investment assets are those held outside of tax-qualified vehicles. In a perfect world, investment assets will continue to accumulate throughout one's lifetime. They may supplement spending, in addition to retirement assets.

Some financial planners recommend spending investment assets before drawing retirement assets. This strategy allows retirement assets to continue growing without current taxation. Other advisors recommend the opposite.

What makes the most sense will depend upon your tax bracket in retirement. The higher your tax bracket, the more you might wish to delay retirement plan withdrawals. If your tax bracket is low, you may want to balance your withdrawals more evenly.

IRA ROLLOVERS

When you retire, most 401(k), profit sharing, and many pension assets will be rolled into IRAs. IRAs allow their owners to delay taxation until funds are withdrawn. "Minimum distributions" must be withdrawn each year, once the owner reaches age 70 1/2. Minimum annual withdrawals are a percentage of total IRA assets, as determined at the end of each calendar year. The minimum percentage withdrawal is set by Congress. The percentage increases each year, with age. Withdrawals are based upon life expectancy. The general objective is to have the owner spend her last retirement dollar on the date of death.

If a 401(k) balance is large enough, you can opt to leave the assets inside your employer's plan. This might make sense if the plan has better and less expensive investment options than you can find on your own. These funds will still be subject to the minimum distribution rules. Here is a Web link that explains them.

https://www.irs.gov/Retirement-Plans/Plan-Participant,-Employee/Retirement-Topics-Required-Minimum-Distributions-(RMDs)

SUMMARY

When you retire, you must determine your assets, income, savings, expenses and your objectives.

Then you can run simulations to determine what rate of return you must earn to keep from outliving your money.

Let's examine the financial modeling calculations for John and Mary.

Example - Assets in Retirement at Various Rates of Return - $75,000/Yr.

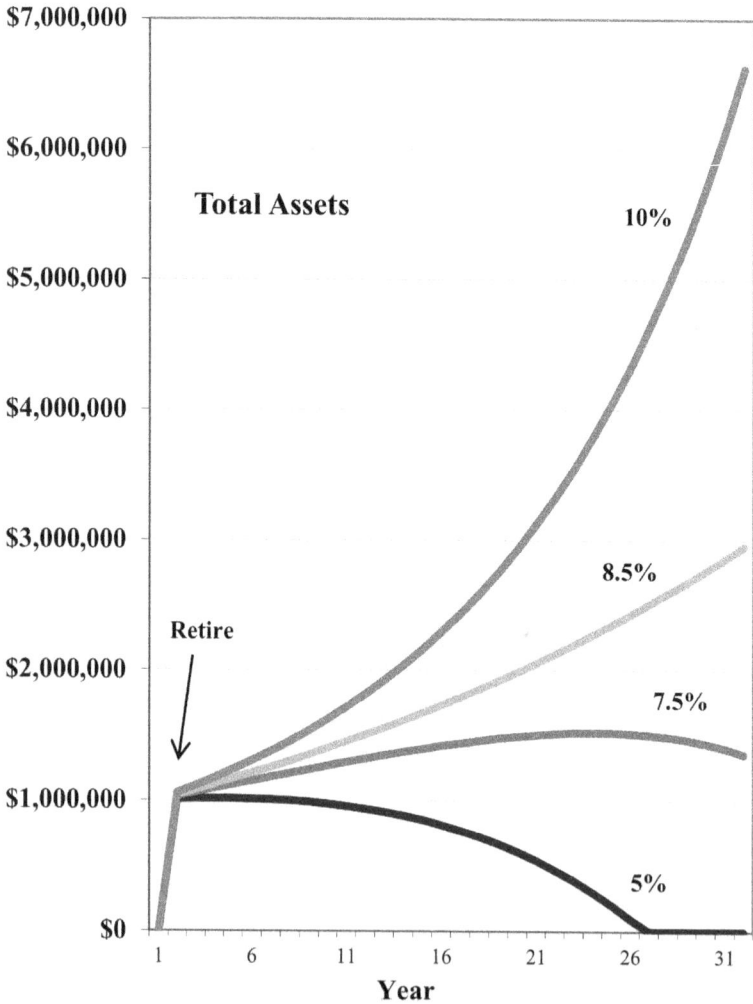

John and Mary's retirement calculations begin with an income goal of $75,000 per year. With an average investment rate of 5%, John and Mary would run out of money before the end of their life expectancy.

As of this writing, the average corporate bond yield is just 2.86%. The interest rates on cash are negligible.

http://www.bloomberg.com/markets/rates-bonds/corporate-bonds/

To earn 5%, John and Mary would be forced to assume more investment risk than they would prefer.

The stock market is highly unpredictable. Because of market risk, if John and Mary own a high percentage of stocks, they could potentially run out of money long before this illustration shows.

There are calculators that can run *Monte Carlo* calculations. These are hundreds of simulated portfolios (using random historical data) that can quantify any portfolio risk. For example, you can design a portfolio that will give you a 98% chance of maintaining assets over your life expectancy.

The greatest risk is that a bad stock market, particularly in the early years of retirement, could shorten the time that any investment portfolio will last.

If John and Mary earn 7.5% on their investments, they would avoid spending all they have. This illustration assumes a consistent stock market, which is impossible. Even at this return, there is a reasonable chance that John and Mary will outlive their money.

John and Mary decided that a $75,000 income in retirement requires too much portfolio risk.

John and Mary reviewed their budget again. They concluded that they could still live comfortably on $65,000 per year. New calculations were run, showing how their money would behave at different rates of return.

Example - Assets in Retirement at Various Rates of Return - $65,000/Yr.

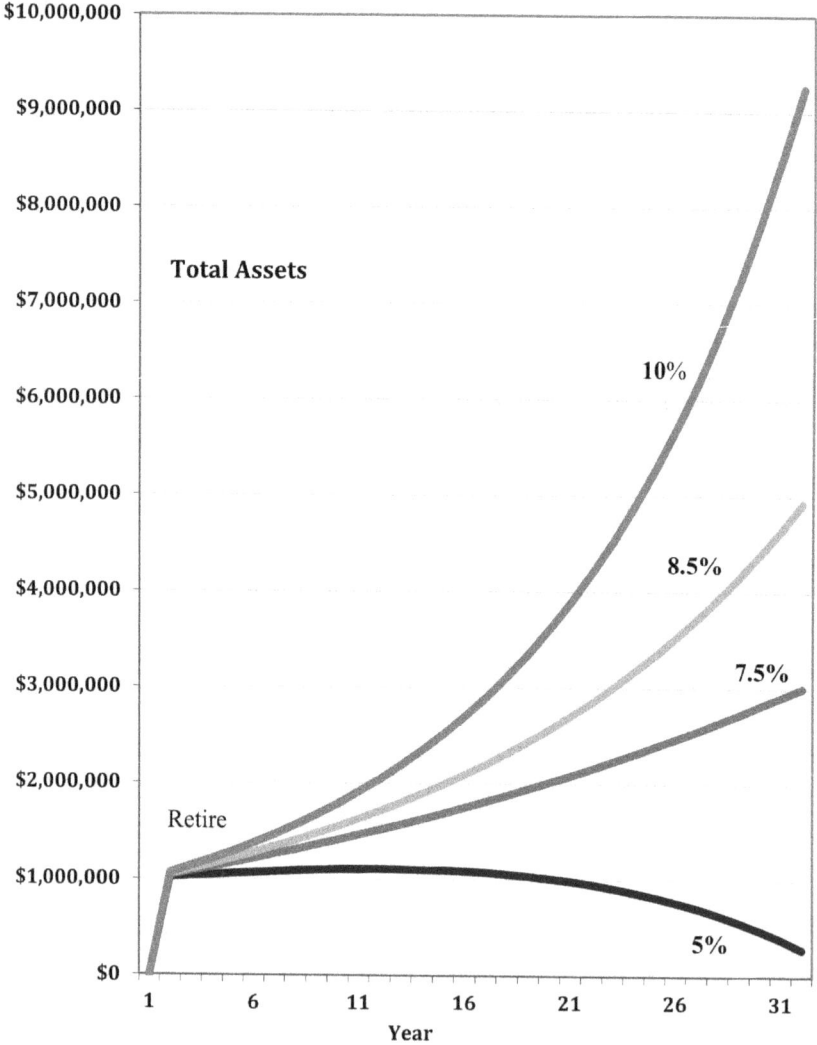

Total Assets

10%

8.5%

7.5%

Retire

5%

Year

Assumes investable assets of $1,015,000, with a retirement income of $65,000. 3% inflation, with 1% Social Security & Pension Growth.

By lowering their income to $65,000 per year, John and Mary reduce the chances that they will outlive their money. A consistent 5% return on investments would allow John and Mary to keep their assets to age 95.

With a 7.5% return, their investments would consistently grow. A balanced portfolio of 60% stocks and 40% bonds might be expected to deliver this type of long-term return.

For example: Let's assume that stocks will earn their historical 10% compound return, and that bonds will yield their normal 5% return. A portfolio consisting of 60% stocks and 40% bonds would produce the following net return.

$$60\% \times 10\% = 6\%$$

$$40\% \times 5\% = \underline{2\%}$$

8% Portfolio yield.

If you reduce by .5% for expenses, this delivers a net return of 7.5%.

This illustration does not account for certain unexpected events. Social Security benefits may be reduced for individuals with substantial assets or other incomes. Social Security benefits may not increase by the projected 1%, as happened in 2016. The stock market may enter a prolonged slump and investment values could be significantly reduced. John or Mary might require a long-term care facility, at considerable extra expense.

Many things can happen to influence a plan in retirement. Having sufficient assets makes plan changes easy. Being short on funds never is.

Example - Assets in Retirement at
Various Rates of Return - $57,200/Yr.
(Using Formula of Total Assets Divided By 25)

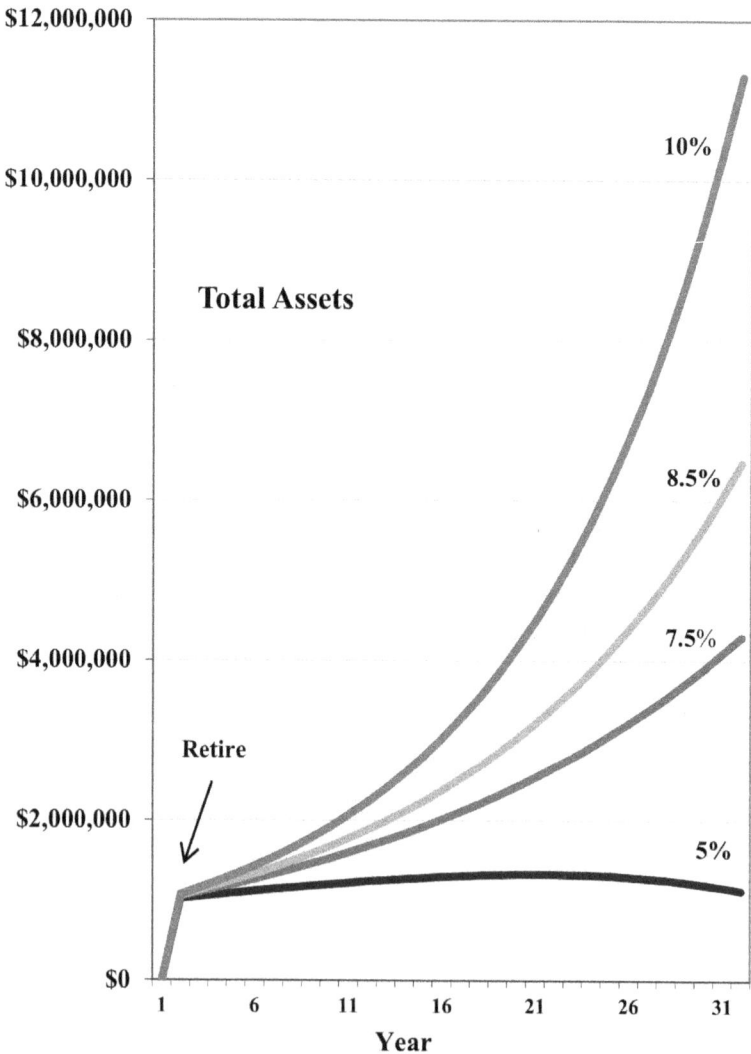

John and Mary sharpened their pencil one more time. They decided that they could maintain their lifestyle with $57,200 per year, with a few easy adjustments.

$57,200 simulates the simplified formula of never taking an income of more than 4% of investment assets.

This strategy gives John and Mary a much better chance of maintaining their investments in retirement, without taking much risk. The 4% strategy has a long-proven track record of allowing individuals to avoid outliving their money.

This strategy would allow John and Mary to own a portfolio that consists of 40% stocks and 60% bonds. Given historical returns, their portfolio might be expected to earn the following:

40% stocks x 10% = 4%
60% bonds x 5% = <u>3%</u>
7% Net Return

If you take away .5% for expenses, this yields a net return of 6.5%. Later, we will run calculations that assume expenses of 1%.

If stocks return less than the long-term 10%, and bonds produce yields that don't match the historical average of 5%, their portfolio might earn less. Here is an example showing John and Mary's portfolio earning 8% with stocks and 4% with bonds.

40% stocks x 8% = 3.2%
60% bonds x 4% = <u>2.4%</u>
5.6% Net Return

If you take away .5% for expenses, this yields a net return of 5.1%. With 1% expense, our net return falls to 4.6%

Don't worry if this is confusing. It always is, at first. The following pages will explain the process in greater detail. This book will also show you how to design your own financial plan.

Example - Assets in Retirement at
Various Rates of Return - $72,000/Yr.
(Using Formula of Total Assets Divided By 20)

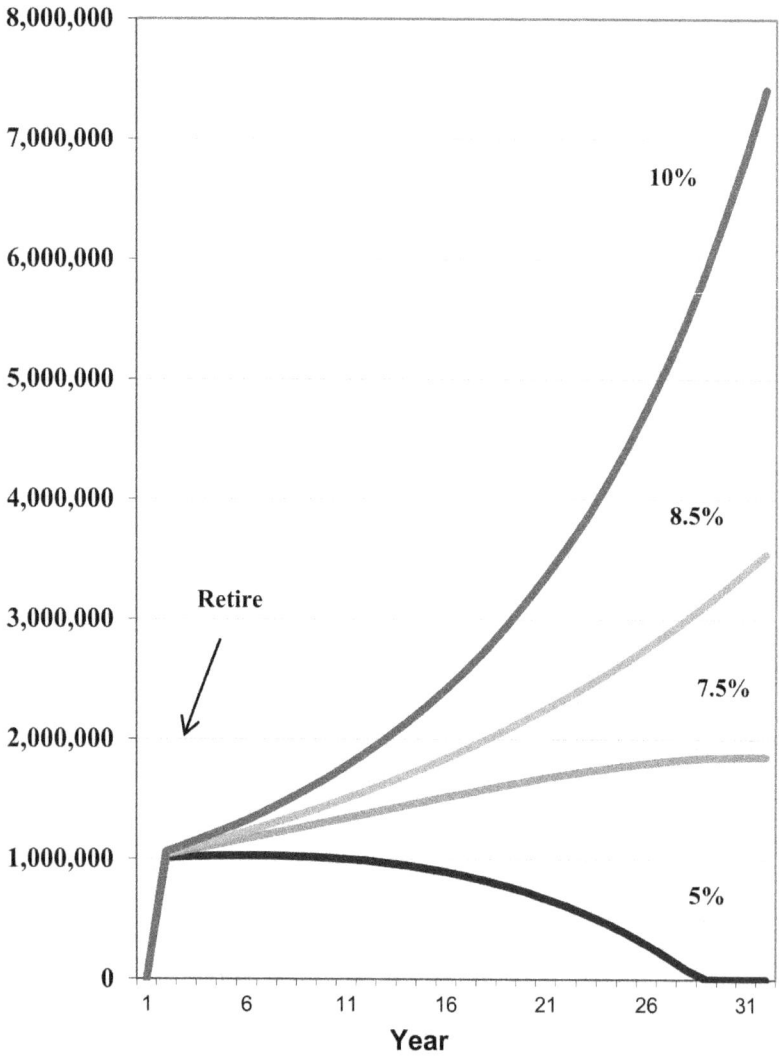

This illustration shows John and Mary taking an average income of 5% from investments. A 5% (after tax) return assures that John and Mary will lose their money before their estimated life expectancy. A 7.5% return on investments would be sufficient to maintain John and Mary's assets over time, assuming the stock market behaves.

John and Mary would need to be aggressive with their portfolio. They would also require more "luck" with the stock market, by earning historical returns, which are not guaranteed.

This chart illustrates a retirement income closer to the aggressive end of our suggested range of income withdrawal. John and Mary will need a portfolio with close to 40% stock and 60% bonds. Otherwise, they will run out of money. The next few pages discuss this in greater detail.

WHAT'S NEXT?

Some experts predict that long-term stock market returns are trending downward. Persistent regulations from Washington—environmental, financial and social all have costs. U.S. GDP growth has slowed to 1.8% per year during this century. It averaged 3.4% per year during the prior two decades. Source: http://www.world-bank.org/

Many U.S. companies spend more on lawyers than they do on research and development.

An analysis by Stanford University showed that smartphone manufacturers spent more than $20 Billion on patents and litigation in one year alone. The New York Times reported that Apple and Google spend more on lawyers than they do on research and development. Pharmaceutical companies make large payouts to claimants. Industrial companies face environmental lawsuits. Coal companies, once providing more than 50% of the nation's energy, have been replaced by less efficient biofuels and other clean energy. Financial institutions have paid hundreds of billions in fines to the U.S. Government. Money that banks would normally lend to companies is now kept in reserve. The cost of doing business in the U.S. is more expensive than ever. Removing all of this capital from businesses reduces their long-term growth potential.

Other experts shrug their shoulders and say that there have always been challenges. These analysts claim that global markets will continue to expand. Growth will occur outside of the western industrialized nations. China and India won't sign climate agreements. They will continue to grow, as western economies outsource their pollution. Large companies, such as Disney, Google and Facebook will continue to import tech workers who work for lower wages. Companies will replace older workers with younger ones. Technology will accelerate worldwide, and productivity will follow. Employees will be replaced by cheaper machines, but new jobs will be created. Business will move on as it always has.

http://www.latimes.com/business/hiltzik/la-fi-hiltzik-20150802-column.html

http://www.newyorker.com/news/john-cassidy/skeptical-note-paris-climate-deal

Some financial "improvements" present a human cost to the economy, the American workforce and to our way of life. Unemployment and underemployment are never fun. It may not be fair or just. We don't like it, but we don't ever do much about it. This has always been the case. Business moves on. People must adapt.

The only thing certain about investments is the past. The past tends to repeat itself. Using long-term returns is a good guide for the long-term future. Still, you should plan for a little less return.

Limiting retirement income withdrawals to 4% should be a goal. Expecting more from your portfolio will involve taking excess risk. Sometimes risk pays off, but not always.

If you have a long time to plan, the choice is yours. The following graphs were used to produce the preceding charts. Notice how different rates of return and the income withdrawn can radically alter investment assets in retirement.

Retire At 65 With $75,000/Year

John's Current Age	65
Mary's Current Age	64
Funds Available for Financial Independence	$1,015,000
Annual Income Need	($75,000)
Retirement Age	65
Take SS at Age	65
Annual Savings	$34,000
John's Social Security	$21,420
Mary's Social Security	$10,924

Projected Inflation Rates	
Projected Rate of Inflation	3.00%
Social Security Growth Rate	1.00%
Pension Growth Rate	1.00%

	John Age	Mary Age	Year Beg.	Income Need	John's SS Inc.	Mary's SS Inc.	Annual Savings	Annual Surplus/ (Shortfall)	1st ROR 3.00%	2nd ROR 5.00%	3rd ROR 7.50%	4th ROR 8.50%	5th ROR 10.00%
0	65	64	2015	(75,000)	21,420	0	0	(53,580)	990,263	1,009,491	1,033,527	1,043,141	1,057,562
1	66	65	2016	(77,250)	21,634	10,924	0	(44,692)	973,938	1,013,039	1,062,997	1,083,317	1,114,157
2	67	66	2017	(79,568)	21,851	11,033	0	(46,684)	955,072	1,014,673	1,092,537	1,124,747	1,174,221
3	68	67	2018	(81,955)	22,069	11,144	0	(48,742)	933,520	1,014,228	1,122,080	1,167,466	1,238,027
4	69	68	2019	(84,413)	22,290	11,255	0	(50,868)	909,131	1,011,527	1,151,552	1,211,508	1,305,874
5	70	69	2020	(86,946)	22,513	11,368	0	(53,065)	881,748	1,006,385	1,180,873	1,256,910	1,378,090
6	71	70	2021	(89,554)	22,738	11,481	0	(55,335)	851,205	998,603	1,209,954	1,303,709	1,455,030
7	72	71	2022	(92,241)	22,965	11,596	0	(57,679)	817,331	987,970	1,238,695	1,351,943	1,537,086
8	73	72	2023	(95,008)	23,195	11,712	0	(60,101)	779,947	974,262	1,266,989	1,401,648	1,624,684
9	74	73	2024	(97,858)	23,427	11,829	0	(62,602)	738,866	957,243	1,294,716	1,452,865	1,718,290
10	75	74	2025	(100,794)	23,661	11,947	0	(65,185)	693,891	936,660	1,321,745	1,505,632	1,818,415
11	76	75	2026	(103,818)	23,898	12,067	0	(67,853)	644,819	912,248	1,347,934	1,559,991	1,925,618
12	77	76	2027	(106,932)	24,137	12,188	0	(70,608)	591,437	883,722	1,373,125	1,615,980	2,040,511
13	78	77	2028	(110,140)	24,378	12,309	0	(73,453)	533,524	850,783	1,397,148	1,673,642	2,163,764
14	79	78	2029	(113,444)	24,622	12,433	0	(76,390)	470,848	813,112	1,419,815	1,733,019	2,296,112
15	80	79	2030	(116,848)	24,868	12,557	0	(79,423)	403,168	770,374	1,440,922	1,794,152	2,438,358
16	81	80	2031	(120,353)	25,117	12,682	0	(82,554)	330,233	722,211	1,460,246	1,857,084	2,591,384
17	82	81	2032	(123,964)	25,368	12,809	0	(85,787)	251,780	668,246	1,477,544	1,921,857	2,756,158
18	83	82	2033	(127,682)	25,621	12,937	0	(89,124)	167,536	608,078	1,492,551	1,988,516	2,933,737
19	84	83	2034	(131,513)	25,878	13,067	0	(92,569)	77,216	541,285	1,504,982	2,057,103	3,125,286
20	85	84	2035	(135,458)	26,136	13,197	0	(96,124)	(0)	467,419	1,514,521	2,127,662	3,332,077
21	86	85	2036	(139,522)	26,398	13,329	0	(99,795)	(0)	386,005	1,520,831	2,200,236	3,555,511
22	87	86	2037	(143,708)	26,662	13,463	0	(103,583)	(0)	296,543	1,523,541	2,274,868	3,797,120
23	88	87	2038	(148,019)	26,928	13,597	0	(107,493)	(0)	198,502	1,522,251	2,351,601	4,058,590
24	89	88	2039	(152,460)	27,198	13,733	0	(111,529)	(0)	91,322	1,516,527	2,430,479	4,341,767
25	90	89	2040	(157,033)	27,470	13,871	0	(115,693)	(0)	(0)	1,505,897	2,511,543	4,648,681
26	91	90	2041	(161,744)	27,744	14,009	0	(119,991)	(0)	(0)	1,489,849	2,594,834	4,981,560
27	92	91	2042	(166,597)	28,022	14,149	0	(124,425)	(0)	(0)	1,467,830	2,680,393	5,342,848
28	93	92	2043	(171,595)	28,302	14,291	0	(129,002)	(0)	(0)	1,439,241	2,768,260	5,735,231
29	94	93	2044	(176,742)	28,585	14,434	0	(133,724)	(0)	(0)	1,403,431	2,858,472	6,161,658
30	95	94	2045	(182,045)	28,871	14,578	0	(138,596)	(0)	(0)	1,359,698	2,951,066	6,625,368

Retire At 65 With $65,000/Year

John's Current Age: 65
Mary's Current Age: 64
Funds Available for Financial Independence: $1,015,000
Annual Income Need: ($65,000)
Retirement Age: 65
Take SS at Age: 65
Annual Savings: $34,000
John's Social Security: $21,420
Mary's Social Security: $10,924

Projected Inflation Rates
Projected Rate of Inflation: 3.00%
Social Security Growth Rate: 1.00%
Pension Growth Rate: 1.00%

Yr	John Age	Mary Age	Year Beg.	Income Need	John's SS Income	Mary's SS Income	Annual Savings	Surplus/(Shortfall)	1st ROR 3.00%	2nd ROR 5.00%	3rd ROR 7.50%	4th ROR 8.50%	5th ROR 10.00%
0	65	64	2015	(65,000)	21,420	0	0	(43,580)	1,000,563	1,019,991	1,044,277	1,053,991	1,068,562
1	66	65	2016	(66,950)	21,634	10,924	0	(34,392)	995,156	1,034,879	1,085,626	1,106,265	1,137,587
2	67	66	2017	(68,959)	21,851	11,033	0	(36,075)	987,854	1,048,745	1,128,268	1,161,156	1,211,664
3	68	67	2018	(71,027)	22,069	11,144	0	(37,815)	978,540	1,061,477	1,172,237	1,218,826	1,291,234
4	69	68	2019	(73,158)	22,290	11,255	0	(39,613)	967,095	1,072,956	1,217,570	1,279,445	1,376,783
5	70	69	2020	(75,353)	22,513	11,368	0	(41,473)	953,391	1,083,058	1,264,305	1,343,200	1,468,841
6	71	70	2021	(77,613)	22,738	11,481	0	(43,394)	937,296	1,091,647	1,312,479	1,410,290	1,567,991
7	72	71	2022	(79,942)	22,965	11,596	0	(45,381)	918,673	1,098,579	1,362,131	1,480,926	1,674,872
8	73	72	2023	(82,340)	23,195	11,712	0	(47,433)	897,377	1,103,703	1,413,300	1,555,340	1,790,183
9	74	73	2024	(84,810)	23,427	11,829	0	(49,554)	873,257	1,106,856	1,466,026	1,633,777	1,914,691
10	75	74	2025	(87,355)	23,661	11,947	0	(51,746)	846,156	1,107,866	1,520,351	1,716,504	2,049,239
11	76	75	2026	(89,975)	23,898	12,067	0	(54,011)	815,910	1,106,548	1,576,316	1,803,805	2,194,751
12	77	76	2027	(92,674)	24,137	12,188	0	(56,350)	782,347	1,102,708	1,633,963	1,895,988	2,352,241
13	78	77	2028	(95,455)	24,378	12,309	0	(58,767)	745,287	1,096,137	1,693,336	1,993,385	2,522,821
14	79	78	2029	(98,318)	24,622	12,433	0	(61,264)	704,543	1,086,617	1,754,477	2,096,351	2,707,713
15	80	79	2030	(101,268)	24,868	12,557	0	(63,843)	659,921	1,073,912	1,817,432	2,205,271	2,908,257
16	81	80	2031	(104,306)	25,117	12,682	0	(66,507)	611,217	1,057,776	1,882,244	2,320,559	3,125,925
17	82	81	2032	(107,435)	25,368	12,809	0	(69,258)	558,218	1,037,944	1,948,960	2,442,662	3,362,334
18	83	82	2033	(110,658)	25,621	12,937	0	(72,099)	500,702	1,014,137	2,017,625	2,572,060	3,619,258
19	84	83	2034	(113,978)	25,878	13,067	0	(75,033)	438,438	986,058	2,088,286	2,709,274	3,898,647
20	85	84	2035	(117,397)	26,136	13,197	0	(78,063)	371,186	953,395	2,160,989	2,854,863	4,202,642
21	86	85	2036	(120,919)	26,398	13,329	0	(81,192)	298,694	915,813	2,235,782	3,009,434	4,533,595
22	87	86	2037	(124,547)	26,662	13,463	0	(84,422)	220,700	872,960	2,312,712	3,173,637	4,894,090
23	88	87	2038	(128,283)	26,928	13,597	0	(87,757)	136,931	824,463	2,391,826	3,348,180	5,286,966
24	89	88	2039	(132,132)	27,198	13,733	0	(91,201)	47,102	769,925	2,473,172	3,533,822	5,715,341
25	90	89	2040	(136,096)	27,470	13,871	0	(94,755)	(0)	708,928	2,556,798	3,731,388	6,182,645
26	91	90	2041	(140,178)	27,744	14,009	0	(98,425)	(0)	641,029	2,642,752	3,941,765	6,692,642
27	92	91	2042	(144,384)	28,022	14,149	0	(102,213)	(0)	565,757	2,731,079	4,165,914	7,249,472
28	93	92	2043	(148,715)	28,302	14,291	0	(106,122)	(0)	482,617	2,821,829	4,404,874	7,857,685
29	94	93	2044	(153,177)	28,585	14,434	0	(110,158)	(0)	391,082	2,915,046	4,659,767	8,522,280
30	95	94	2045	(157,772)	28,871	14,578	0	(114,323)	(0)	290,596	3,010,778	4,931,807	9,248,752

Retire At 65 With $57,200/Year: Assets At 25x Income

John's Current Age	65	
Mary's Current Age	64	
Funds Available for Financial Independence	$1,015,000	
Annual Income Need	($57,200)	
Retirement Age	65	
Take SS at Age	65	
Annual Savings	$34,000	
John's Social Security	$21,420	
Mary's Social Security	$10,924	

Projected Inflation Rates

Projected Rate of Inflation	3.00%
Social Security Growth Rate	1.00%
Pension Growth Rate	1.00%

Yr	John Age	Mary Age	Year Beg.	Income Need	John's SS Income	Mary's SS Income	Annual Savings	Surplus/ (Shortfall)	1st ROR 3.00%	2nd ROR 5.00%	3rd ROR 7.50%	4th ROR 8.50%
0	65	64	2015	(57,200)	21,420	0	0	(35,780)	1,008,597	1,028,181	1,052,662	1,062,454
1	66	65	2016	(58,916)	21,634	10,924	0	(26,358)	1,011,706	1,051,914	1,103,276	1,124,164
2	67	66	2017	(60,683)	21,851	11,033	0	(27,800)	1,013,423	1,075,320	1,156,138	1,189,555
3	68	67	2018	(62,504)	22,069	11,144	0	(29,291)	1,013,656	1,098,330	1,211,360	1,258,886
4	69	68	2019	(64,379)	22,290	11,255	0	(30,834)	1,012,306	1,120,871	1,269,065	1,332,436
5	70	69	2020	(66,310)	22,513	11,368	0	(32,430)	1,009,272	1,142,863	1,329,382	1,410,507
6	71	70	2021	(68,300)	22,738	11,481	0	(34,081)	1,004,447	1,164,221	1,392,449	1,493,422
7	72	71	2022	(70,349)	22,965	11,596	0	(35,788)	997,719	1,184,855	1,458,411	1,581,533
8	73	72	2023	(72,459)	23,195	11,712	0	(37,552)	988,972	1,204,668	1,527,423	1,675,219
9	74	73	2024	(74,633)	23,427	11,829	0	(39,377)	978,083	1,223,555	1,599,649	1,774,889
10	75	74	2025	(76,872)	23,661	11,947	0	(41,264)	964,924	1,241,406	1,675,264	1,880,983
11	76	75	2026	(79,178)	23,898	12,067	0	(43,214)	949,361	1,258,102	1,754,454	1,993,980
12	77	76	2027	(81,554)	24,137	12,188	0	(45,229)	931,256	1,273,516	1,837,417	2,114,395
13	78	77	2028	(84,000)	24,378	12,309	0	(47,313)	910,461	1,287,514	1,924,362	2,242,784
14	79	78	2029	(86,520)	24,622	12,433	0	(49,466)	886,826	1,299,950	2,015,513	2,379,750
15	80	79	2030	(89,116)	24,868	12,557	0	(51,691)	860,189	1,310,672	2,111,109	2,525,944
16	81	80	2031	(91,789)	25,117	12,682	0	(53,990)	830,384	1,319,516	2,211,403	2,682,070
17	82	81	2032	(94,543)	25,368	12,809	0	(56,366)	797,239	1,326,308	2,316,665	2,848,889
18	83	82	2033	(97,379)	25,621	12,937	0	(58,820)	760,571	1,330,862	2,427,183	3,027,224
19	84	83	2034	(100,301)	25,878	13,067	0	(61,356)	720,192	1,332,981	2,543,264	3,217,967
20	85	84	2035	(103,310)	26,136	13,197	0	(63,976)	675,902	1,332,456	2,665,234	3,422,081
21	86	85	2036	(106,409)	26,398	13,329	0	(66,682)	627,497	1,329,063	2,793,444	3,640,608
22	87	86	2037	(109,601)	26,662	13,463	0	(69,477)	574,761	1,322,565	2,928,265	3,874,677
23	88	87	2038	(112,889)	26,928	13,597	0	(72,363)	517,470	1,312,712	3,070,094	4,125,511
24	89	88	2039	(116,276)	27,198	13,733	0	(75,345)	455,389	1,299,236	3,219,356	4,394,430
25	90	89	2040	(119,764)	27,470	13,871	0	(78,424)	388,274	1,281,852	3,376,502	4,682,867
26	91	90	2041	(123,357)	27,744	14,009	0	(81,603)	315,871	1,260,261	3,542,016	4,992,371
27	92	91	2042	(127,058)	28,022	14,149	0	(84,887)	237,914	1,234,144	3,716,414	5,324,620
28	93	92	2043	(130,869)	28,302	14,291	0	(88,277)	154,126	1,203,160	3,900,248	5,681,433
29	94	93	2044	(134,796)	28,585	14,434	0	(91,777)	64,220	1,166,953	4,094,106	6,064,777
30	95	94	2045	(138,839)	28,871	14,578	0	(95,390)	(0)	1,125,141	4,298,620	6,476,785

Retire At 65 With $72,000/Year
Assets At 20x Income

John's Age	65
Mary's Age	64
Funds Available for Financial Independence	$1,015,000
Annual Income Need	($72,000)
Retirement Age	65
Take SS at Age	65
Annual Savings	$34,000
John's Social Security	$21,420
Mary's Social Security	$10,924

Projected Inflation Rates	
Projected Rate of Inflation	3.00%
Social Security Growth Rate	1.00%
Pension Growth Rate	1.00%

Yrs	John's Age	Mary's Age	Year Beg.	Income Need	John's SS Income	Mary's SS Income	Annual Savings	Annual Surpl/ (Shortf)	1st ROR 3.00%	2nd ROR 5.00%	3rd ROR 7.50%	4th ROR 8.50%
0	65	64	2015	(72,000)	21,420	0	0	(50,580)	993,353	1,012,641	1,036,752	1,046,396
1	66	65	2016	(74,160)	21,634	10,924	0	(41,602)	980,303	1,019,591	1,069,786	1,090,201
2	67	66	2017	(76,385)	21,851	11,033	0	(43,501)	964,906	1,024,895	1,103,256	1,135,670
3	68	67	2018	(78,676)	22,069	11,144	0	(45,464)	947,026	1,028,402	1,137,127	1,182,874
4	69	68	2019	(81,037)	22,290	11,255	0	(47,492)	926,520	1,029,956	1,171,358	1,231,889
5	70	69	2020	(83,468)	22,513	11,368	0	(49,588)	903,240	1,029,387	1,205,903	1,282,797
6	71	70	2021	(85,972)	22,738	11,481	0	(51,753)	877,032	1,026,516	1,240,711	1,335,683
7	72	71	2022	(88,551)	22,965	11,596	0	(53,990)	847,734	1,021,153	1,275,726	1,390,638
8	73	72	2023	(91,207)	23,195	11,712	0	(56,301)	815,176	1,013,094	1,310,882	1,447,756
9	74	73	2024	(93,944)	23,427	11,829	0	(58,688)	779,183	1,002,127	1,346,109	1,507,139
10	75	74	2025	(96,762)	23,661	11,947	0	(61,154)	739,570	988,022	1,381,327	1,568,894
11	76	75	2026	(99,665)	23,898	12,067	0	(63,700)	696,146	970,538	1,416,449	1,633,135
12	77	76	2027	(102,655)	24,137	12,188	0	(66,331)	648,710	949,418	1,451,377	1,699,983
13	78	77	2028	(105,734)	24,378	12,309	0	(69,047)	597,053	924,389	1,486,005	1,769,565
14	79	78	2029	(108,906)	24,622	12,433	0	(71,852)	540,957	895,164	1,520,214	1,842,018
15	80	79	2030	(112,174)	24,868	12,557	0	(74,749)	480,194	861,436	1,553,875	1,917,488
16	81	80	2031	(115,539)	25,117	12,682	0	(77,740)	414,528	822,881	1,586,845	1,996,126
17	82	81	2032	(119,005)	25,368	12,809	0	(80,828)	343,711	779,155	1,618,968	2,078,099
18	83	82	2033	(122,575)	25,621	12,937	0	(84,016)	267,485	729,896	1,650,073	2,163,579
19	84	83	2034	(126,252)	25,878	13,067	0	(87,308)	185,583	674,717	1,679,973	2,252,754
20	85	84	2035	(130,040)	26,136	13,197	0	(90,706)	97,723	613,212	1,708,462	2,345,822
21	86	85	2036	(133,941)	26,398	13,329	0	(94,214)	3,614	544,948	1,735,316	2,442,995
22	87	86	2037	(137,959)	26,662	13,463	0	(97,835)	(0)	469,468	1,760,292	2,544,499
23	88	87	2038	(142,098)	26,928	13,597	0	(101,573)	(0)	386,290	1,783,124	2,650,575
24	89	88	2039	(146,361)	27,198	13,733	0	(105,430)	(0)	294,903	1,803,521	2,761,482
25	90	89	2040	(150,752)	27,470	13,871	0	(109,412)	(0)	194,766	1,821,167	2,877,496
26	91	90	2041	(155,275)	27,744	14,009	0	(113,521)	(0)	85,307	1,835,720	2,998,913
27	92	91	2042	(159,933)	28,022	14,149	0	(117,762)	(0)	(0)	1,846,805	3,126,049
28	93	92	2043	(164,731)	28,302	14,291	0	(122,138)	(0)	(0)	1,854,017	3,259,244
29	94	93	2044	(169,673)	28,585	14,434	0	(126,654)	(0)	(0)	1,856,915	3,398,860
30	95	94	2045	(174,763)	28,871	14,578	0	(131,314)	(0)	(0)	1,855,022	3,545,288

Chapter Eight

R

The Number

THE NUMBER

This book used the retirement of John and Mary to illustrate the interplay between assets and retirement income over time. Now, this book will focus on YOU.

Every individual should have a *target retirement number*. Your number is the **minimum amount of money you will need at retirement to provide the income you want, for as long as you need it**.

Achieving this number should be the goal of everyone, especially participants in a retirement plan.

RETIREMENT RULE OF 4%

repetitio est mater studiorum

When planning retirement income, many professionals use a simple rule of thumb. The rule states: Take no more than 4% from your portfolio in any given year.

If a diversified portfolio earns 7.5%, and a retiree draws 4%, this leaves additional funds to accumulate. This helps offset future inflation. With normal, long-term investment returns, this strategy can allow portfolio assets and income to increase over time.

There is an easy way to test this strategy. Choose a balanced mutual fund, or a diversified mix of funds, from any well-established mutual fund company. Make sure the fund has been in existence for thirty years or more. Use the mutual fund website (or your advisor) to run a hypothetical retirement illustration, starting at least thirty years ago. Set the illustration to withdraw 4% of the portfolio value each year and see what the numbers say. Long-term past performance might give you a reasonable idea of future performance. Past performance is no true guarantee of future performance, but it's the most important clue we've got. Now, run the same illustration using a 5% withdrawal. See the difference? It can be dramatic.

The following is an actual, historical illustration of a well-known balanced fund. There was a $1,000,000 deposit in year 1. Each year a 4% withdrawal was taken from the fund. If you run an illustration, you should get a table showing year-by-year returns and withdrawals. You should also get a chart that looks like the one on the next page.

Over the course of thirty years, this balanced fund would have returned $3,952,376 in income. Income in year thirty was $228,262. This is far more than the initial, 4% withdrawal of $40,000. The final fund value was $6,105,499. This fund would have generated $10,057,875 of income & principal in thirty years. Not bad.

Please note: The average return for this fund was more than 11%. This return should *not* be expected in the next thirty years. Your future experience could be far different. Much of your result will depend upon what happens in the early years of your retirement.

When ten-year rolling averages are analyzed, the worst average ten-year return for this fund was about 4%. If this had occurred during the first decade of retirement, the total returns illustrated here would have been significantly lower.

Hypothetical Example
Using Actual Mutual Fund
$1,000,000 invested on 12/31/1985
4% of year-end value withdrawn each year,
beginning 12/31/1986.

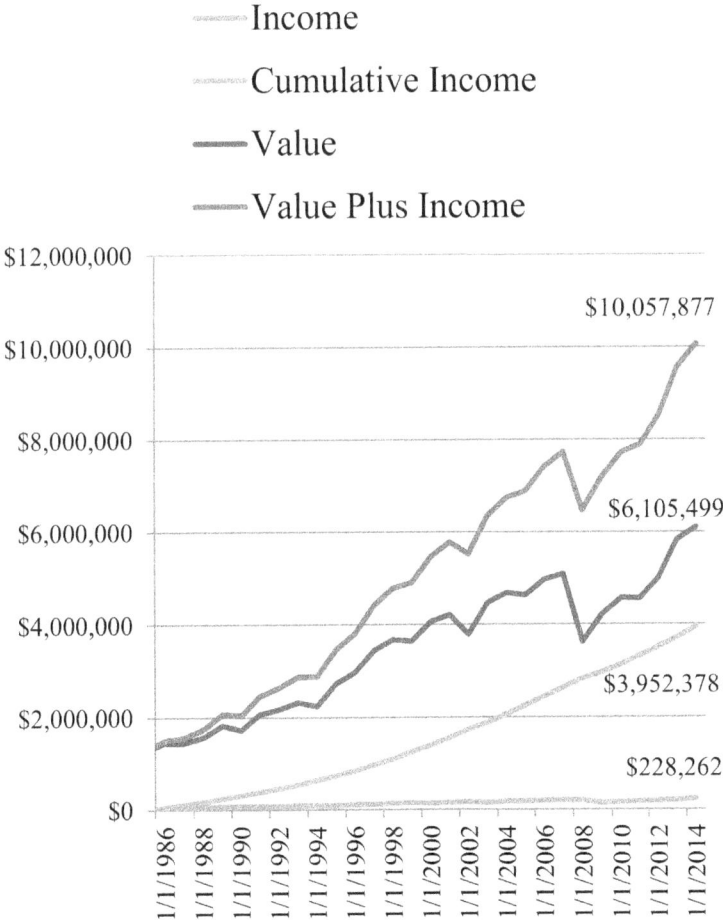

Income

Cumulative Income

Value

Value Plus Income

Down market years can happen at any time. That is why it is critical to limit withdrawal percentages.

By limiting withdrawals to 4%, and earning historical, long-term diversified investment returns, an individual should have a reasonable chance of not outliving their money.

There are many variables that can change return expectations. As of this writing, bond yields are historically low. This is primarily due to loose monetary policy, implemented to stimulate the economy, shore up the banking system and avoid recession. The stock market has been positive, but volatile. Dividends are below historical norms. Welcome to world of investing. Things are never "normal."

CRITICAL CHOICE

Everyone should make a choice, a critical decision that can determine their security in retirement. Everyone should create a target, a real-dollar number.

4% is the safe place to limit income. In the case of John and Mary, this would have initially produced a retirement income of about $72,000 per year (including Social Security) to begin. But John and Mary would not have been able to maintain this income with inflation.

With average investment returns, a beginning income of $57,200 would keep them within 4% each year, for the remainder of their retirement. The difference occurs because Social Security represents a sizable portion of John and Mary's income. Social Security is projected to grow at just 1%. This is lower than the projected inflation of 3%.

Over time, John and Mary will increasingly rely on their investments for income. The percentage of income they must draw from their portfolio will grow. Therefore, John and Mary must increase their investment assets in the early years of their retirement, so money will be there when they need it.

John and Mary chose to budget $57,200 per year. This will allow them to maintain their lifestyle (with a few sacrifices), and still create a safety cushion for their money to grow.

If you want a safety cushion, you must accumulate more, or plan to live on less.

RETIREMENT ACCUMULATION GOAL

With 4% as a target withdrawal, each individual's retirement number should be approximately *25 times* the desired retirement income. (25 x 4% = 100%) This is *the number*.

For example: If you need your investments to produce $100,000 per year, you will need $2.5 million when you retire ($100,000 x 25). This would be *your* number. 4% of $2.5 million is $100,000.

Remember that your number (target accumulation) must be adjusted for inflation and other income sources, like Social Security. You will need to earn about 7.5% per year on your retirement assets to match inflation. We will examine how to make adjustments shortly.

CALCULATING YOUR NUMBER

This book has presented a data/profile example for John and Mary.

Now let's create your profile.

To calculate a retirement accumulation number, you must:

- *Determine the investable assets you currently own.* This should exclude your home, if you have one.

- *Deduct* major *expected future expenses* from your investable assets. Such expenses might be a new car, home improvements, education expenses, and wedding expenses.

- Add annual savings to investable assets each year.

- Assume an expected rate of return on investment assets

until retirement. This amount may be greater in the early years and less as retirement approaches. With less time to retirement, investors tend to grow more conservative.

NOTE TO EMPLOYERS:

A 401(k) PLAN ALSO HAS A NUMBER

The target number for a 401(k) plan is the cumulative numbers of your employees. Talk to your financial advisors and plan provider about calculating a number for your plan.

VARIABLES TO THE NUMBER

The 4% rule is a simple, but viable target. This target can be affected by many outside factors. For example, someone who wants to retire at 55 will need more at that age than someone who plans to work until age 70. Low investment returns will also increase the number. Below, you will find some of the variables that may be considered when fine-tuning one's number, and determining an investment strategy. A qualified financial advisor can help you model how these factors might alter your target number.

LIFESTYLE

Timing of Retirement - What Target Age?

Lifestyle in Retirement

Inflation Assumptions

Tax Projections

Current Savings/Investment Rate

Years In Retirement

Non-qualified Assets (taxed differently than qualified assets)

Qualified Assets (no current taxation)

Health

Married or Not

Leave Money for Children?

Long-term Care Needs

Fifteen Percent—This is the minimum amount that everyone should save annually.

Eighty Percent — Try to plan on an inflation-adjusted income that represents 80% of your pre-retirement income.

INVESTMENTS:

Rate of Return Assumptions

Risk Tolerance

Long, Short, Mid-term Risk

Dollar Cost Averaging

Stocks

Bonds

Mutual Funds

Inflation

Chances of Outpacing Inflation By Asset Class

Bucket Theory (Invest money in five-year buckets. Assets to be used in the next five years are kept very safe. Those to be used in years 5-10 are invested for more growth. Assets needed for years 10-15 are invested more aggressively, and so on.)

This book will teach you how to make good estimations for the assets and income you will need for retirement. This book can get you close—by using reasonable assumptions. Further fine-tuning is up to you.

NUMBER EXAMPLE:

Let's assume that I am 35 years old. I want to retire at age 65. I earn $100,000 per year and would like to maintain my lifestyle when I retire. (Note: If you are earning $50,000 per year, you can divide these numbers in half. If you earn $30,000/year, multiply these numbers by .3, and so on.)

My number is a function of my target income, the number of years I wish to receive that income, an assumed inflation rate, and a rate of return to retirement, and a more conservative rate of return once retirement begins.

RETIREMENT INCOME PERCENTAGE

When I reach retirement age, I should be able to live on about 80% of my pre-retirement income. Any children are probably out of the house. I'm usually throwing out more stuff than I am buying. I'm done saving for retirement. I can live on less.

If I want to travel the world in first class hotels, I will need more than 80% of my pre-retirement income. If I have large medical expenses, or need long-term care, I will need to adjust my plan.

This is *your* plan, and you can customize it for your own personal needs.

In this case, I am going to plan for 80% of my $100,000 income. This is an $80,000 retirement income, adjusted for inflation. I will review and manage my plan annually and hope for the best.

INFLATION

In a normally functioning economy, prices increase gradually over time. As this book goes to press, the Federal Reserve is target-ing 2% as its annual inflation goal. www.federalreserve.gov, 2012 Too much or too little inflation will upset our nation's financial balance.

Too much inflation causes large ripples through the economy, as well as government programs like Social Security, Medicare and Medicaid. In the 1960s and 1970s, we faced runaway inflation. In 1980 alone, inflation was 14%. For over two decades, inflation averaged more than 6%.

Lower prices (deflation) are a death knell to any advanced economy. Lower prices cause lower earnings, which mean lower government tax revenues. Servicing our national debt (over $18 trillion at this time) would become impossible with sustained deflation. The Federal Reserve would need to print a lot of money to fund the government. This would eventually cause inflation. Inflation is ideal for the government, as long as it is managed.

The long-term U.S. Inflation rate (since 1913) is 3.2%. Source: U.S. Treasury, Inflationdata.com, http://inflationdata.com/Inflation/ Inflation_Rate/HistoricalInflation.aspx.

During the 1970s, inflation averaged 7.06%. In the 1980s, it averaged 5.51%. Since the turn of the 21st century, inflation has averaged a little less than 2.5%. What is your guess for inflation?

Many experts expect inflation to rise soon, resulting from the Federal Reserve's unprecedented monetary stimulation. Other experts think that inflation is substantially tamed. The Fed targets 2%.

This book's calculations plan for 3% inflation—the long-term historical average. If inflation is lower than 3%, you may have a surplus of funds. If inflation returns to its long-term average, you will be right on track.

Hypothetical Example
$80,000 Income With 3% Inflation Over 30 Years

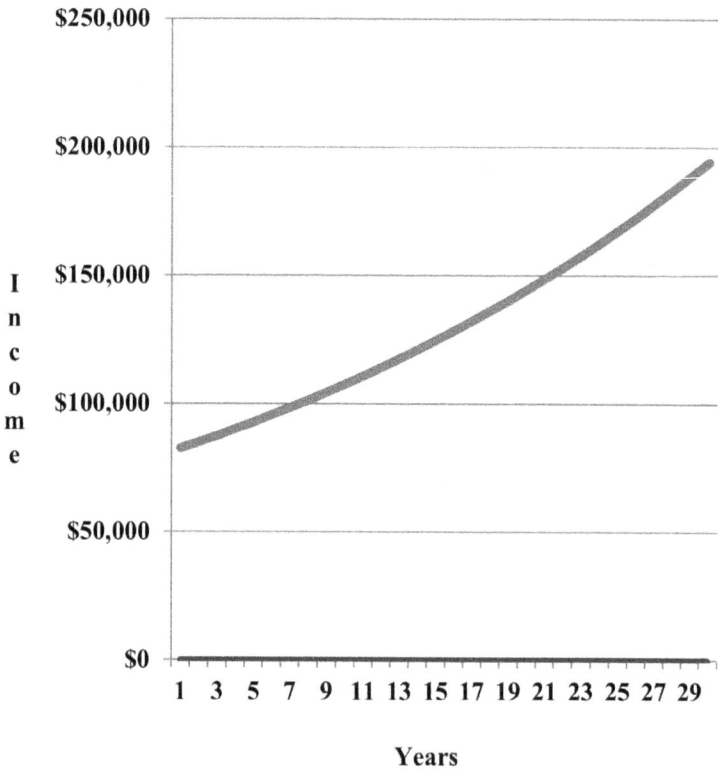

When I retire, I won't need just $80,000 per year in the future. I will need an *inflation-adjusted* $80,000. Assuming a long-term inflation rate of 3%, in 30 years it will take $194,181 to provide the same purchasing power as $80,000 today.

So my *target retirement income* is **$194,181 Per Year.**

My number is twenty-five times my target retirement income. My initial target number is $4,854,525.

Note: The closer you are to retirement, the less inflation will impact your number. For example, if I want to retire today, with $80,000 per year, my number is about $2 million, rather than nearly $5 million.

DON'T PANIC!

The initial number may cause some people to begin hyperventilating. Others will look at this figure and quit planning, even before they start. **Don't panic. And don't quit. You can do this...**at least better than you are right now.

If you are young, this sum *can* be achieved. If you are close to retirement, you will need to make adjustments if you have not saved enough.

REDUCTIONS

My target investment number will be **reduced by the value of Social Security**, any assets I might inherit, and any other fixed income streams I might receive, such as a pension.

HOW LONG?

How long will I need my income? We reviewed how long people live in retirement. Most of us should plan for at least 30 years.

In this example, if I am married, I will need my income for 30 years or more. If I am single, I may shave a few years off this total, depending upon health and family history.

This income will need to increase with inflation. This means that I can't just leave my money in the bank and hope it will be enough. That just won't work.

In order for my investments to last, they must grow over time. This means maintaining a diversified portfolio, with some *risk* still involved. This book has demonstrated the historical, long-term return expectation of a portfolio that consists of a 60/40 mix of stocks and bonds. It has shown what might be expected with a 40/60 mix.

If I don't want to assume investment risk in retirement, I will need far more than 25 times my planned retirement income. We have already seen what happens to John and Mary's million dollar nest egg if they withdraw too much, while earning just 5%. Their money vanishes before they do.

Calculating Your Retirement Need

- Take Your Current Income (Or An Increased Income If Your Earnings Track Is Upward).

- Inflate Your Income To Retirement (Suggestion: Use 3%).

- Retire With 70% - 80% Of Your Inflated Income Amount. (Suggestion: 80%)

- Determine Your Social Security Benefits. (Suggestion: Use No More Than 1% Growth. Younger People Might Consider Planning For No Social Security At All.)

- Determine Any Pension or Other Benefits.

- Make Up Shortfalls With Investments.

    o Grow Your Current Investments at a Rate Of Return. Suggestion: Use no more than 8%. Assume lower rates the closer you are to retirement. 7.5% is a reasonable long-term expectation for a growth-oriented, balanced portfolio.

    o Invest monthly to make up any shortfall.

SUMMARY

In order to maintain my $100,000 lifestyle 30 years from now:

- I will need approximately 80% of my current income annually, adjusted for inflation. This is 194,181.

- I will reduce this by fixed income sources, such as Social Security, pensions & annuities. I may also reduce it by future inheritance amounts.

- I should plan on having this income for at least 30 years.

- My income will need to grow with inflation.

- I must decide whether or not I want to have anything left for my family once I pass away. If I want to leave an inheritance, I must preserve principal. Therefore, I may need more.

- I can make adjustments for expected inheritance amounts. An expected receipt date can be modeled, with planned investment returns.

- The future value of my target income stream, plus anything I want to leave for my family, will help create my final number.

Once I know my number, and what I want to leave my children, it is simple mathematics to determine how to get there.

I know the current investments I have today. I can estimate future Social Security. I will assume a target rate of return, based upon historical averages. **I can now estimate my target value based upon my target retirement date.**

SURPLUS OR SHORTFALL

Once I know my number, I can determine my current surplus or (in most cases) shortfall at retirement.

I make up for any shortfall with *annual contributions* to savings, investments and retirement plans. If I have no savings today, this example shows that I will need to invest 18% of my earnings each year to achieve an inflation-adjusted, $80,000/year in retirement. This means an $18,000 deposit in year one. I increase my savings along with inflation, and invest it at 7.5% per year.

Few employees have accumulated enough toward retirement. This is why retirement plans, like a 401(k), are so valuable.

In a few pages, this book will help you determine how much you need to save each month to achieve your personal goal.

Before we do that, let's get back to John and Mary, and see how investing *in* retirement can affect our planning.

Example: Calculating Retirement Income At Age 65 $57,200/Yr.

SOURCES

INVESTMENTS AFTER SOCIAL SECURITY

Social Security
$1,785/mo
$910/mo

$415,000 Present Value

Monthly
Income
$5,417/mo

Pension
$0

$ 1,015,000

$15,000

$10,000

$5,000

$0

$1,015,000 for Investing

Investments
$1,015,000

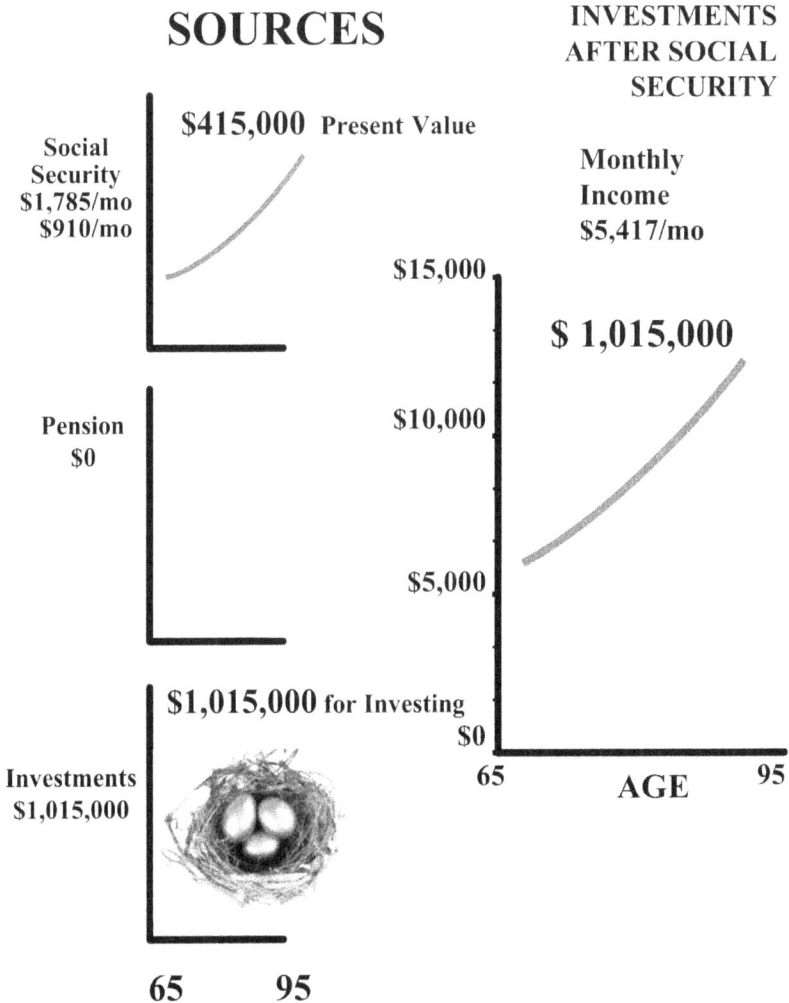

65   95

65   AGE   95

65   95

SEE HOW LONG WILL THE MONEY LAST CALCULATIONS

John and Mary have investable, retirement assets of $1,015,000. They also have Social Security income. Each item has a value today. Assets have a stated value. Income has *present value*.

John and Mary's retirement income will come from both sources, Social Security plus income from their assets.

When planning, it can be helpful to treat income and assets in the same manner. By creating an "apples to apples" comparison, the assets can be combined to determine our target *number*.

PRESENT VALUE

Any income stream can be converted to what is called a *discounted present value*. The present value of an income stream is the *lump sum of cash that it would take, today, to provide the promised future income.*

The present value formula is a function of age, the income benefit (which may include inflation adjustments) and rate of return assumptions. This calculation will help you estimate the current value of an income stream, such as Social Security.

The preceding chart shows the financial picture of John and Mary. In year-two, both John and Mary will have full Social Security benefits—of $1,785 & $910 per month, or $32,558/year. The discounted present value of John and Mary's income stream is approximately $415,000. In other words, if they had $415,000 of cash, it would provide the same income stream as John and Mary's Social Security benefits. The present value figured is estimated by taking John & Mary's combined Social Security income ($32,558) and projecting it with 1% annual increases for 33 years. An annual discount rate of 7% is factored into these calculations. You can run your own free calculations at the NYU Stern School of Business website:

http://people.stern.nyu.edu/igiddy/calculators/financialcalculators.htm

John and Mary also have $1,015,000 in investments.

John and Mary's final retirement goal of $57,200 works out to $4,767 per month.

If we add the investment assets of $1,015,000 to the present value of Social Security assets ($415,000), John and Mary have achieved a "number" of $1,430,000. 4% of this number is $57,200 per year. 5% of this number is $71,500 per year.

Historical analysis demonstrates that taking 5% does have a possibility of getting John and Mary through retirement. But there is still a plausible chance that John and Mary would go broke. This depends upon their returns, which are subject to chance because investments are unpredictable. They chose a more conservative 4% income withdrawal from their portfolio.

This book will show you how to make your own calculations by hand. It will also teach you how to use the free, Yahoo Finance calculator to make alternative calculations.

These calculations will provide an estimate only. Financial advisors have access to more sophisticated software. This can help you design a more comprehensive financial plan that adjusts over time.

PLANNING ONLY AS GOOD AS YOUR ASSUMPTIONS

Many things in finance are not guaranteed—inflation, investment returns, Social Security... Planning is only as good as your assumptions and your actual investment returns. Approximations can be enough to give you a good idea of how much you need to save and invest for your retirement. Sometimes, this works out better than a detailed analysis with incorrect assumptions. Don't overinflate your returns or underestimate expenses and inflation in retirement.

PROJECTING SOCIAL SECURITY BENEFITS

Projecting Social Security benefits can be easy. It can also be complicated. The challenge is making the right assumptions. Here is the problem: Nobody knows the future of Social Security payments. You have seen the present value of all U.S. promises, plus its current debt profile. Our country's promises are massive. Where do you think Social Security increases will rank in federal importance, especially once the nation's IOU has been depleted?

The following Web address will bring you to the government's Social Security Quick Calculator.

http://www.socialsecurity.gov/OACT/quickcalc/index.html

Here, you can enter your current income. The calculator will project your Social Security income at retirement. You can choose to calculate this benefit in "today's dollars," or in "future dollars." The future dollars calculation assumes that your pay will increase over time, and that all "promised" benefits will be paid. This assumes future inflation increases, no change in eligibility dates and no future means testing. This is highly optimistic, probably unrealistic.

BENEFIT STATEMENT

From time to time, the Social Security Administration will send "benefit statements." The benefit statement shows your credited work history and your projected Social Security benefits. You can request a statement at any time. You may also establish an online account with Social Security by going to the following Web address:

http://socialsecurity.gov/myaccount/?utm_source=google&utm_medium=cpc&utm_content=my-social-security&utm_campaign=CM-myss-14&gclid=CIr9n7vd6cQCFVY8gQodib4AkQ

BE CAUTIOUS

This book reviewed how the United States is in debt. It explored the flaws in Social Security's design. There is no money saved for you, and there are few people supporting beneficiaries. When deciding what benefits to expect from Social Security, choose a conservative number. Your most optimistic assumption should be something between the "current" and the "projected" results.

If you are just beginning your career, you might not want to rely on Social Security at all. Remember, your Social Security income will be paid by the employees of the future. Intelligent robots, working twenty years from now, may rebel against paying into the Social Security system.

You can also use Yahoo Finance to project your Social Security benefits. If you follow this link, it will take you to the Yahoo calculator.

http://finance.yahoo.com/calculator/retirement/ret04/

With the Yahoo calculator, you can choose a Social Security inflation rate. The default rate is 2.5%. If you enter 1% instead, you may get a *more realistic benefit figure*. There was no increase in 2016 benefits.

If you accumulate enough to retire using a low Social Security inflation figure, you will have a better chance of maintaining your investments in retirement. This would allow you to invest more conservatively in retirement. This will lower the volatility and the risk of your portfolio.

DEFINED BENEFIT

If you are enrolled in a defined benefit pension plan, you should ask your benefit administrator to prepare a retirement projection. A defined benefit plan is designed to pay an income stream in lieu of a fixed sum at retirement. Some plans allow the annuity stream to be converted to a lump-sum payment. This sum is determined by the *present value* of your future income, as outlined in the plan document. A companion book entitled, *Making Cent$ of Retirement Plans*, explains such plans in greater detail.

Once you have calculated your fixed income sources in retirement, you will be able to determine your investment needs. You can then calculate how much you should save annually, and what rate of return you will need on your investments until, and during retirement.

YAHOO EXAMPLE:

The following example illustrates an individual planning for retirement. This person:

- Is age 35.

- Earns $80,000/year.

- Wants to retire with 80% of current income, adjusted for inflation.

- Plans to earn 7.5% on investments until retirement.

- Plans to earn 5.5% on investments during retirement.

- Assumes Social Security grows at 1%, not the projected 2.5% inflated rate.

- Plans to live for 30 years.

Here is the Yahoo Finance Web address:

http://finance.yahoo.com/calculator/retirement/ret02/

This link will bring you to a screen that looks like what you see on the next page. Many of the questions are self-explanatory.

You don't want to spend years saving, only to find out you didn't save enough. This book includes suggestions that can help you avoid that crisis. Use the following suggestions as a starting point.

After you enter your data, you will receive a three-page illustration similar to the one printed after the data entry page. These three pages show the Yahoo results.

Yahoo Finance calculates that our sample individual needs to save 14.6% of income to achieve The Number. Remember, this illustration assumes that you will spend your last dollar on the day you die. There is little "wiggle room" here. If you want more safety, you will need to save more or earn more.

Yahoo Finance:
Simplified Retirement Calculator
(How much to save for retirement)

- Retirement Information and Assumptions

- Your current age: Use Age 35.

- Current annual income: Use $80,000.

- Spouse's annual income (if applicable):

- Current retirement savings: Enter your own investment total.

- Expected inflation: (Suggestion: Use At Least 3%.)

- Desired retirement age: (Suggestion: Age 67. Beware of Social Security Limitations.)

- Number of years of retirement income: (Suggestion: If Married or Female, Plan For At Least 30 Years.)

- Income replacement at retirement: (Suggestion: 80%)

- Pre-retirement investment return: (Suggestion: 7.5%, No More Than 8%)

- Post-retirement investment return: (Suggestion: 5.5%, No More Than 7.5%)

- Include Social Security (SS) benefits? Yes (Suggestion: Try Planning Without Social Security. Then Run With Projected Income From Social Security Website.)

- Marital status (For SS purposes only) Married Or Single

- Social Security override amount: (Suggestion: Run With Projected Income From Social Security Website.)

- Social Security Override: (Use a figure between current and projected. Monthly amount in today's dollars. This example uses $1855.)

The Calculator Can Be Found At This Web Address:
http://finance.yahoo.com/calculator/retirement/ret02/

HOW MUCH WILL I NEED TO SAVE FOR RETIREMENT?   YAHOO! FINANCE

Date: March 11, 2015

INTRODUCTION

Retirement can be the saddest or happiest day of your life. This pre-retirement calculator will help you determine how well you have prepared and what you can do to improve your retirement outlook. It is important that you re-evaluate your preparedness on an ongoing basis. Changes in economic climate, inflation, achievable returns, and in your personal situation will impact your plan.

ANALYSIS

To provide the inflation-adjusted retirement income you desire, you may need to save 14.6% of your yearly income (less any employer match, if applicable). This year, for example, the amount would be $11,671 or $973 a month. The total amount needed for retirement, including amounts already saved, is $2,078,898.

If you wait just one year to start saving for retirement you may need to save 16% of your annual income, which amounts to $12,760 in the first year. Save Now and Save Less!!!

Retirement Analysis

Legend: Retirement Balance, Retirement Income

Age	Annual Salary increasing @ 3%	Beginning Retirement Balance	Earnings Pre-Ret 7.5% Post-Ret 5.5%	Estimated Annual Savings	Retirement Income Replace 80%	Annual Social Security Income	Annual Retirement Account Withdrawal	Ending Retirement Balance
37	$80,000	$50,000	$3,750	$11,671	$0	$0	$0	$65,421
38	82,400	65,421	4,907	12,021	0	0	0	82,349
39	84,872	82,349	6,176	12,382	0	0	0	100,907
40	87,418	100,907	7,568	12,753	0	0	0	121,229
41	90,041	121,229	9,092	13,136	0	0	0	143,457
42	92,742	143,457	10,759	13,530	0	0	0	167,746
43	95,524	167,746	12,581	13,936	0	0	0	194,263
44	98,390	194,263	14,570	14,354	0	0	0	223,187
45	101,342	223,187	16,739	14,785	0	0	0	254,711
46	104,382	254,711	19,103	15,228	0	0	0	289,043
47	107,513	289,043	21,678	15,685	0	0	0	326,406
48	110,739	326,406	24,480	16,156	0	0	0	367,042
49	114,061	367,042	27,528	16,640	0	0	0	411,211
50	117,483	411,211	30,841	17,140	0	0	0	459,191
51	121,007	459,191	34,439	17,654	0	0	0	511,284
52	124,637	511,284	38,346	18,183	0	0	0	567,814
53	128,377	567,814	42,586	18,729	0	0	0	629,128

Age								
54	132,228	629,128	47,185	19,291	0	0	0	695,604
55	136,195	695,604	52,170	19,869	0	0	0	767,644
56	140,280	767,644	57,573	20,466	0	0	0	845,682
57	144,489	845,682	63,426	21,079	0	0	0	930,188
58	148,824	930,188	69,764	21,712	0	0	0	1,021,664
59	153,288	1,021,664	76,625	22,363	0	0	0	1,120,652
60	157,887	1,120,652	84,049	23,034	0	0	0	1,227,735
61	162,624	1,227,735	92,080	23,725	0	0	0	1,343,540
62	167,502	1,343,540	100,766	24,437	0	0	0	1,468,743
63	172,527	1,468,743	110,156	25,170	0	0	0	1,604,068
64	177,703	1,604,068	120,305	25,925	0	0	0	1,750,299
65	183,034	1,750,299	131,272	26,703	0	0	0	1,908,274
66	188,525	1,908,274	143,121	27,504	0	0	0	2,078,898
67	0	2,078,898	114,339	0	155,345	54,031	101,314	2,091,924
68	0	2,091,924	115,056	0	160,005	55,652	104,353	2,102,626
69	0	2,102,626	115,644	0	164,805	57,321	107,484	2,110,787
70	0	2,110,787	116,093	0	169,749	59,041	110,708	2,116,172
71	0	2,116,172	116,389	0	174,842	60,812	114,030	2,118,531
72	0	2,118,531	116,519	0	180,087	62,637	117,451	2,117,600
73	0	2,117,600	116,468	0	185,490	64,516	120,974	2,113,094
74	0	2,113,094	116,220	0	191,055	66,451	124,603	2,104,711
75	0	2,104,711	115,759	0	196,786	68,445	128,341	2,092,128
76	0	2,092,128	115,067	0	202,690	70,498	132,192	2,075,004
77	0	2,075,004	114,125	0	208,770	72,613	136,157	2,052,971
78	0	2,052,971	112,913	0	215,034	74,791	140,242	2,025,643
79	0	2,025,643	111,410	0	221,485	77,035	144,449	1,992,603
80	0	1,992,603	109,593	0	228,129	79,346	148,783	1,953,414
81	0	1,953,414	107,438	0	234,973	81,727	153,246	1,907,605
82	0	1,907,605	104,918	0	242,022	84,178	157,844	1,854,679
83	0	1,854,679	102,007	0	249,283	86,704	162,579	1,794,108
84	0	1,794,108	98,676	0	256,761	89,305	167,456	1,725,327
85	0	1,725,327	94,893	0	264,464	91,984	172,480	1,647,740
86	0	1,647,740	90,626	0	272,398	94,743	177,655	1,560,711
87	0	1,560,711	85,839	0	280,570	97,586	182,984	1,463,566
88	0	1,463,566	80,496	0	288,987	100,513	188,474	1,355,588
89	0	1,355,588	74,557	0	297,657	103,529	194,128	1,236,018
90	0	1,236,018	67,981	0	306,586	106,635	199,952	1,104,047
91	0	1,104,047	60,723	0	315,784	109,834	205,950	958,819
92	0	958,819	52,735	0	325,258	113,129	212,129	799,425
93	0	799,425	43,968	0	335,015	116,522	218,493	624,901
94	0	624,901	34,370	0	345,066	120,018	225,048	434,223
95	0	434,223	23,882	0	355,418	123,619	231,799	226,306
96	$0	$226,306	$12,447	$0	$366,080	$127,327	$238,753	$0

SUMMARY OF INPUT

Your current age	37	Current annual income	$80,000
Spouse's annual income (if applicable)	$0	Current retirement savings	$50,000

Expected inflation	3.00%	Desired retirement age	67
Number of years of retirement income	30	Income replacement at retirement	80.00%
Pre-retirement investment return	7.50%	Post-retirement investment return	5.50%
Include Social Security (SS) benefits?	Yes	Marital status (For SS purposes only)	Single
Social Security override amount (monthly amount in today's dollars)	$1,655		

$&¢

Chapter Nine

R

The Number: Hand Calculations

NUMBER EXAMPLE

Detailed financial modeling isn't easy. It takes years to fully understand how subtle alterations make significant changes to one's outcome. However, markets are so unpredictable that even fine-tuned plans will go awry. Reasonable estimations can often be as effective as the most sophisticated planning.

The critical part to good long-term planning is the assumptions. If you assume an investment rate of return that is too high, you will never achieve your goals because you won't save enough. If you assume a low rate of return, and achieve better, you will have more money than you expected.

You should have a good understanding of what your financial numbers mean. This way, you will have the best chance to achieve your goals, with a safety cushion.

This book has shown you how to plan online with the Yahoo free calculator. It will now show you how to plan by hand. Nothing teaches better than hands-on experience.

SAMPLE PLAN

This book illustrated financial calculations for a sample individual—age 35, with an income of $100,000. The retirement goal was $80,000 per year.

In thirty years, it will take $194,181 to provide the same living standard as $80,000 today. To achieve this income, our sample individual has a "number" of $4,854,525. This sum, invested in retirement, at 5.5%, should produce the desired income.

This individual must save approximately 18% of income to achieve the number. If this sum is deferred into a 401(k), it will represent a deferral of $18,000 today. This will achieve the target number with a long-term investment return of 7.5%.

An 18% savings rate gives our sample client a reasonable chance of having money throughout life expectancy. If this individual earns more than 7.5% during the accumulation phase, this would reduce the required contributions. If this individual earns more than 5.5% in retirement, it would reduce today's required saving amount. Alternatively, higher returns could produce a more comfortable retirement.

If there is no employer match, 18% must be saved annually.

If the individual is married, $18,000 in savings may be achieved with each spouse saving a portion of the total. If each spouse earns the same, they may each defer 9% and achieve the accumulation goal.

An employer match of 3%, for one spouse, would leave a shortfall of 6% for that spouse. If the other spouse's plan has a 3% match, the out-of-pocket needed will be reduced again. With equal incomes and a 3% match, each spouse must defer 6% of their pay to achieve the number needed to produce an inflation-adjusted $80,000 income in retirement. Anything more would help our sample employees overfund their retirement savings.

In an effectively designed 401(k), average employee deferrals of 12% are quite normal.

Now let's learn how to make these calculations by hand.

HANDS ON EXPERIENCE—A NEW EXAMPLE

There is nothing that will help someone understand complicated retirement concepts better than hands-on experience.

YAHOO EXAMPLE BY HAND

Yahoo Finance calculated the monthly investments needed to achieve a retirement goal for someone, age 35, earning $80,000 today. This resulted in a target investment number of $2,078,898. The annual savings needed was $11,671, or 14.6%.

Now, we will do this on paper. As you do your own calculations, you will develop a better idea of how the process works.

Our hand calculations will be made for the same individual, age 35, with a current income of $80,000.

These calculations should help you obtain results similar to those you receive from Yahoo Finance, or approximate quick calculations that might be prepared by a highly-skilled financial advisor. Hands-on calculations will help you take something that is theoretical and make it more tangible and real.

Let's begin. This example illustrates an individual, age 35, with a current income of $80,000.

- Choose a target date for your retirement. Follow this link and you will find the date when you can retire with full Social Security benefits.
  http://www.socialsecurity.gov/OACT/ProgData/nra.html

  For example, if you were born in 1957, you can receive full Social Security benefits at age 66 1/2.

- Choose your retirement date. This gives you a *target date*.

- Go to the **Factor One Table** (just a few pages ahead). Take your *target retirement income* and multiply it by the *factor* next to the *number of years* you have left until retirement.

This example uses current earned income as the initial target retirement income.

Factor One increases retirement need at an inflation rate of 3%.

In our example, we are planning for retirement thirty years from now. The Factor One Table yields a factor of 2.43. If our target income at retirement is $80,000, we will need $194,400 in thirty years to provide the same benefit.

- We now *reduce* this figure by *20%* in retirement. To get this, we multiply our adjusted retirement income by 80% (.8). This gives us our retirement figure (80% of our pre-retirement income) equal to $155,520.

- Now we *subtract* our annual *Social Security* and/or *retirement benefits from this sum*.

  http://www.socialsecurity.gov/OACT/quickcalc/index.html

If you know your projected monthly Social Security benefit, multiply this figure by 12 to get your *annual benefit*. We discussed how to determine and adjust your Social Security benefits just a few pages back. The above link will get you to the Social Security Quickcalc calculator.

Try to be conservative with your estimations. Congress has been moving the goalposts on Social Security. Full retirement benefits used to be earned by age 65. Now, if you were born after 1959, you will need to wait to age 67 for full benefits. This is important, especially if you have many years to retirement. Consider adjusting the Social Security calculations downward to prepare for future benefit reductions. This illustration assumes 3% annual benefit increases in retirement, so start with a conservative number.

- Once we subtract Social Security and pensions from our adjusted target income, we will get the *income shortfall* to be made up by investments.

- Now *multiply* this *income shortfall* by a *number between 20 and 25*.

  Multiplication by 25 means that you will be taking *4%* per year from your portfolio in retirement. This figure has been used as a useful rule-of-thumb for decades, as a way to maintain long-term solvency in retirement.

  By taking withdrawals greater than 4%, you will increase the risk of depleting principal. If you multiply by 20, you will be taking 5% from your portfolio. This leaves you little room for error, and will require that you assume greater risk with your investments in retirement.

- Use a factor of 25 in your planning. It is more conservative and safer. Don't use a multiplication factor less than 20 (an income withdrawal in excess of 5% of principal). This is asking for trouble.

- When you *multiply your income shortfall by 25*, you will get the target amount that you will need to achieve to produce your retirement goals.

- If you have current investments, these should grow over time. This book's calculations assume an after-tax growth rate of 7.5%. To achieve this, you must invest for growth. This usually means having a portfolio with *at least* 60% stocks.

- *Multiply your existing investment assets by the appropriate figure from Factor Two*.

  This will be the number beside the *number of years* you have until retirement. The result gives you an *accumulation amount for your existing investments at retirement*.

Make sure to invest your assets for long-term balanced growth. If you put your money in the bank, it will lose to inflation. Our example assumes $50,000 in current investments. At 7.5%, these assets would grow to $437,500 by year thirty. This should require a portfolio with at least 60% stocks.

Now, **subtract this figure from your adjusted accumulation goal.** This gives you the amount you must achieve with your ongoing investments. Our example gives us a target of **$2,100,500.**

- Now, all you need to know is how much to save each month.

- **Divide your target amount by Factor 3.** This assumes a monthly investment, earning a return of 7.5% per year. If you plan to retire in 30 years, you would use a growth factor of 145.89.

- Our example gives an **annual savings goal** of $14,398 per year to reach our retirement objective. This is 18% of an $80,000 income.

A higher investment growth rate would reduce the annual savings need. So would a company match and spousal deferrals.

A husband and wife could defer 9% each and achieve the target amount. Employer matching contributions would lower the target minimum deferrals.

SUMMARY OF STEPS

$80,000 INCOME: Simplified Retirement Planning Calculations – Target Income & Shortfall With 4% Annual Withdrawal

- <u>Choose</u> A Target Retirement Income Based Upon Today's Dollars. This may be your current income.

- <u>Choose</u> A Retirement Date. This Example Illustrates A Retirement Date In 30 Years.

- Look At <u>Factor One</u>. <u>Multiply</u> Your Retirement Income By The Inflated Value.

    o Example: $80,000 In 30 Years Would Be $194,400 ($80,000 x 2.43 using Factor One).

- <u>Reduce</u> This Amount By 20% for retirement lifestyle.

    o Example: **$155,520** ($194,400 x .8).

- <u>Subtract</u> Projected Social Security & Pension:

http://www.socialsecurity.gov/oact/ProgData/nra.html

http://www.socialsecurity.gov/OACT/quickcalc/index.html

    o The first Web address will give you the age when you can receive full Social Security benefits. For Example: 1957 – Age 66 and 6 months.

    o Example: $2,243/Mo. x 12 = $26,916 (Projected Social Security Benefits With Current $80,000 Income In 30 Years). This Assumes "**Today's Dollars**," With No Social Security Increases.

- o Example: $6,777/Mo x 12 = $81,324 (Projected Monthly Benefits With Current $80,000 Income In 30 Years). This Assumes "**Future Dollars**" in the Social Security Calculator.

  - Note: With Fewer Than Two Workers Supporting Each Retiree In 2030, Achieving The "Future Dollars" Projection Is Doubtful. Be Conservative In Your Planning.

- o <u>Split</u> The Difference: Example Uses $4,500/Month Social Security, or **$54,000/Year**.

◊ Shortfall: The Income <u>Shortfall</u> That We Must Provide With Investments Is: **$101,520** ($155,520 Target Income - $54,000 Social Security).

- <u>Multiply</u> The Target Shortfall By A Factor Of 20 Or 25 (Using A Factor Of 25 Will Give You A Better Chance Of Keeping Your Assets In Retirement).

- Factor Of 25: $101,520 x 25 = **$2,538,000**

- <u>Multiply</u> Existing Assets By <u>Factor Two.</u>
  - o Assume $50,000 In Investable Assets.
  - o $50,000 Growing At 7.5% /Year For 30 Years Would Become **$437,500** ($50,000 x 8.75).

- The Target Asset Amount From Annual Investments is **$2,100,500** ($2,538,000 <u>minus</u> $437,500).

- <u>Divide</u> The Target Amount By <u>Factor 3</u>. $2,100,500 divided by 145.89 = **$14,398/Year**. (This assumes 3% increases in annual investments, and a 7.5% after tax return on investments).

SIMPLIFIED RETIREMENT PLANNING CAL-
CULATIONS CONTINUED – INVESTING FOR
SHORTFALL (MORE AGGRESSIVE 5% WITH-
DRAWAL WITH HIGHER CHANCE OF DEPLET-
ING ASSETS)

SHORTFALL HAND CALCULATIONS: These calculations assume an accumulation rate of 7.5%
until retirement. They assume a 6.5% return on
assets *in* retirement.

- Target <u>Shortfall</u>: **$101,520/Year** ($155,520 Target
  Income - $54,000 Social Security).

- <u>Multiply</u> Target Shortfall By A Factor Of <u>20</u> Or
  25 (Using A Factor Of 20 Will Give You Less Of A Chance Of
  Keeping Your Assets In Retirement).

- Factor Of 20: $101,520 x 20 = **$2,030,400**

- <u>Multiply</u> Existing Assets By <u>Factor Two.</u>
  - o Assume $50,000 In Investable Assets.
  - o $50,000 Growing At 7.5% /Year For 30 Years
    Would Become **$437,500** ($50,000 x 8.75).

- <u>Subtract</u> assets from target shortfall. The Target Asset Amount From Annual Investments is
  $1,592,900 ($2,030,400 minus $437,500).

- <u>Divide</u> Target Amount By <u>Factor 3</u>.
  $1,592,900/145.89 = **$10,918/Year**. (This assumes 3% increases in annual investments, and a
  7.5% after tax return on investments).

This represents a savings need of 13.6%/year of an $80,000 income.

o The Yahoo Finance calculator produces a savings requirement of $11,671/year. This is a 14.6% savings rate. Yahoo's result comes after adjusting Social Security to the "split the difference" estimate. With Yahoo's savings need of $11,671/year, all assets would be depleted in 30 years with a 5.5% return in retirement.

o The default Social Security amount in the Yahoo illustration is $67,740/year. Using the default calculations for Social Security, Yahoo produces an estimated current savings need of $9,671, or 12.1%.

o No one can predict Social Security or investment returns. If you have many years to retirement, you should rely less on Social Security, as it will become more and more difficult for taxpayers to fund.

If an annual savings goal of $14,398 seems out of reach, you may adjust your calculation formula. If we multiply our shortfall by a multiple of 20 (rather than 25), we end up with annual savings goal of $10,918. This is about $300 per month less into your ongoing investments, and represents a savings rate of 13.6%. This represents the lowest savings rate in this book's recommended range.

If you have a company match, or are married, all of the sources can be added together to achieve your ultimate retirement goal.

With our example, the *Yahoo Finance calculator* comes up with an annual savings amount needed of *$11,671*. This is *after* adjusting Yahoo's Social Security calculation to our "split the difference" figure.

Using Yahoo's full Social Security estimate (2.5% annual growth), the software comes up with an annual savings need of $9,671. This represents a savings rate of 12.1%.

Yahoo makes calculations based upon ***running out of money*** at life expectancy. This also assumes a ***static, 5.5% level investment return***. If you have ever owned stocks, or a mutual fund, you understand that this isn't how the stock market behaves.

Example: If, in the year you enter retirement, there is a stock market fall of 40%, the Yahoo strategy might not work. If all of your investments are in stocks, it will take a future stock market gain of 80%, just to return to your retirement day value. In the meantime, you may be liquidating investments at fire sale prices.

Conversely, if you enjoy a bull market during the first five years of your retirement, you may end up having more than you had hoped.

Investing in retirement can be like rolling dice. Sometimes you win. Sometimes you lose. If you save enough, your portfolio can be designed to remain intact through nearly every financial storm.

SUMMARY:

Calculations reveal that most people need to save somewhere between 12% and 18% of income over their career. A company match and spousal deferrals may reduce this saving need.

Invested at a net return of 7.5%, such annual 401(k) deferrals would allow someone to maintain the same lifestyle as their current income.

Just like John and Mary Smith, you can make choices. You can save at a higher rate and increase the chances of a comfortable retirement. You can invest for greater gains. You can reduce or increase your target retirement income. Repeat these calculations annually. It is like taking the temperature of your retirement health.

Summary Of Steps

Here are the hand steps required to determine your annual savings requirement.

- Choose A Target Retirement Income = X.

- Multiply By Factor One For Your Planned Retirement Year. This gives you your inflation-adjusted retirement income. Example: Multiply By 2.43 Times For A Retirement 30 Years From Now.

- Reduce To 70%, 75% or 80%. This Depends Upon Your Lifestyle Goal: For Example: (2.43 times X) multiplied by .8 gives you the future income required to provide 80% of your current income.

- Subtract Projected Social Security & Pension (2.43 *times* Target Income *times* .8 *minus* Social Security & Pension Income). This gives your income shortfall.

- Multiply Income Shortfall By 20-25 times. The higher the number, the more you will need to save. The more you save, the better your retirement chances (2.43X x .8 – (Social Security & Pension) x 25).

- Multiply Existing Assets By Factor 2. Example: Assets x 8.75 in 30 years.

- Subtract Result of Assets Times Factor: (2.43X x .8) Minus Social Security/Pension x 25 – (Assets times 8.75).

- Divide Target Investment Accumulation By Factor 3. This gives your annual savings need. (Use Factor 4 if you think your income and annual investment savings will be growing faster than inflation. Factor 4 uses 5% growth rather than 3%.)

    o ((2.43X x .8) – Social Security x 25 – (Assets times 8.75)) / 145.89.

What Is Your Number?

Use This Table To Estimate Your Savings & Investment Needs.
Tables 1, 2, 3 Should Be Used For These Calculations

		Multiplication or Subtraction Amount Or Factor	Total
1	**Choose Target Income**		
2	**Multiply By Factor One**		
3	**Reduce By Lifestyle (Multiply by .7, .75 or .8)**		
4	**Subtract Projected Social Security**		
5	**Multiply Shortfall By 20-25**		
6	**Multiply Existing Assets By Factor 2**		
7	**Subtract Results From Step 6 From 5**		
8	**Divide Result By Factor 3**		

Example: Your Number

Example: Individual Earning $80,000/Year. Retiring In 30 Years With 80% Of Income. Goal of 7.5%/Year Investment Returns Until Retirement. Investment Returns of Approximately 6.5% In Retirement Are Needed To Achieve Income Goals. Returns Are Not Guaranteed.

		Multiplication or Subtraction Amount Or Factor	Total
1	**Choose Target Income**	$80,000	$80,000
2	**Multiply By Factor One**	2.43 (30 Years)	$194,400
3	**Reduce By Lifestyle (Multiply by .7, .75 or .8)**	.8 (80% of Current)	$155,520
4	**Subtract Projected Social Security http://www.socialsecurity.gov/cgi-bin/benefit6.cgi**	$54,000 (Using middle of current & projected)	$101,520
5	**Multiply Shortfall By 20-25**	25 (4% Withdrawal)	$2,538,000
6	**Multiply Existing Assets By Factor 2 (Ex. $50,000 x 8.75)**	$437,500 (Grows Current Assets)	− $437,500
7	**Subtract Results From Step 6 From 5**	Target	$2,100,500
8	**Divide Result By Factor 3**	145.89 (Year 30)	Savings Need $14,398/Yr

The preceding table shows the summary of simple steps to determine your retirement number.

The blank table is designed to help you make *your* plan. Make copies and try different retirement scenarios. Choose the strategy that is best for you.

The completed table is filled in using our $80,000 example. You can practice by doing the math, and using the tables with the sample case. See if you can get the numbers to match. If you earn $40,000 per year, your target number would be 50% of this total.

Once you understand the concepts, it will be easy to create planning strategies for yourself, by using the What Is Your Number page.

Conduct this exercise regularly. This will keep you on target with your savings and investments.

Remember: A financially secure retirement doesn't happen by accident. It is a decision. The earlier you plan, the more successful you will become.

The most important part of planning is your *assumptions*. Assuming high rates of return before, and during, retirement will decrease your projected savings requirement. If you plan by using high return figures, you will decrease the chance of reaching your financial goals.

Factor One
Inflation Multiplier For Retirement Calculations: Illustrates Inflation At 3%.

Years	Multiplier	Years	Multiplier
1	1.03	26	2.16
2	1.06	27	2.22
3	1.09	28	2.29
4	1.13	29	2.36
5	1.16	30	2.43
6	1.19	31	2.50
7	1.23	32	2.58
8	1.27	33	2.65
9	1.30	34	2.73
10	1.34	35	2.81
11	1.38	36	2.90
12	1.43	37	2.99
13	1.47	38	3.07
14	1.51	39	3.17
15	1.56	40	3.26
16	1.60	41	3.36
17	1.65	42	3.46
18	1.70	43	3.56
19	1.75	44	3.67
20	1.81	45	3.78
21	1.86	46	3.90
22	1.92	47	4.01
23	1.97	48	4.13
24	2.03	49	4.26
25	2.09	50	4.38

FACTOR ONE

Factor One illustrates inflation at 3%. Every year, goods and services grow more expensive. The United States' long-term inflation rate is right around 3%. This is the figure used here, and a good one for your planning.

Factor One shows what things will cost in the future, with a 3% inflation rate. For example, in ten years, it will take $134 to buy what $100 buys today.

In recent years, inflation has been slightly lower than 3%. This is normal during times of low economic growth and the early stages of loose monetary policies. As growth expands, wages and prices normally increase. This creates more money vying for the available goods and services. This drives prices upward. As the economy responds to monetary stimulus, inflation occurs.

During recent years, the Federal Reserve has "printed" a great deal of money. The "Fed" has been purchasing government debt, and stimulating the economy with historically low interest rates. These policies usually stimulate an economy. Growth in the money supply normally causes inflation, as the economy recovers and expands.

The future of inflation is anybody's guess. The U.S. government has significant long-term incentives to maintain price, wage and inflation growth. We owe $18 trillion and growing. We have over four times that amount in unfunded promises. If this debt gets repaid with inflated dollars, it will cost the taxpayers less in "real money."

The U.S. Federal Reserve has set a target inflation rate of 2%. Unfortunately, many factors that can cause inflation (such as budget deficits) are out of the Fed's control. You should plan for inflation. It isn't going away.

Factor Two
Growth Of Existing Investments At 7.5%

Years	Multiplier	Years	Multiplier
1	1.08	26	6.56
2	1.16	27	7.05
3	1.24	28	7.58
4	1.34	29	8.14
5	1.44	30	8.75
6	1.54	31	9.41
7	1.66	32	10.12
8	1.78	33	10.88
9	1.92	34	11.69
10	2.06	35	12.57
11	2.22	36	13.51
12	2.38	37	14.52
13	2.56	38	15.61
14	2.75	39	16.79
15	2.96	40	18.04
16	3.18	41	19.40
17	3.42	42	20.85
18	3.68	43	22.42
19	3.95	44	24.10
20	4.25	45	25.90
21	4.57	46	27.85
22	4.91	47	29.94
23	5.28	48	32.18
24	5.67	49	34.60
25	6.10	50	37.19

FACTOR TWO

Factor Two is used to project the growth of your existing investments until retirement.

Factor Two can help you estimate the ultimate value of your current investments on your target retirement date. Multiply (the total of) your existing investments by the multiplier beside the number of years you have until retirement. You will subtract this total from your initial target number. This gives you the amount that you must accumulate with your ongoing investments.

Note: Factor Two projects investment growth at 7.5% after taxes. This illustrates a year-end value and is rounded to the nearest tenth of a percent. For example, the factor to the nearest 1000th for year one would be 1.075.

The underlying growth for each year illustrated is 7.5%. The running total is accurate, although the year-end factor gets adjusted slightly by rounding. This is a minor adjustment that won't materially affect your planning numbers.

Factor Three
Investing $83.33/Month ($1,000/Yr.)
Increase Investments By 3%/Yr.

Year	Growth Factor	Year	Growth Factor
1	1.04	26	101.42
2	2.18	27	111.27
3	3.45	28	121.92
4	4.84	29	133.44
5	6.37	30	145.89
6	8.05	31	159.35
7	9.89	32	173.89
8	11.91	33	189.61
9	14.12	34	206.58
10	16.53	35	224.91
11	19.17	36	244.69
12	22.04	37	266.05
13	25.17	38	289.10
14	28.59	39	313.98
15	32.30	40	340.81
16	36.34	41	369.76
17	40.73	42	400.97
18	45.50	43	434.64
19	50.68	44	470.93
20	56.30	45	510.06
21	62.39	46	552.24
22	69.00	47	597.70
23	76.16	48	646.69
24	83.92	49	699.48
25	92.33	50	756.36

FACTOR THREE

Factor Three is used to project the accumulation of monthly investments made toward retirement. Factor Three uses the same 7.5% growth rate.

Factor Three takes current monthly investments and accumulates them at a level return of 7.5% per year. This factor also assumes that you will increase your savings/investment amount with inflation, at 3% per year.

If you multiply your Current Monthly Investment by the Growth Factor beside the number of years to retirement, you will see your final total.

Note: You may notice that the factor for year one is only 1.04, versus 1.08 in Factor Two. This happens because only part of your annual investments are working for you during the year. This is because you are making investments monthly, not annually. For example, only 1/12th of your annual investment amount earns a return in month one.

The factor totals are rounded to the nearest 10th of 1% (the nearest 1000th).

From this table, you can see that $1 invested this way each month, at 7.5% per year, will grow to $145.89 in thirty years.

Factor Four
Investing $83.33/Month ($1,000/Yr.)
Increase Investments By 5%/Yr.

Year	Growth Factor	Year	Growth Factor
1	1.03	26	90.25
2	2.15	27	98.40
3	3.39	28	107.15
4	4.75	29	116.53
5	6.23	30	126.57
6	7.85	31	137.33
7	9.62	32	148.85
8	11.54	33	161.17
9	13.63	34	174.36
10	15.90	35	188.46
11	18.37	36	203.54
12	21.04	37	219.65
13	23.93	38	236.87
14	27.06	39	255.26
15	30.44	40	274.89
16	34.09	41	295.86
17	38.04	42	318.23
18	42.29	43	342.09
19	46.87	44	367.55
20	51.80	45	394.70
21	57.11	46	423.64
22	62.82	47	454.50
23	68.96	48	487.37
24	75.56	49	522.40
25	82.64	50	559.72

© EJ L

If you are the kind of person that has trouble taking risk with your investments, you might consider using the Factor Four table rather than the Factor Three table. This illustrates the growth of ongoing investments at 5% rather than 7.5%.

Chapter Ten

_____R_____

401(K)

The Creation of 401(k)

In 1978, the U.S. government provided a way for every worker to save part of their salary and avoid current taxation. This benefit is detailed in subsection K of Section 401 of the Internal Revenue Code. This type of plan is known as a 401(k).

401(k) is the retirement plan over which individuals have the most control.

What You Can Do

You have learned how to determine your NUMBER. You know how to calculate your Social Security benefits. You can calculate the monthly deferrals needed (at a 7.5% return) to achieve financial independence.

This book will now review how to invest for retirement. The best place to invest for retirement is in a retirement plan.

repetitio est mater studiorum Repetition is the mother of studies.

There are a number of important concepts that you should understand as you invest for financial independence. Some of these have been reviewed already. Others may be new to you.

Since nearly all employees and business owners have access to a 401(k), or similar type plan, this book reviews 401(k)s in some detail. If your employer does not offer this kind of plan, an IRA will probably be your retirement vehicle of choice. If you are retired, or not currently working, read on. This section is not overly long.

401(k)s are retirement plans. Therefore, they address many of the concepts we have addressed in this book. The following 401(k) bullet points highlight the principal objectives for all retirement plan participants.

If you are eligible for a 401(k), you should:

- Understand The Important Features.
- Know Why It Is Important That You Participate As Soon As Possible.
- Learn How To Prepare & Invest Appropriately.

How To Plan For Retirement:

- With Social Security Uncertain You Must Act Today.
- Retirement Can Last For Many Years. You Should Prepare For A Long Retirement.
- You Should Account For Inflation In Retirement.
- Take A Long-term View Toward Investing.
- Use A Balance Of Investments To Manage Risk.
- Stick To An Asset Allocation. Don't Chase Performance.

These are the guiding principles of retirement investing. Let them guide you on your journey.

We have reviewed the importance of starting your planning today. We explored how inflation impacts your plans. You have learned how to determine your number. Now, let's discuss how to invest your money.

Whenever possible, you should use a 401(k). Here's why:

The Advantages Of A 401(k)-type Plan:

- You can save before you spend.
- Investing is easy and painless. You won't feel it.
- Contributions are *not* subject to Federal Income Taxes.
  Note: You must still pay Social Security and Medicare Taxes.
- Most states do not tax 401(k) contributions.
- Investment gains inside the plan are not subject to current taxation. They will be taxed when withdrawn.
- Your employer may match deposits (deferrals) that you make.
- The investments in the plan are designed to outpace inflation.
- Investment professionals helped choose your plan's investments, from thousands of available options.
- Education and financial advice is often available to help you tailor a savings and investment program that is right for you.

Let Uncle Sam Help Subsidize Your Retirement

Deferrals Into Your Retirement Plan Not Currently Taxed By Federal Or State Government

The Immediate Benefit of Participation:

Saving Outside   vs.   Inside 401(k)

Outside Plan: **Inside Plan:**

$133 Earned*	$133 Earned
$ 33 Taxes	$133 Contributed
$100 Saved	$ 33 25% Company Match
	$166 Saved!

A 66%+ return on your money from day one!

* Assumes a 25% tax bracket. Yours may be lower or higher.

CONGRESS HELPS SUBSIDIZE RETIREMENT PLANS

Deferrals into a 401(k) are not subject to federal or (most) state taxation. Check with your plan's advisor, or with your state, if you are not sure about state tax deferrals.

The preceding page shows the power of saving inside a retirement plan versus saving outside a plan.

With a 25% tax bracket on the last dollars you make, in order to save $100 you must earn $133.

Inside the plan, the whole $133 is saved and contributed because there are no current taxes.

Many companies provide some sort of matching contribution. This example illustrates a 25% match on the income you defer.

By contributing $133, you now have $166 in your account versus $100 outside the plan. This is like getting a 66% on your money from day one. This is a no brainer.

$&¢

Chapter Eleven

_____R_____

IRAs

IRAs

IRAs are individual retirement arrangements. IRAs were created so that individuals could have the same retirement advantages as employees covered under company qualified plans.

The major features of IRAs are as follows:

- An IRA is an Individual Retirement Arrangement/Account.
- IRAs are always owned and controlled by the individual, not by an employer.
- IRAs can be formed and funded by individuals for themselves.
- IRAs can also be part of an employer-sponsored retirement plan and funded by employers.

In most cases, individuals can take a tax deduction for funds that are contributed to an IRA. Contributions grow tax-deferred. They are taxed when they are withdrawn from the account.

As with anything having to do with favorable tax treatment, there are rules and regulations regarding the deductibility for income tax purposes. There can also be tax penalties for removing money before a certain age (59 1/2), or for not taking minimum distributions beyond a certain age (70 1/2).

This book does not go into great depth regarding IRAs. Our focus is on how IRAs interface with qualified plans provided by employers.

Deductibility

The deductibility of IRA deposits is affected by whether or not an employee is *participating* in a company-sponsored plan. Deductibility is also affected by a taxpayer's *adjusted gross income*. Adjusted gross income is the amount of income used by the IRS to determine tax liability.

Destination

Most of the money that is held inside qualified retirement plans will eventually find its way into an individual IRA. This normally happens when an employee terminates service with a company. When an employee leaves a company, they will have the option to transfer their retirement funds from a tax-qualified plan to an IRA. By moving the funds from a qualified vehicle to an IRA, employees can avoid the immediate taxation of benefit proceeds. All taxation is avoided with a transaction called a "trustee to trustee" transfer.

If a 401(k) distribution is made in the form of a check, the check must be deposited into an IRA within 60 days. Any amount that is not deposited into the new IRA will be taxed in the year received.

If your employer issues a check, there is a mandatory withholding of 20%, even if you intend to roll the entire amount into an IRA. This 20% can be made up with personal funds to avoid taxation on the 20% withholding. If you are under age 59 1/2 , there is an additional 10% tax on amounts that are not rolled to an IRA.

A Brief IRA History

Because IRAs are a retirement tool that is constantly changing, it is helpful to review their legislative history. IRAs have evolved significantly over time.

IRAs were created with the enactment of the Employee Retirement Income Security Act (ERISA), in 1974.

In the beginning, individuals were allowed to contribute up to $1,500 per year into an IRA, provided they were not covered by a qualified retirement plan.

The Economic Recovery Tax Act of 1981 (ERTA) expanded the use of IRAs. This act removed the qualified plan restriction, allowing all taxpayers (under the age of 70½) to contribute to IRAs. ERTA raised the maximum annual contribution to $2,000, and allowed participants to contribute $250 for a nonworking spouse. At that time, all IRA contributions were tax deductible, and were taxable when withdrawn.

The Tax Reform Act of 1986 created phase out provisions for IRA contributions made by high-earning employees (or their spouses) that were covered by employment-based retirement plans.

The Small Business Job Protection Act of 1996 raised the limit for contributions on behalf of nonworking spouses from $250 to $2,000.

The Taxpayer Relief Act of 1997 created the *Roth IRA*.

- Roth IRA contributions are not deductible for income tax purposes.
- The growth of Roth IRA assets is tax free.
- Withdrawals from a Roth IRA are tax free.

Besides creating the Roth, the Taxpayer Relief Act of 1997 made significant changes to IRAs. The act increased the income threshold, above which deductible contributions were phased out. It also made adjustments to the eligibility of taxpayers who were covered (and whose spouses were covered) by an employment-based plan.

The Economic Growth and Tax Relief Reconciliation Act of 2001 raised the limit on contributions beginning in 2002. It also allowed for catch-up contributions to be made by people age 50 and above. The provisions of this act, (as well those of the Jobs and Growth Tax Relief Reconciliation Act of 2003) were extended until 2012.

The American Taxpayer Relief Act of 2012 gave permanency to most of the EGTRRA changes. It lifted many of the restrictions on Roth conversions within 401(k) plans. It also allowed individuals to make tax-free charitable contributions from an IRA, of up to $100,000 per year.

EVER CHANGING

As you can see, Congress has made many changes to IRAs over the years, and will continue to do so. Some people have personal or rollover IRAs while they are working. Others will have them when they retire.

IRA DEDUCTIBILITY RULES

The deductibility of IRA contributions is affected by two factors:

- Participation (including spouses) in company-sponsored retirement plans.
- Adjusted gross income.

Complete details of the deductibility are available each year through IRS Publication 590:

https://www.irs.gov/publications/p590a/index.html

2015 Combined Traditional and Roth IRA Contribution Limits:

For someone under 50 years of age: The maximum contribution that can be made to a traditional or Roth IRA is the lesser of $5,500 or the amount of taxable compensation for 2015. This limit can be split between a traditional IRA and a Roth IRA. Regardless of the split, the combined limit is always $5,500. The maximum deductible contribution to a traditional IRA, and the maximum contribution to a Roth IRA, may be *reduced* depending on modified adjusted gross income. (See government tables.)

For someone 50 years of age or older: The maximum contribution that can be made to a traditional or Roth IRA is the smaller of $6,500 or the amount of taxable compensation for 2015. This limit can also be split between a traditional IRA and a Roth IRA. The combined limit is $6,500. The maximum deductible contribution to a traditional IRA and the maximum contribution to a Roth IRA may be *reduced* depending on modified adjusted gross income.

See government tables: http://www.irs.gov/pub/irs-pdf/p590.pdf

$&¢

Chapter Twelve

R

Investment Risk

A Discussion of Risk

When it comes to investments, there are two major forms of risk:

- Investment Risk, &

- Inflation Risk.

INVESTMENT RISK: Investment risk is the chance that your investments will lose value before you need them.

INFLATION RISK: Inflation risk involves the *purchasing power* of your investments. The lower the investment risk, the lower your long-term returns. *Low investment returns* produce *high inflation risk*.

TRUE RISK: **The greatest you face with investments risk is not achieving your long-term investment and retirement objectives.**

REAL RISK

Risk wears many faces. Sometimes risk fools us.

For example, over the course of a full working career, the investments with the *greatest short-term investment risk* have proven to have the *lowest long-term inflation risk*.

This is important: Over the course of a working career, the investments with the *greatest short-term risk* have always proven to have the *lowest long-term risk*.

When it comes to maintaining *purchasing power over time*, the greater the time frame, the more "risky" low risk investments become, and the less risky "high risk" investments become. It is critical that you understand this as you invest for retirement.

RISK REVIEW

Risk is the chance of losing money. There are two ways you can lose money as you save toward retirement.

- Your investments can fall in value. This is market risk.
- Your investments can lose purchasing power relative to inflation. This is inflation risk.

In the short run, the risk of losing money in stocks is greater than in the long run. The *longer* the time frame, the *lower* the risk in stocks. Over a period of 20 years, the historical risk in stocks is lower than the risk of bonds or cash.

If you don't take short-term risk with your investments, there is a good chance that your investments will *lose* purchasing power against the inflating cost of retirement.

If you are investing for retirement, you should take a long-term view with regard to your investments.

HOW BIG IS MARKET RISK?

Market risk is the chance that your investments will fall in value. How often does this happen?

- Common Stocks produce the *greatest long-term return* and have the *greatest short-term risk*. The chance of losing actual money in stocks in any particular year is about one in four—**5 times every 20 years**. Losses can be large.

- Bonds pay a set income. They are less risky and less volatile than stocks. They lose value about **3 times every twenty years**. Losses are usually not very large.

- Traditionally, the 91-day T-bill issued by the United States Treasury is considered the safest of all investments. A 91-day T-bill is purchased by investors at a discount to the note value. In 91 days, the investor receives 100% of the note value. T-bills never lose money if you hold them to retirement.

    As of this writing, short-term T-bills are "yielding" .04%. This represents only four one hundredths of one percent. This is below the actual inflation rate. T-bills are losing purchasing power.

INFLATION RISK

- Inflation risk considers the actual purchasing power of your investments. If your investments grow, but at a rate that is lower than inflation, your money will buy less (when adjusted for inflation) than when it was invested.

- When planning for retirement, risk is needed to accumulate sufficient assets to retire.

TRUE RISK

- When planning for retirement, your true risk is not achieving the sum you will need to retire as you desire.

$&¢

Chapter Thirteen

R

Inflation Risk

Many people make the mistake of assuming that prices will stay level in retirement. This isn't the case. Those nearing retirement today can remember gasoline at 25 cents a gallon, five cent candy bars, 15 cent hamburgers and 25 cent movie matinees.

If a retiree does not take inflation into account, disaster may be on the horizon.

This book has reviewed how inflation impacts your retirement number. Understanding inflation is critical to effective retirement planning. So, let's review inflation in greater detail.

The opposing chart illustrates how inflation will impact purchasing power over time. As you can see, even small changes in inflation can have a significant impact on what a dollar will buy in the future.

With an inflation rate of 3%, someone retiring in 30 years will need $243 to buy what $100 buys today. In 40 years, ten years into retirement, those same goods would cost $326. With 4% inflation, in 40 years it would take $480 to buy what $100 buys today.

With 6% inflation, as the U.S. experienced from the late 1960s to the 1990s, a dollar would purchase far, far less.

As you prepare your retirement plan, you must understand that adjusting for inflation is crucial to all saving and investment strategies.

Inflation
How It Erodes Your Future Purchasing Power

How much future money will you need to equal $100 today?

Purchasing Power Erodes With Inflation

Year	2%	3%	4%	5%	6% Inflation
10	$121	$134	$148	$163	$179
20	$149	$181	$219	$265	$321
30	$181	$243	$324	$432	$574
40	$221	$326	$480	$704	$1,029

In 40 years, at 3% inflation, it will take $326 to buy what $100 buys today.

Inflation and Retirement
With 3% inflation, what income will be needed to replace a $25,000 income?

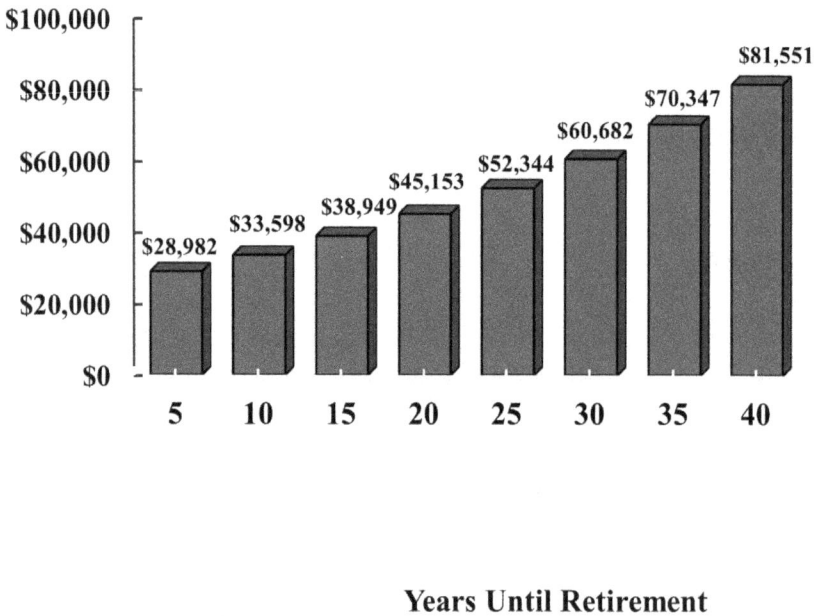

Years Until Retirement

In 30 years, at 3% inflation, it will take $60,682 to buy
what $25,000 buys today.

This illustration shows the inflation-adjusted income that will be needed in retirement to replace $25,000.

With an inflation rate of 3%, someone retiring in forty years would need over $81,000 to buy what $25,000 buys today.

Put another way, if you plan to retire with $25,000 per year in today's dollars, you should plan on having enough money to provide an income of $81,000 forty years from now.

If you need $50,000 per year in today's dollars, you will need $162,000 per year, forty years from now.

The Rule of 72

- The Rule of 72 Is A Financial Constant

- Money Doubles When The Net Rate Of Return Multiplied By The Number Of Years Invested = 72

Doubling Examples:

- Money invested at 6% will double in 12 years (6 x 12 = 72). It will be worth 4 times as much in 24 years. 8 times as much in 36 years.

- Money invested at 8% will double in 9 years (9 x 8 = 72). It will be worth 4 times as much in 18 years, 8 times as much in 27 years.

- Money invested at 12% will double in 6 years (12 x 6 = 72). It will be worth 4 times as much in 12 years, 8 times as much in 18 years, and 16 times as much in 24 years. It will be worth 64 times as much in 36 years

Note: Bonds yield a more constant return. Bond values change less than stocks. Stocks will have an "average rate of return," but their value is more volatile each year. The Rule of 72 is a useful trick to help you plan your wealth accumulation.

Compounding Comparison:

Invested at 6%, $1 would grow to $8 in 36 years.

Invested at 12%, the same dollar would grow to $64 in 36 years.

This shows the power of compounding. Doubling the investment return produces *eight times* the investment in 36 years.

Chapter Fourteen

R
_____

The Rule of 72

Understanding the Rule of 72 can be helpful to any investor. This "rule" is a simple mathematical constant that will allow you to determine how fast your money can grow over time. Here is how it works.

When you multiply the number of *years* an investment is held by the average rate of *return*, you get a number (product). When this number equals *72*, your money has *doubled*.

For example, if you earn 4% per year, it will take 18 years for your investments to double in value (4 x 18 = 72).

Over the long-term, small stocks have grown at a rate close to 12% per year. Money invested at 12% will take just six years to double.

In eighteen years, money invested at 12% will double three times, and be worth 800% of the original amount.

A 12% return is an unreasonable expectation for diversified, long-term growth. But it does give you an idea how money can compound over time.

You can create your own estimates of asset growth in the future. For example: If you have thirty-six years until retirement:

- With **6%** growth, your money will double *three* times in 36 years. (6% x 12 years = 72, 36 years / 12 years = 3 times). Doubling three times would cause your investment to grow by 800%.

- If you earned **12%**, your money would double every six years. In 36 years, your money would double six times (36 years / 6 = 6 times). Doubling six times would cause your money to be worth **sixty-four times** its current value.

You may not think that earning a few percent more on your investments is worth the added risk. But, over time, even small return increases can magnify investment growth. If you are young, adding risk to your portfolio can increase your chances of retirement success.

Chapter Fifteen

R

Dollar Cost Averaging

Dollar Cost Averaging: Not Magic, Just Math

Dollar cost averaging is a proven strategy, where you invest the same amount of money on a regular schedule. When the market falls, share prices fall. The same investment amount will purchase more investment shares when the price is low. When the market rises, fewer shares are purchased, because the purchase price is higher.

If prices vary, but stay level, in the long-run your average *cost* per share, will be significantly lower than the average *price* per share. You will have a built-in gain, even though the price is where it started.

In the following example, we invest $100 every three months. If our initial purchase price is $10 per share, we buy 10 shares.

If the stock market falls, and our investment now costs $5, we purchase 20 shares with our $100.

The market begins to climb back up. By the time we make our third purchase, our stock (or fund) price has risen to $7.50 per share. This time we purchase 13.3 shares with $100.

Our stock then returns to its original price. We buy 10 more shares.

We have invested $400. We have purchased 533 shares.

At $10 per share, our total investment *value* is $533. Our investment was $400. This represents a *33% gain*, even though the stock price is *right where it started*.

This is the brilliance of dollar cost averaging. It is an example of "buying low."

THE MATH OF DOLLAR COST AVERAGING WITH MUTUAL FUNDS

- EXAMPLE 1: Let's assume you decide to invest $100 every 3 months.

Investment:	Price/Share:	# of Shares Purchased:
$100	$10.0	10
$100	$ 5.00	20
$100	$ 7.50	13.3
$100	$10.00	10
$400	$10.00	53.3 shares

DOLLAR COST AVERAGING EXAMPLE

- You have invested every quarter for a year.
- Your total investment into the program is $400.
- Your 53.3 shares are worth **$533** with the current price of $10/share.
- This gives you a gross profit of 33%.
- Even though the value of your fund has not increased since your original purchase date, your investments *have* increased in value.
- This is the brilliant math of dollar cost averaging.

Long-Term Gains Require Short-Term Pain

Buying when the stock market is low, or falling, is emotionally difficult, even for aggressive investors. Dollar cost averaging is a time-tested investment practice that can reduce your buying stress.

If you are saving for retirement many years from now, understanding this concept will help you feel less fear over market lows. Think of a bad stock market as a great buying opportunity. Really!

Markets rise and fall. *What matters is how much money you have in the end.*

Stock market swoons present great buying opportunities for the long-run, especially if they are deep and long. Let the math work for you.

401(k) investing is a perfect way to take advantage of dollar cost averaging.

EXAMPLE #2: Continue investing as the market goes up, and then down.

What does our profit picture look like now?

Investment:	Price/Share:	# Shares Purchased:
$100	$10.00	10.0
$100	$ 5.00	20.0
$100	$ 7.50	13.3
$100	$10.00	10.0
$100	$15.00	6.7
$100	$10.00	10.0
$600 Investment	$10.00	70 Shares

$600 investment buys 70 shares. These are now worth $10/share. You have invested $600 and your investments are worth $700.

You still have a tidy profit of nearly 17%. With a 401(k) company match you would have even more.

DOLLAR COST AVERAGING MAY BE THE MOST INFALLIBLE METHOD EVER DESIGNED FOR STOCK MARKET INVESTING. IT IS A METHOD YOU CAN PRACTICE TODAY.

Here is what happens to dollar cost averaging if the stock price rises and then falls back down.

If the share price rises to $15, we buy only 6.7 shares. If the price then falls back down to $10, we have experienced a loss, a gain, and a leveling of stock prices. The price is right where it was when we started investing.

We have invested $600. We have purchased 700 shares. Our shares are worth $10 per share, or $700. This produces an investment gain of nearly 17%. The overall "market" *hasn't changed from where it started.* But we have still made money.

Our stock price started at $10. It went down, up, and then down. It is back to where it started, at $10. Yet, we have a substantial investment gain.

Let the math of dollar cost averaging work for you in your retirement planning.

When the markets really fall, view it as a buying opportunity rather than an investment calamity. Think about buying as much as you can.

S&C

Chapter Sixteen

_____R_____

Compounding

MONEY MAKES MONEY.

Anyone who is planning for retirement must understand that money compounds upon itself as it grows.

This book introduced compounding during its discussion of the Rule of 72. Now, let's review this concept in greater detail.

Compounding occurs when investors earn positive returns on their investments. If your investments grow in value, and then grow again, they are compounding.

For example: If you earn a 10% return on $1,000, you will have $1,100. If you earn 10% on this amount, you won't have $1,200 ($100 gain twice), you will have $1,210. You have earned an additional 10% on your $100 of gain.

Over time, growth on your investment earnings can become quite significant. The following pages illustrate how compounding can affect your retirement planning.

The Magic Of Compounding
Future Values: 4% and 6%*
Compound Annual Growth

Assumes contributions of 10% of $30,000 income. 5% salary increases/year thereafter. * Investment returns and income growth are not guaranteed and will be different.

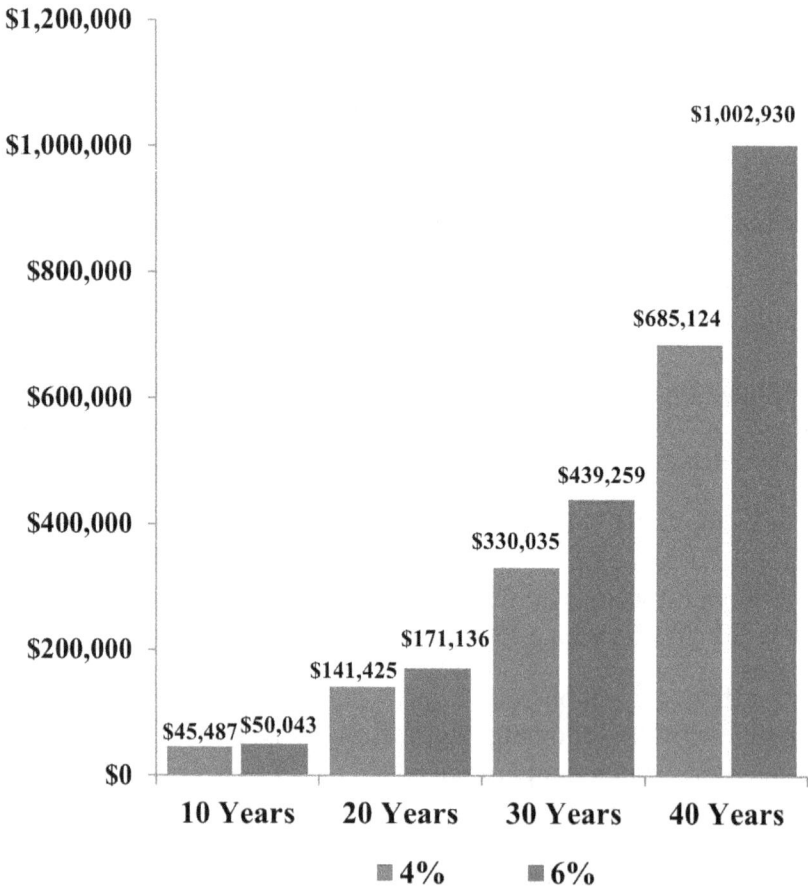

	10 Years	20 Years	30 Years	40 Years
4%	$45,487	$141,425	$330,035	$685,124
6%	$50,043	$171,136	$439,259	$1,002,930

The preceding example shows annual 401(k) deferrals of 10%, beginning with an income of $30,000 per year. The deferral would be $3,000 in the first year. The deferral amount grows at 5% per year. There is no company match.

With an average investment return of 4%, this investor would accumulate more than $330,000 in 30 years.

With a 6% return, the investment fund would grow to more than $439,000. In 40 years, the accumulations exceed $1 million.

An investment return of 6% versus 4%, yields $109,000 more dollars in 30 years. This is the power of compounding. In 40 years, the difference between the accumulation amounts exceeds $300,000.

Investment results cannot be guaranteed. You must assume some risk to achieve greater returns. History and time work in your favor. Use them to help you retire comfortably.

The Magic Of Compounding
Future Values: 8% and 10%*
Compound Annual Growth

Assumes contributions of 10% of $30,000 income. 5% salary increases/year thereafter. * Investment returns and income growth are not guaranteed and will be different.

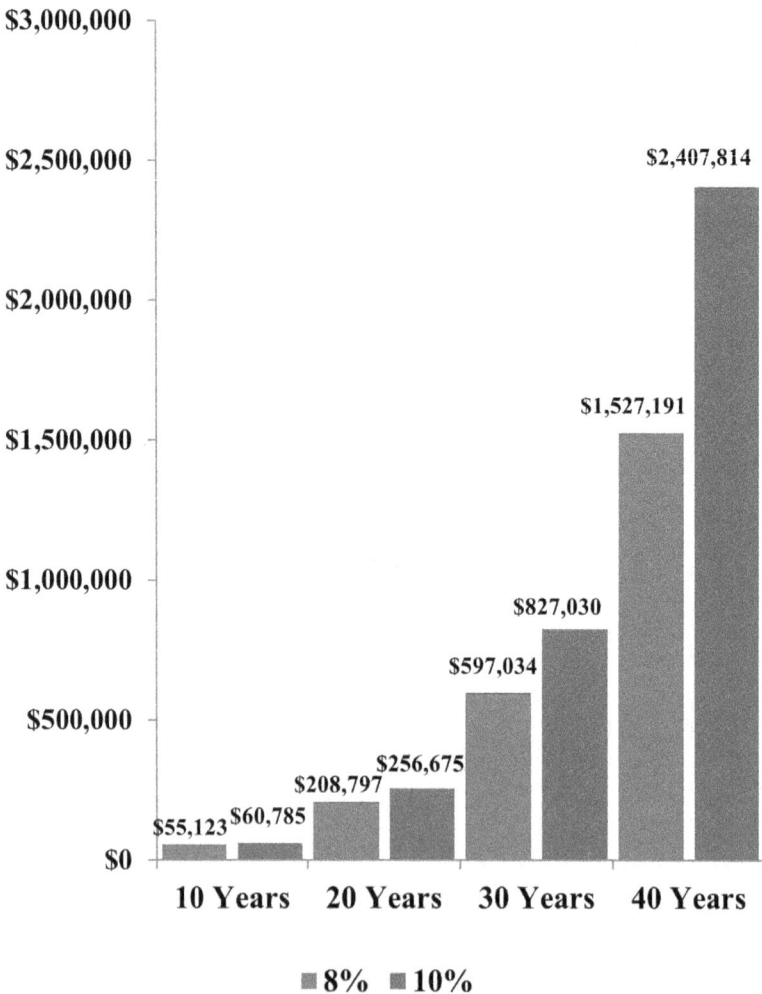

	10 Years	20 Years	30 Years	40 Years
8%	$55,123	$208,797	$597,034	$1,527,191
10%	$60,785	$256,675	$827,030	$2,407,814

■8% ■10%

The first compounding chart illustrated growth at 4% and 6%. Did you notice how much impact that a higher rate of return will have on retirement accumulation?

The second chart illustrates how even higher investment returns increase accumulations over time.

Remember the rule of 72? These charts show the rule in action. The differences in accumulation values become more significant as rates of return increase.

In forty years, earnings growth of 4% results in an accumulation of $685,124. A growth rate of 10% results in an accumulation of $2,407,814. Compounding investments at 10% accumulates far more than compounding at 4%.

By taking more risk, an investor would have earned nearly **four times more in retirement assets** over an investing career.

There are good years for stocks. There are bad years. There are good decades. There are bad decades. Over time, common stocks have grown at about 10% per year. There is no guarantee that they will behave this way in the future. That's why there is a high return potential.

Can a retirement plan investor be rewarded for taking risk? Absolutely.

Assets *must* be subject to the potential for loss in order to achieve gain. This is a simple law of investing. But the *longer* the time horizon, the *lower* the inflation-adjusted risk.

The focus of this book will now shift to investments themselves — the assets that will allow you to earn the returns you need on your savings to retire comfortably.

$&¢

Chapter Seventeen

R
_____

Investment Characteristics

INVESTMENT CHARACTERISTICS

Like people, investments come in many shapes and sizes. There is no perfect person. There is no perfect investment.

With investments, for every benefit you receive, you must sacrifice somewhere else.

If you want an investment that will grow in value over time, you must risk having it lose value in the short run. If you want high income, you will have to sacrifice growth and safety. If you want an investment that is extremely safe, you will sacrifice income and growth potential. Let's look more closely.

FIVE MAJOR INVESTMENT CATEGORIES

Most investments come with five major characteristics.

- **Liquidity:** Liquidity represents the ease in which an investment can be sold. Some investments, like a stock or mutual fund, can be sold any day and time that the stock market is open. Others, like an office building or an oil well, take more time to sell.

- **Income:** Many investments pay an income, some more than others. Investments that pay the highest income usually aren't the safest, or the most tax friendly. Investments that pay tax free income generally have little or no potential for growth.

- **Taxes:** Every investment has certain tax characteristics. These characteristics are determined by politicians in Washington. If Congress wants to create incentive for certain investments, they endow them with favorable tax treatment. Here are three examples:

Example #1: Municipal bonds are debt instruments issued by government entities, both federal and state. These bonds are used to fund municipal projects, like roads or schools. The income on municipal bonds is usually protected from taxation. This is legislated so municipal entities can pay lower interest than taxable bonds.

Some states tax federal municipal debt, but they don't tax income on bonds issued by municipalities in their own state.

Example #2: Retirement plans have favorable income tax treatment because Congress wants to help people save for retirement.

Example #3: Gains on stocks that were owned for more than one year are taxed at long-term capital gains rates, which are less than the rates on ordinary income.

- **Growth:** Many investments are designed for long-term growth. Some growth investments pay no income at all. These usually have significant short-term risk, and high potential return. The objective of growth investments is appreciation over time.

  Some growth investments, such as stocks, have good liquidity. Others, like rare coins, art, or land may not.

- **Safety:** Every investment has a particular safety profile. Generally, high safety means low or little growth potential. It means low or moderate income, and either low taxes (municipal bonds) or high taxes on everything else that isn't sheltered.

Now, think of every investment as having the potential to hold *20 ounces of water*. This allocates an *average* of 4 ounces for each of these five investment characteristics.

Investment Characteristics
Liquidity, Income Taxes, Growth, Safety

20 Potential Ounces

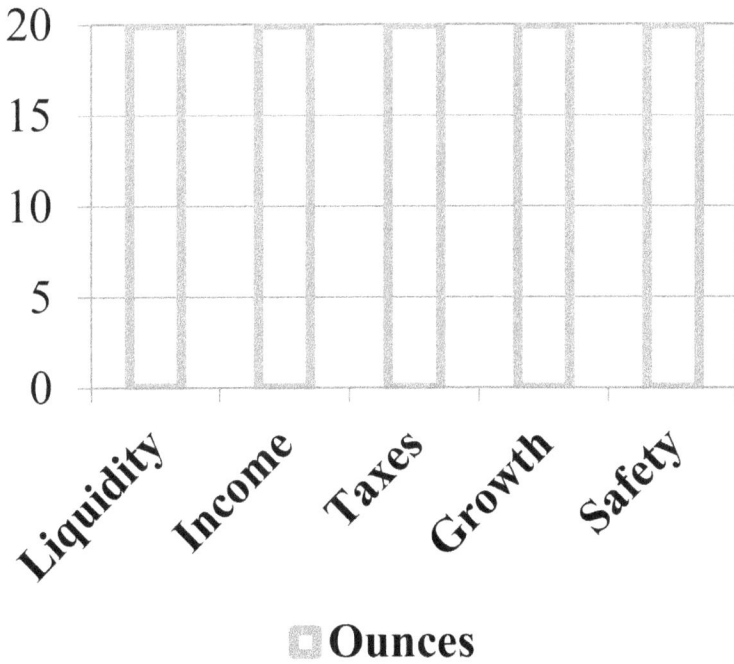

Ounces

Few, if any, investments have equal parts of each characteristic. They usually have one or two dominant features.

If we desire a lot of one particular investment characteristic, we must be willing to sacrifice somewhere else. They are all relative. Let's look at some examples:

GROWTH STOCK OR GROWTH MUTUAL FUND

A growth stock, or a growth mutual fund, has more appreciation potential than a municipal bond. It has less safety, too.

Let's say that the stock or fund we choose takes *10 ounces of growth* from our total of twenty. This leaves 10 ounces to be allocated among the other four characteristics.

Growth stocks and growth mutual funds pay little or no income. This example gets a 1 for income. Growth is volatile in the short run. Volatility means risk. Growth stocks get a low 1 for safety.

If we hold a stock for longer than one year, it qualifies for special tax treatment, known as long-term capital gains. In mutual funds, net capital gains and income are passed through to shareholders each year. Capital gain rates are lower than the tax rates on ordinary income.

Interest and dividends are taxed at ordinary income rates, which grow higher as your income increases. This example gets a 3 for tax advantages, although this could be higher in some cases.

Finally, liquidity is high. This is because publicly traded stocks (as well as mutual funds) can be sold any day that the stock market is trading. We give liquidity a 5.

Investment Characteristics
Liquidity, Income, Taxes, Growth, Safety
Growth Mutual Fund

20 Potential Ounces

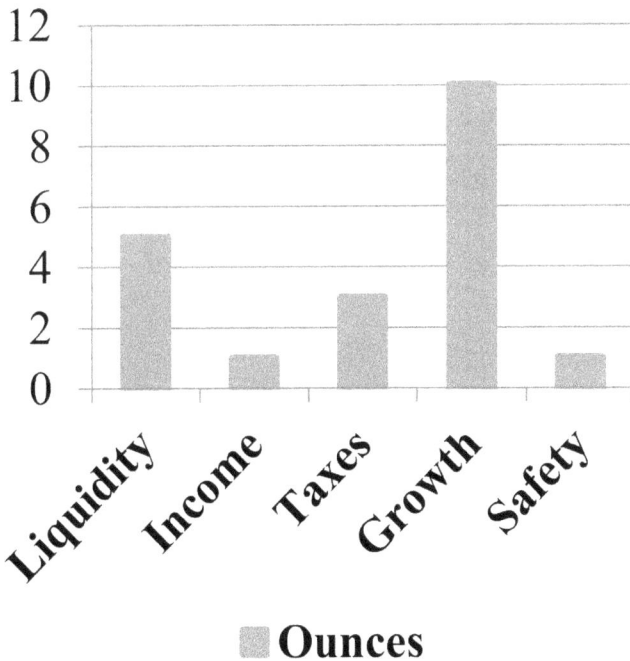

Ounces

BALANCED FUND

Balanced mutual funds own a mix of stocks and bonds. This makes them less risky than growth stocks or growth funds. They also pay more income.

Investors (outside a retirement plan) must pay higher income taxes with balanced funds than with growth funds. This is because interest and dividends are greater, and taxed at higher rates. Long-term growth is normally lower than with growth funds.

In this case, our prime objectives are equal—for income and growth. Each gets a 6.

We give this example a 2 for taxes, as this value is low relative to the other objectives.

The liquidity value is higher than taxes or safety. It gets a 4.

Volatility is still fairly high, so safety still gets a 2.

Investment Characteristics
**Liquidity, Income, Taxes, Growth, Safety
Balanced Mutual Fund**

20 Potential Ounces

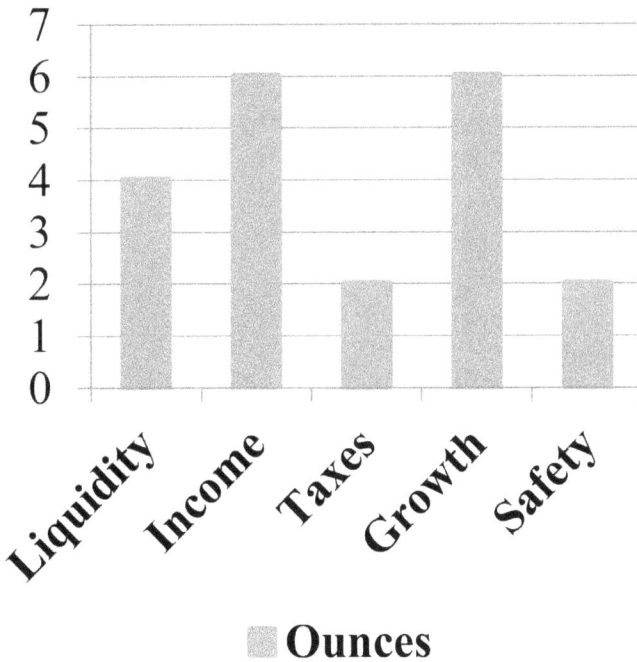

Ounces

GROWTH FUNDS IN A RETIREMENT ACCOUNT

This chart illustrates a growth fund or growth asset allocation model in a retirement plan. This book will review asset allocation shortly.

This example illustrates a dominant characteristic of growth. We give it an 8.

There are no current taxes in a 401(k), so our tax benefits are high. This earns a 6.

Our investment has a little income. We give it a 1.

A model, or fund, can be sold on market trading days. But it cannot be withdrawn from a retirement plan without penalty (or as a loan). Assets held within tax-favored retirement plans, such as a 401(k), have penalties for early withdrawal. This makes liquidity low. It receives a 1.

Short-term safety is minimal, as the goal is long-term growth. It gets a 3.

Investment Characteristics
Liquidity, Income, Taxes, Growth, Safety
401(k) Growth Model

20 Potential Ounces

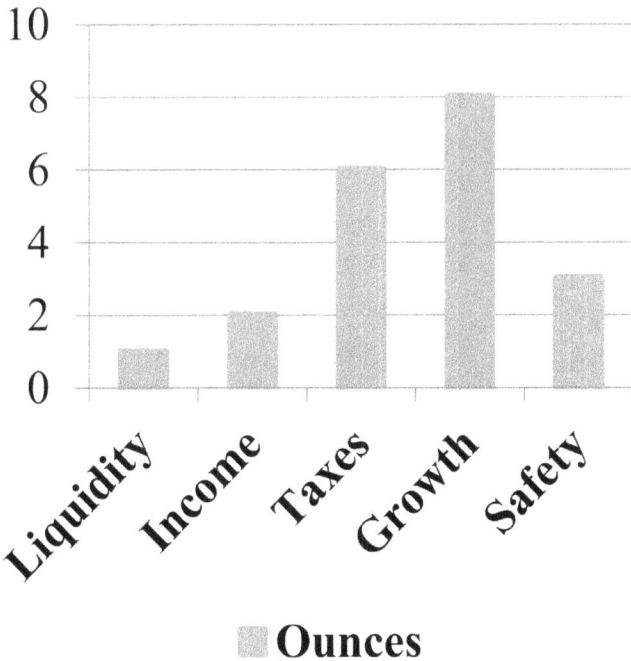

Ounces

Summary

Nothing is absolute when it comes to investments. But each investment class has characteristics that can be profiled and understood. The 20 ounce model can be a helpful guide as you plan and understand your investment strategy.

Investments are like everyday life. There are trade-offs. You must define the characteristics you desire, and then invest to achieve them.

The safer the investment in the short-run, the less it will produce in the long-run. Stocks have higher risk and greater return potential than bonds. Historically, they grow more over time. But there are bumps, even craters, along the way.

When yields (interest rates) *rise* in the marketplace, stocks become less attractive. Can you figure out why? Think of our 20 ounces. Higher interest rates put more water in the income portion of the model. High interest rates usually lead to lower business growth. This leads to lower corporate earnings growth, and lower stock value estimates. When interest rates rise, short-term growth potential is reduced. Stock prices normally fall as interest rates rise.

Stocks often perform poorly in the early stages of a recession. This is because stocks are priced relative to current and *expected* (future) earnings. Recessions mean lower earnings. As recessions start, stock prices fall. When stocks rebound, they do so quite rapidly. They can catch us by surprise. You can't miss out. If you miss the turnaround, your long-term return potential plummets.

The following pages discuss stocks and bonds in greater detail.

The information will be presented in different ways — sometimes in words — sometimes with pictures. Important concepts will be repeated. This may seem redundant to some. Others will find that such layering helps.

Chapter Eighteen

R

Types Of Investments

When you put your money to work, there are different types of investments to choose from. Investments come in many variations, with different goals, characteristics and risk profiles.

Investment choices outside a retirement plan are more diverse than those inside retirement plans.

There are few restrictions placed upon how an individual may invest his *personal* money. You want to buy gold? No problem. Pork belly futures? No problem. Oil drilling partnerships? No problem. A convenience store? No big deal.

You won't find exotic investments inside a corporate retirement plan. Why? To whom much is given, much is expected.

Congress has given special tax considerations to qualified retirement plans, such as a 401(k). Money put into qualified plans usually goes in *before* federal taxes. Assets accumulate without current taxation.

In order to receive such special tax treatment, retirement plan fiduciaries (the people in charge of the plan) must follow certain rules. One rule limits the type of investments that are allowed in retirement plans. The major types of investments that you will use for retirement planning are explained in the following pages.

Major Types Of Investments

- Common Stocks
- Mutual Funds
    - Domestic & Foreign
    - Large, Mid & Small
    - Growth, Value & Blend
- Bonds
    - Government & Corporate
    - Low, Moderate & High Risk
    - Short, Long & Mid-term Duration
- Target Funds
- Asset Allocation Models
- Indexes
- Derivatives

Chapter Nineteen

R

Stocks

TWO BASIC TYPES

There are two basic types of stocks: **common and preferred**.

Most shares of stock have voting rights in the issuing company. Voting allows shareholders to elect a board of directors.

The directors elect a chairman of the board, who is ultimately in charge of the company.

The chairman, or the board of directors, will appoint an executive officer to carry out the daily tasks of managing the business. This person is usually called the CEO or the president.

The CEO (and perhaps the board, or the chairman) will select the next level of corporate officers, such as a chief operating officer, chief financial officer, chief technology officer, or senior and executive vice presidents.

Common Stocks — What They Are

A common stock represents an ownership share in a publicly traded company. If you own a share of stock, you are part owner of that company.

Each corporation has a number of "outstanding" shares, shares in the hands of owners. If you multiply the stock price by the number of outstanding shares, you will get the company's "market capitalization." This is the total market value of the company.

At the time of this writing, Apple, Inc. had the largest market capitalization in the world (approaching $1 trillion). Apple had close to $200 billion in cash, more than the U.S. Government keeps on hand. Note: By the time this book was edited, Apple stock had lost more than $200 billion of its market capitalization. Apple's market cap was only $50 billion more than Alphabet, Inc., the parent of Google and its related companies. By the second editing, Alphabet had overtaken Apple in total market value.

The price of a stock is determined somewhat like an auction on eBay. There are sellers of shares and buyers of shares. The seller has an asking price. The buyer has a bid price. When a buyer's price meets a seller's price, a transaction takes place.

At any given time, there are both buyers and sellers. Someone is willing to sell shares of stock if the price is high enough. Somebody is willing to buy if the price is low enough.

When demand increases—after such events as an earnings increase, a new product launch (think iPhone), a fall in interest rates, or if the unemployment rate falls dramatically—buyers might be willing to pay more for a stock, because they expect higher earnings. More willing buyers cause higher stock prices—just like an auction.

Conversely, when there is bad news because of recession fears, interest rate rises, the loss of a patent or the failure of a new product—buyers become scarcer at current prices. Sellers become more willing to sell. This causes prices to fall.

Some corporations include their own company stock as an investment option in their retirement plans. This is regulated by ERISA laws, created to protect plan participants.

Common Stocks — Facts To Know

- Common stock shares may or may not pay a dividend. Dividends are cash payments to shareholders. Younger companies like to keep their cash while they grow, and often pay no dividends. Larger, and older companies, usually pay ongoing dividends to their shareholders. Dividends can be increased or lowered at any time by the board of directors. They can also be made on a one-time basis.

- Stocks have value based upon what someone else will pay for them.

- Stocks of larger companies are often traded on exchanges, such as the New York Stock Exchange. (NYSE)

- The NYSE used to run like an actual auction on a trading floor. Today, most (but not all) trades occur electronically.

- The NYSE is based on Wall Street.

- Many stocks, particularly those of high tech companies, like Apple and Microsoft, are traded on NASDAQ. NASDAQ shares are sold through computer networks.

- Stocks gain or lose value in many different ways. Their value comes from the income they pay (dividends), their earnings and perceived earnings growth, and their underlying assets. Most importantly, stock prices are determined by what someone will pay for them.

- A single stock can gain or lose 40%, or more, in any given year. But over the long run, stocks have fared well against other investment vehicles.

The following pages illustrate how stocks are traded.

THE ANATOMY OF A COMMON STOCK

1. A company issues shares in an Initial Public Offering (IPO). The shares then trade publicly through trading networks. The New York Stock Exchange is the largest trading network. The NYSE is based on Wall Street. NASDAQ is the second largest trading network, followed by the London Stock Exchange Group.

2. The investor (you or a mutual fund manager) buys a stock through an auction, electronic or computer-generated trade. This transaction can happen anywhere stocks are traded. Most large stocks trade through networks based in New York (Wall Street).

3. Companies often pay quarterly dividends on their shares. These go to share owners. Stock owners also earn net capital gains or losses on their shares.

4. Over time, public stocks have been one of the most trusted ways to accumulate assets for retirement.

Stocks

Investor Owns Shares

$ Goes To Company

1.
Company Management Issues Stock Through Wall Street (IPO)

Investor Buys & Sells Stock Through Wall Street

2.

Investor Receives Net Capital Gains or Losses, Dividends & Interest

3.

Wealth Grows To Create Nest Egg

4.

PREFERRED STOCKS

Preferred shares are commonly issued before a company becomes public. Preferred shares can be quite complicated. But there are some basic characteristics that investors should understand.

- Preferred stock shares generally pay a stated dividend. This dividend is almost always higher than the dividends paid on the company's common stock. In the event of a company's failure, and subsequent liquidation, the holders of preferred shares are usually paid before the holders of common shares. This is usually a "par value," a stated price per share.

  - Preferred shares are usually sensitive to interest rate changes. They increase in value when interest rates fall. They fall in value when interest rates rise.

  - Most preferred stocks have less gain or loss potential than common stocks. They don't normally increase much in value, unless they are convertible into common shares.

  - Some preferred shares are convertible. Most are not.

  - Some preferred shares are "cumulative." If preferred dividends are skipped, all back unpaid preferred dividends must be satisfied before common shareholders receive any future dividends.

Different Kinds Of Common Stocks

- Common stocks of public companies are classified by size — Large-Cap, Mid-Cap & Small-Cap. There are no strict definitions of size — only generalizations. Individual stocks can jump from one classification to another and then back again.

- Large Capitalization Common Stocks — Large-cap stocks are shares of very big companies. An example would be the companies that comprise the Dow Jones 30 Industrials. Large cap stocks generally have market capitalization over $3.5 billion. They are usually worth more than $5 billion. They often pay dividends. This reduces price fluctuations relative to the overall stock market. Large company stocks tend to be less volatile than the stocks of smaller companies.

- Medium Capitalization Common Stocks — Mid-Cap stocks are typically well-established companies. They are often in a growth (or rebuilding) mode. They generally have a market capitalization between $2 billion and $10 billion. They could be worth as little as $1 billion. They usually range from $1-$5 billion in value.

- Small Capitalization Common Stocks — Small-Cap stocks usually have less than $1-$2 billion in market capitalization. They are often in a rapid growth or contraction phase. Small stocks are the most volatile over the short run. They may provide the greatest opportunity for gain over the long run.

- Companies with market capitalizations below $300 million are called *micro-cap* stocks.

- International Stocks — International stocks are ownership shares of companies domiciled outside the U.S. In the U.S., international stocks are typically traded with shares known as American Depository Receipts (ADRs).

- The prices of international stocks, especially those from emerging markets, can be unusually volatile. This is because investors buy shares in dollars. But a company from Singapore or China may conduct business with their own currency. Earnings will have to be adjusted for currency fluctuations. This can magnify gains or losses.

- Many foreign markets, and foreign companies, are less regulated than companies from America. Less oversight increases the risk that a company can misrepresent their sales and earnings growth. Other factors can be hard to anticipate.

- Emerging-market stocks represent those of companies from developing countries. They often represent the greatest investment risk.

Large, small and mid-cap stocks are defined by range. Because of their volatility, by definition, a stock could be a mid-cap one day and a large-cap the next. And then back the day after.

This book will review other attributes of common stocks. First, let's talk a little about bonds.

Chapter Twenty

_____R_____

Bonds

Bonds = Debt

- When a corporation, government, or government agency borrows money, they go to two primary places to obtain it:

  1. A Bank or Bank-like Institution, or

  2. The Investing Public.

- When borrowing from investors, the borrower usually backs the bonds with collateral.

- With corporations, the collateral used will generally be assets of the company.

- For cities and towns, collateral might be a revenue stream from something being built, such as a toll-road, bridge, tunnel, or sewer system.

- A municipal issue may also be backed by the taxing power of the entity. This is known as a general obligation bond.

- Many bonds are issued by the federal government, especially to finance ongoing budget deficits. Many such bonds have a federal guarantee of principal and/or interest.

- Some bonds are partially backed by the government. Such government support lowers the default risk and keeps interest rates reasonable.

  o For example, many mortgages are purchased by the Federal National Mortgage Association (Fannie Mae) and the Federal Home Loan Mortgage Corporation (Freddie Mac). The mortgages are then bundled together into pools and resold, as bonds.

Some of these mortgage pools may have certain insurance arrangements to reduce the credit risk. Overall, these bonds have no government guarantees. FHA and VA mortgages are primarily pooled and guaranteed by the Government National Mortgage Corporation (Ginnie Mae). Ginnie Mae provides government guarantees that lower the risk for investors. Lower risk reduces the interest rates paid by homeowners for their mortgages.

Bonds – Characteristics

- If a corporation goes bankrupt and is liquidated, bondholders stand first in line (after the IRS and other taxing authorities) for most proceeds.

    o Common stockholders usually stand last in line.

- Because of their collateral, bonds are a comparatively safe place to invest.

- Bonds are rated according to credit quality. There are three primary credit rating agencies—Standard & Poors, Moody's Investors Services and Fitch. Bonds with the highest credit quality are rated AAA (Aaa with Moody's). Investment grade bonds are rated BBB- or better with S&P or Fitch, and Baa3 with Moody's. Bonds that are not investment grade or above are considered various levels of junk bonds.

- There are two primary types of bonds.

    ◊ There are those that pay a regular, stated interest rate. These are often called *vanilla bonds*.

    ◊ There is another form of bonds, usually called *zero coupon bonds*. These bonds are issued at a sizable discount to their stated, par value, but will be redeemed at 100% of par value.

    ◊ Zero coupon bonds pay no current interest. Each year they gain value, as the full redemption date approaches. Zero coupon bonds can be unusually volatile when market interest rates change. This is because they have no "current interest," only a future gain when redeemed.

- Vanilla bonds pay interest for a specific duration of time. Interest is normally a fixed percentage of the original offering price, such as 5% of face value.

- Treasury Inflation-Protected Securities (TIPS) are bonds issued by the federal government that adjust principal and interest for inflation. Every 6 months, principal and interest are adjusted relative to the Consumer Price Index (CPI). This protects investors against losing income and purchasing power to inflation. TIPS don't outpace inflation; they just match it.

- Bonds fluctuate in value on a regular basis. The primary cause of daily value changes is interest rates. As interest rates rise, the value of the bonds you are holding will decline. As interest rates fall, the value of your bonds will normally increase.

- Other factors can cause bonds to fluctuate in value. Changes in financial strength, government policies and international events can all affect bond prices.

- Bond interest rates are affected by several factors:
    o Credit quality,
    o The length of time until principal is repaid, and
    o The prevailing interest rates.

- Each bond has a stated face value. Bonds are normally issued at, or close to, face value. Interest is paid as a percent of face value. For example: If face value is $1,000 and the interest rate is 5%, annual interest is $50. In most cases, the bond issuer would pay $12.50 every three months to investors.

- When bonds sell at a discount (for less than their face value) or at a premium (more than their face value) this is because something has changed since the bond was first issued. If prevailing interest rates were 8% when a bond was issued, and similar new bonds have a yield of 4%, our old bond will trade at a significant *premium* to its face value. The old bond sells for more because it pays a higher interest rate. When a bond that was purchased at a premium is redeemed by the issuer, the bond holder will receive the face value only, not the higher purchase price. Because there is a theoretical loss in annual principal value, the market will determine a "yield to maturity" for the bond. The yield to maturity amortizes the principal (value) loss over the remaining life of the bond. When combined with the higher current yield, investors will earn essentially the same return as a current bond of similar quality and duration.

- Discounts: If a bond trades at a discount, a theoretical, annual principal gain will be figured into the price. When redeemed, the bond issuer will pay more than the bond's current price.

- In this manner, bonds of similar quality and duration are traded at roughly the same yield to maturity.

Hopefully you are beginning to feel more comfortable with the concepts and terminology of investing. Let's have a little review.

IOU

Bonds represent an IOU from a company or a government entity. In exchange for investors lending money, a bond issuer promises to pay quarterly interest and/or redeem investor principal at some point in the future. Bond investors also have first crack at assets (after taxing authorities) in the event of a company default and liquidation.

YIELD TO MATURITY

Bond prices rise or fall relative to interest rates and credit quality adjustments. Yield to Maturity allows bonds to *equalize* the total return when they are compared to bonds of similar quality, interest and duration. A simple formula would be the following:

Yield To Maturity

Approximate Yield To Maturity $\quad \dfrac{C + ((F-P)/n)}{(F+P)/2}$

C = Coupon

F = Face Value

P = Price

n = Years To Maturity

repetitio est mater studiorum

PRICING A BOND

Bonds are bought and sold between dealers, who represent themselves or their investing clients. Bonds trade much like stocks. But they get valued in different ways. A bond's value is determined by its quality and duration. Equivalent bonds are usually traded on a yield-to-maturity basis.

Yield to maturity determines a current rate of return for a bond that will be held until its maturity date. This number incorporates the current bond interest rate, with appreciation or depreciation of principal, when a bond is redeemed by the issuer. Compounded, amortized capital gains (or losses), plus current interest rates should equal the yield on new debt of similar quality. The above formula shows how to approximate a YTM value.

Yield to maturity creates a level playing field for bonds, especially for those of similar quality.

Some investors prefer to pay a premium for bonds selling at a discount to their redemption value. Other investors value current bond yield over appreciation. This often depends upon the tax status of the purchaser. Qualified plans pay no taxes, so they want current return. Individuals, mutual funds or corporate investors may prefer capital gains over current interest rates, because taxes are lower.

If interest rates fall after a bond is issued, assuming stable creditworthiness, the price of the bond will *rise*. The price increase equalizes the yield to maturity between competing bonds.

If interest rates rise, the price of an existing bond will *fall* in value. The lower price will result in a higher bond appreciation value, making the total bond return equivalent to new bonds being sold with higher yields.

If an issuer becomes less creditworthy, their bond price will fall. This reduction creates a higher yield to maturity for new purchasers of the outstanding debt. If an issuer's credit rating increases, their bond prices might rise to equalize yield to maturity with similar quality bonds. New bond purchasers will accept a lower yield to maturity, because of the increased security financial.

Chapter Twenty-One

R

Stocks, Bonds & Interest Rates

Here are the most important concepts that you should know about how stocks and bonds react to interest rates.

Interest Rates

- Interest rates are a major force on the bond market.
- When interest rates rise, the price of existing bonds declines.
- As interest rates fall, bond prices rise.
- The yield (return) on long-term debt is almost always higher than the yield on short-term debt. The risk of loss is greater over longer time frames.
- The price movement of short-term debt is generally less volatile than the movement of long-term debt.
- There is less chance for bond default over the short run than over long periods of time.
- Bonds with long maturities and high duration have the greatest risk.
- Small interest rate changes can become magnified over long periods of time.

- Interest rates affect economic expansion. Changes in interest rates often affect the price of stocks.
- Higher interest rates make stocks less attractive to own.
- Lower interest rates stimulate business growth and help stock prices rise.
- Lower interest rates make bonds less attractive to own. This helps drive stock prices upward.

INTEREST RATES & INVESTING

Prevailing interest rates have a significant impact on investing.

Low interest rates make it easy to borrow money. This usually leads to economic expansion, as companies borrow at low rates to grow. The same holds true for individuals when they borrow to spend. When interest rates are low, people buy more things like cars, large appliances and homes. People refinance mortgages to get cash to invest or spend. This propels the economy, and lifts stock prices.

High interest rates tend to limit business growth. High interest rates often lead to less lending, lower business growth and lower personal spending. High rates lead to lower economic growth, or even cause recession. High interest rates can keep stock prices down, especially in the early stages of economic slowdowns..

Interest rates have an effect on all investments. The greater the interest rate changes, the greater the investment impact.

Investors purchase common stocks with *future earnings* in mind. If interest rates rise significantly, investors will expect lower business growth. Bonds will become more attractive to own. This can drive down the price of stocks.

Bondholders normally own bonds for the income. Therefore, the prices of existing bonds will react quickly to any changes in prevailing, or expected interest rates. When new bonds have high yields, investors won't want older ones with lower yields.

WHAT CHANGES INTEREST RATES?

Some interest rate changes are determined by market forces. Others are created by governments as they manipulate bond yields to maintain, stimulate or slow economic growth or inflation.

There are a few basic concepts every investor should know.

YIELD

Yield: The yield (interest rate & return) on long-term debt is usually higher than the yield on short-term debt. There is less chance of default in the short run, and more risk over the long-term. As risk increases, so do yield rates.

VOLATILITY

Volatility: The price movement (volatility) of short-term debt is usually less than that of long term debt. Longer terms mean higher risk.

INTEREST IMPACT

Impact: Small interest rate changes become magnified over time. A temporary, one percent change in yield may not materially affect your retirement planning. A one percent change that remains for a decade becomes significant.

Interest Rates
How Bond Prices Move
Relative To Interest Rates

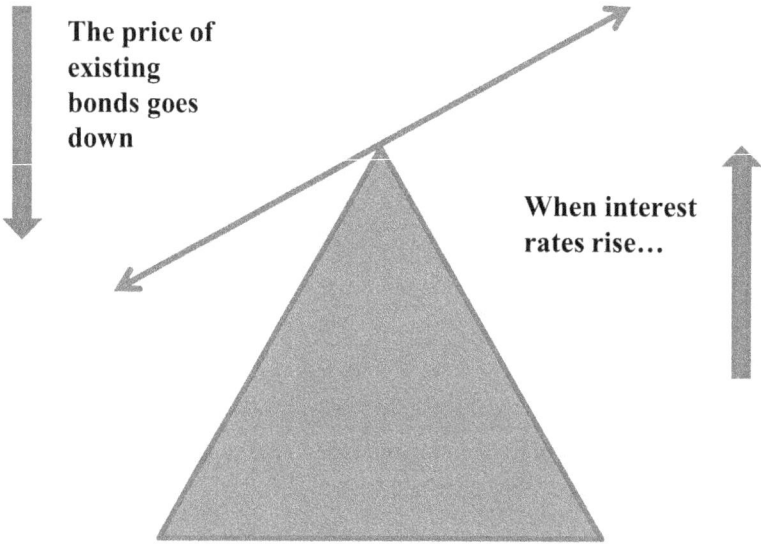

**The price of
existing
bonds goes
down**

**When interest
rates rise...**

RISING RATES

The preceding chart illustrates the impact of rising interest rates on the price of existing bonds. When rates rise, the prices of existing bonds move in the opposite direction. Existing bonds become less competitive as interest rates rise. This is because old bond yields are less than the yields on new bonds. If current rates rise, bond prices must fall, so that the yield to maturities *equalize* between new and existing bonds of similar duration and quality.

FALLING RATES

When rates fall, the prices of existing bonds rise. This is because new bonds have lower interest rates than old bonds. The prices of old bonds increase, so that the yield to maturity of old bonds matches those of new bonds.

BOND RISK & RETURN

When bond risk is high, yields are high.

Interest Rates
How Bond Prices Move
Relative To Interest Rates

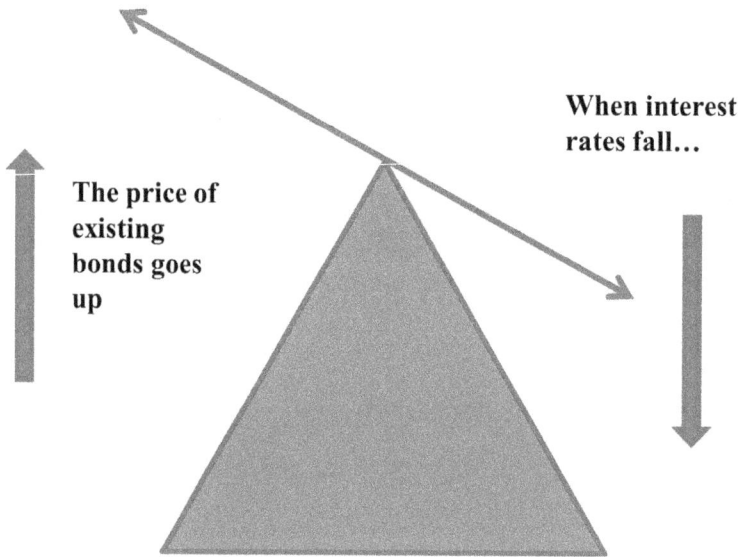

When interest
rates fall...

The price of
existing
bonds goes
up

Risk & Return
The Greater The Short Term Risk, The Greater Expected Long-Term Return

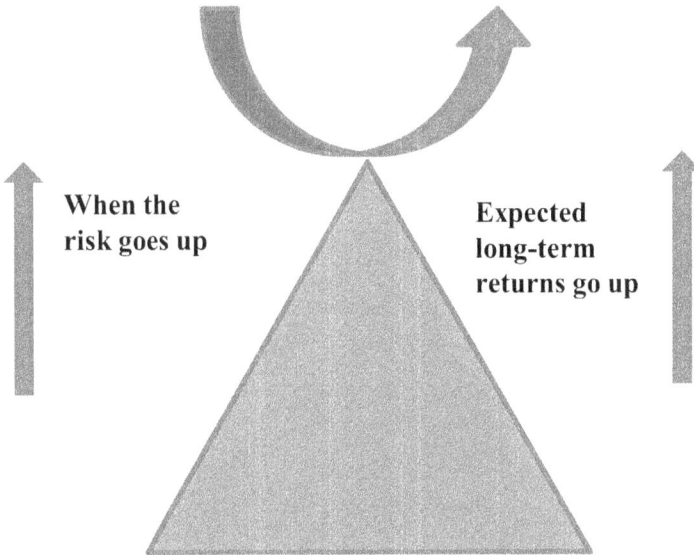

When the risk goes up

Expected long-term returns go up

Let's continue with our charts.

When risk goes down, either by higher credit quality or shorter duration, bond yields fall. When an issuer has a higher credit rating, investors feel safer and demand lower returns. When investors will be repaid in a shorter period of time, risk falls, along with yields.

Risk & Return
The Lower The Short Term Risk, The Lower Expected Long-Term Return

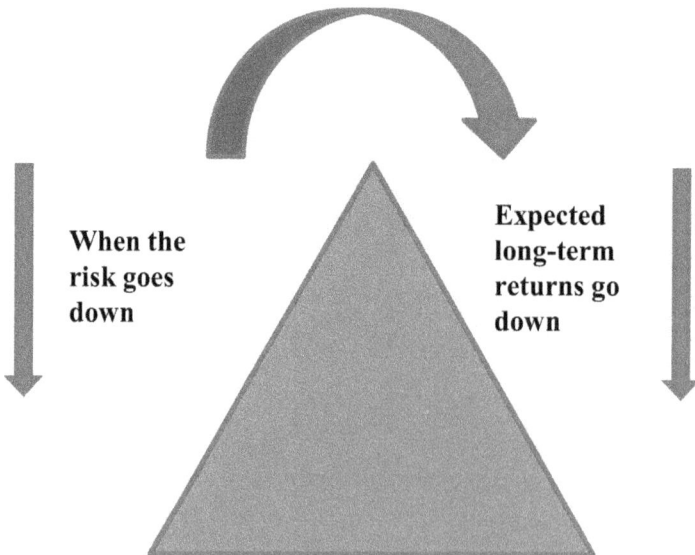

When the risk goes down

Expected long-term returns go down

TYPES OF BOND RISK: Bonds have two primary types of risk:

- Default Risk &

- Duration Risk.

DEFAULT RISK

Default risk is the risk that a company (or government entity) will default on its principal and interest payments.

Many countries, such as Brazil, Argentina, Greece, Spain and Ireland have defaulted on their debt, or had major restructuring (adjustments to the original terms).

Many companies have gone out of business. Others have become mere shells of their former greatness. Dominant computer manufacturers like Wang are gone. The former camera giant, Polaroid, declared bankruptcy in 2001. The energy trading giant, Enron, no longer exists. Global Crossing, an Internet fiber-optics leader, went into bankruptcy, its assets sold to a company controlled by Li Ka-Shing, who also owns the Panama Canal. A123, the high-end battery manufacturer, declared bankruptcy and sold it's assets to another Chinese company. Myspace, Napster and Lycos came and went in a cyber flash. Detroit, and other major U.S. cities, are approaching default. Home prices are so low in Detroit that they can be purchased with a credit card.

Default risk is very, very real.

DURATION

There is a helpful mathematical formula that can be calculated for all bonds. It is called duration. Duration is a measurement that helps investors quantify a bond's risk. Duration represents how the price of a bond reacts to a rise and fall in interest rates. Duration is a function of a bond's:

- Maturity (when the bond matures),

- Yield, (what rate the bond is paying investors now),

- Coupon (the initial interest rate), and

- It's Call Features — when and if the bond issuer can buy its bonds back for a stated price.

Duration is normally measured with a function called the Macaulay Duration, named after Frederick Macaulay who devised the measure. More about the Macaulay Duration can be found here: https://en.wikipedia.org/wiki/Bond_duration#Macaulay_duration

MATURITY

When a company or government entity issues debt, it comes with a due date. At some point in time, the issuer promises to repay the debt in full. Sometimes, the issuer can "call" its debt, and redeem it at a sooner time.

Some bonds can be redeemed early. Interest rates change daily. The credit quality of issuers fluctuates. Duration statistics incorporate these variables and gives a more accurate estimate of when a bond might be repaid — its true maturity date.

MATURITY & DURATION

Stable corporations issue bonds with long maturities. It is not unusual for financially secure companies, and governments, to issue bonds that won't be repaid for thirty years. Until redemption, every three months, these bond issuers will pay interest on their notes. The bondholders receive the income as a return for their investment.

Thirty years is a long time. Many things can go wrong for a company or government before it repays its debt. Such long-term risk *increases* duration.

Bonds with longer maturities, and high durations, tend to be *more volatile* when interest rates change. The bonds with higher duration are more sensitive to interest rate changes. The higher the duration, the more a bond's price will fall when interest rates rise. And vice versa. There are reasons for this. The primary causes are as follows:

- The longer the term, the greater the chance that a company or government entity will default on its debt.

- The shorter the term, the less current interest rates affect the price.

- The higher the yield on a bond, the more it responds to changes in prevailing interest rates.

YIELD & DURATION

Yield is what a bond pays. The higher the yield, the higher the risk, the higher the duration. Lower credit quality means higher yield, and higher duration. The shorter the maturity, the lower the yield and duration.

CALL FEATURES

Call features lower duration. When a bond issuer has the option of paying off (redeeming) its debt before the maturity date, there is a chance it might do so. The likelihood of a redemption changes with interest rates, time and credit quality.

For example: Let's assume that an issuer has a call feature that it can exercise at any time. The initial interest rate is 4% on bonds that mature in thirty years. If interest rates fall to 2%, and the credit quality of the issuer hasn't changed since the issue, the borrower can pay off its 4% notes and issue new ones at 2%. This ability reduces duration. If interest rates rise to 6%, duration (the essential/ expected payoff date) will rise closer to the maturity date.

If the credit quality of the issuer falls significantly, duration will rise. This is because the issuer will find it more difficult to pay off its debt, or redeem it and issue new debt at a rate lower than 4%.

AVERAGE DURATION & BOND MUTUAL FUNDS

When a mutual fund owns bonds, it usually holds many of them. Each bond will have its own set of cash flows, its own duration. A mutual fund's average duration is the *weighted average of the durations of all bonds held by the fund.*

MORTGAGE BONDS: MATURITY & DURATION

Most mortgages are packaged together and sold as bonds. These bonds will have an average duration, plus an average maturity.

The underlying mortgages inside a bond may have different maturity dates. Some could be fifteen year mortgages. Others may be for thirty years. They may be in different stages of repayment.

Over time, some mortgages will remain in place. Others will be paid off, upon sale of the home or after foreclosure. Other mortgages might be paid off due to a refinance by the owner.

As market interest rates fall significantly, average maturities will fall as well. More homes will be sold. More mortgages will be refinanced. As interest rates rise, fewer mortgages will be redeemed. Fewer mortgages will be refinanced and fewer homes will be sold. Average maturity grows longer.

BOND SUMMARY

This book has said the same thing in many different ways. Hopefully, this has helped you gain a better understanding of bonds.

To a professional investor, bonds are quite sophisticated. For the individual investor, bonds must be made simple. Think of this:

Investors give cash to a borrower. The borrower promises to pay quarterly interest, either current or implied with zero coupon, for the length of the bond. When the bond matures, payment will be made in full.

Bonds are bought and sold based upon what they pay now, when they will be paid in full, and the credit quality of the borrower.

The longer the maturity, the higher the duration, the higher the risk. Higher risks mean higher interest rates on bonds. There is also a higher risk that you will lose money. Shorter maturity lowers the risk.

The lower the credit quality of the borrower, the higher the risk. The higher the risk, the higher the yield. The higher the credit quality of the borrower, the lower the risk. The lower the risk, the lower the yield.

Longer maturities and higher interest rates lead to longer duration. High duration means greater price sensitivity to changes in interest rates. The greater the duration, the higher the risk, the higher the yield. To learn more about bonds, try this link: https://www.pimco.com/resources/education/understanding-duration

Convexity

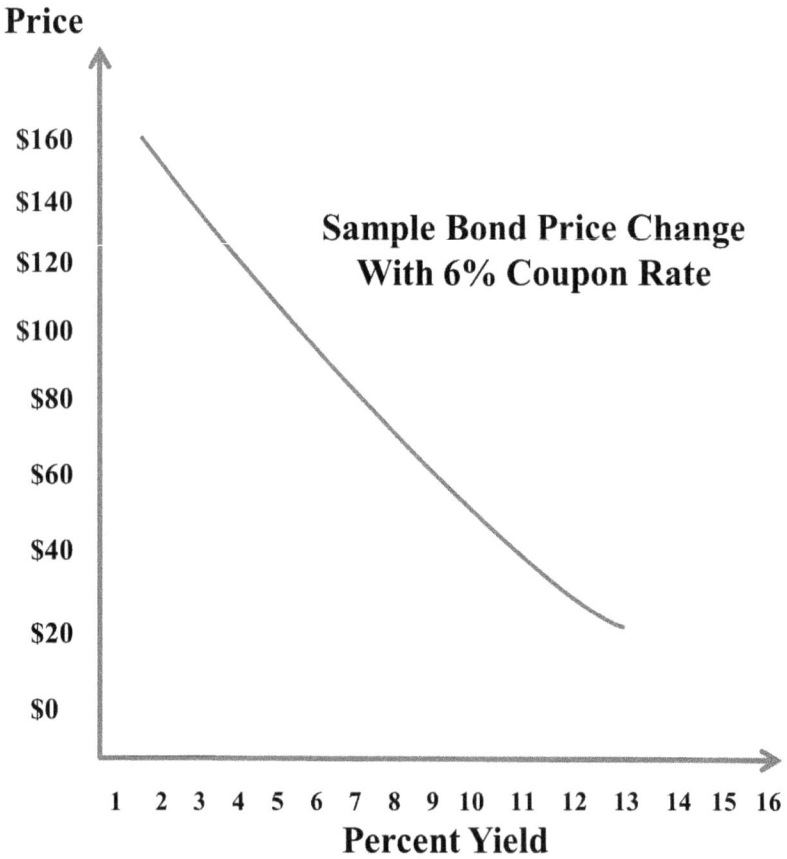

The preceding chart illustrates how bond prices can change relative to prevailing interest rates. This represents the price movement of a sample 15-year, $100 bond with a coupon (interest) rate of 6%. When interest rates are at 6%, the bond price is at 100. As prevailing rates increase (to the right on the chart), the price of the bond will fall. As interest rates fall below 6% (toward the left), the price of the bond will rise.

INVESTOR SUMMARY

For most investors, bonds represent the "low risk" portion of their retirement assets. Excessive bond risk can undermine a long-term accumulation plan. Most individuals that are accumulating for retirement should consider the following:

- A well diversified mix of investment grade bonds, with

- A moderate duration of 5-12 years,

- Held through the ups and downs of interest rate changes and economic cycles.

The following chart illustrates the relationship between duration, credit quality and bond yields. High quality, short-duration bonds will have the lowest yields. T-bills would be on your left. Low quality, long-duration bonds will have the highest yield. Junk bonds and junk international bonds with 30-year maturities would be far to the right. As you can see, the longer the duration and the lower the quality, the higher the yield bond issuers must pay to borrow money.

Note: As of this writing, Triple-C-Rated high yield (junk) bonds have ranged in yield from 10% - 18.6%. Prices have fallen 16% in the past 52 weeks.

http://online.wsj.com/mdc/public/page/2_3022-bondbnchmrk.html

Debt Duration & Credit Quality

Yield Versus Duration & Quality

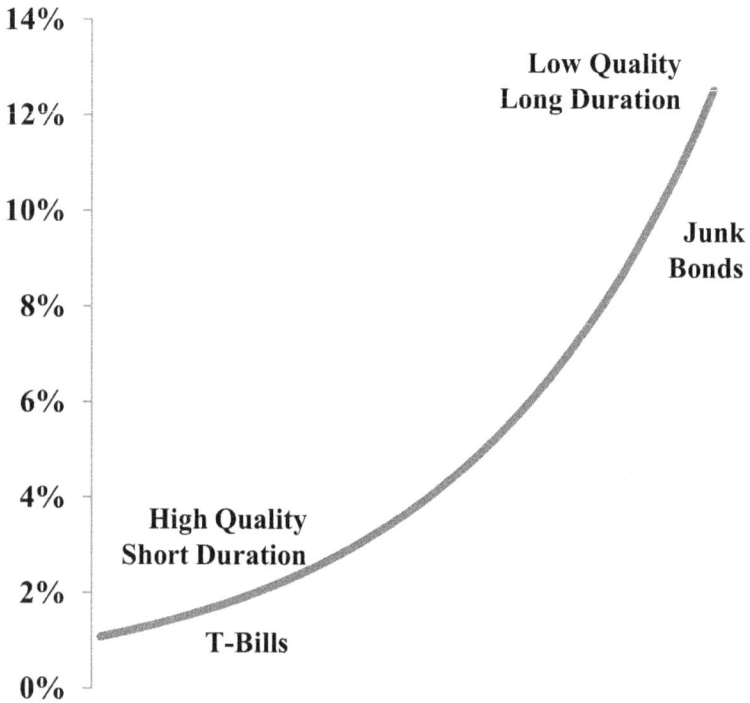

Chapter Twenty-Two

_____R_____

Benchmarks Of Investment Performance

INVESTMENT PERFORMANCE

As you study investments, inside and outside a retirement plan, you need to know how well they perform. Let's say you consider a mutual fund that has grown by _100%_ over the past decade. This performance may look outstanding. But if the _average_ of similar mutual funds grew by _150%_ during the same decade, this fund won't seem as good to own.

Stock and bond returns should be measured against _unmanaged indexes_. Indexes provide independent **benchmarks** that can be used to measure the _relative performance_ of individual stocks, bonds, or managed accounts, like mutual funds.

The following page explains some of the indexes that are used by investors to measure relative performance.

If you watch the news, you will usually hear mention of stock performance, particularly that of the S&P 500 Index, or the Dow Jones Industrial Average.

You will hear less talk of bond market indexes. This does not mean that bonds aren't important. Bonds are very important. The total U.S. bond capitalization is greater than U.S. common stocks. They just aren't spectacular to report. The media likes sensation. Stock market indexes often gain or lose hundreds of points in a day. Bond indexes move in hundredths of points at a time. Big institutions care. The general public doesn't understand the complexities, or pay attention.

Relevant Market Indexes

There are many indexes that measure the performance of domestic stocks. Some of the major indexes are explained below. Indexes are designed to present an *average market capitalization*. There are larger and smaller companies within each index. They are approximations only.

U.S. STOCKS

Large Cap Indexes:

Large cap stocks represent the largest market capitalization of US equities. The indexes that measure the performance of large companies vary in structure. The companies included in these indexes tend to have market capitalization of at least $3.5 billion, usually more.

- The Dow Jones Industrial Average Index represents 30 large US industrial companies (Such as Apple, 3M, IBM, Microsoft & Wall Mart), which are chosen to represent a cross-section of American business.

- The Dow Jones Wilshire Large-Cap Index represents the "large-cap" portion of the Dow Jones Wilshire 5000 Index. This index contains the 750 largest public companies, as measured by total market capitalization.

- The S&P 500 Index represents the 500 largest publicly traded companies.

Mid-Cap Indexes:

As a general rule, mid-cap stocks have market capitalizations more than $1 billion and less than $5 billion. Market cap could be as high as $10 billion.

- The Dow Jones Wilshire Mid-Cap Index is a subset of the The Dow Jones Wilshire 5000 Index. It consists of the US companies that are ranked 501-1,000, as measured by total market capitalization. The larger companies might still be considered large-cap, while the smallest could be considered small cap companies. The average is mid-cap.

- The S&P 400 Mid-Cap Index includes stocks with market capitalizations from (approximately) $750 million to $3.5 billion.

Small Cap Indexes:

Most small-cap stocks have market capitalizations between $300 million and $2 billion.

- The performance of small-cap domestic stocks is measured by the Dow Jones Wilshire US Small-Cap Index. This is comprised of stocks ranked 751-2,500 in the Wilshire 5000 Index.

- The S&P Small-Cap 600 Index measures a narrower range of small-cap stocks.

- The Russell 2000 Index represents the smallest 2,000 stocks of the Russell 3000 Index.

International Stock Indexes

The primary International Stock indexes are measured by Morgan Stanley, a large investment banking firm. They are as follows:

- The MSCI EAFE Index (Europe, Asia, & Far East)
- The MSCI World Index (Large & Mid-cap in 23 Developed Markets)
- The MDCI Emerging Markets Index (Large & Mid-cap in 23 Emerging Market Countries)

NASDAQ

The NASDAQ Index represents companies traded on the electronic NASDAQ system. These stocks often represent high tech companies. The NASDAQ Index is used to measure the broad performance of technology companies.

BONDS

The primary goals of most bond investors are safety of principal and current income. Most individuals are not counting on capital gains with their bond holdings.

The performance of bonds is measured in a number of ways. Bond indexes focus around major broad classes, such as: Global bonds, US corporate bonds, U.S. Government bonds, Emerging Market bonds, High-Yield bonds & Asset-Backed securities.

Within a retirement plan, bonds tend to be from two primary asset classes—government & corporate bonds. High-yield, asset-backed and international bonds may also be part of an expanded retirement plan mix.

The most widely used indexes are Barclays and Lipper.

- The Barclays Capital Aggregate Bond Index measures a very broad mix of bonds. These bonds consist primarily of widely-traded treasury securities, government agency bonds, corporate bonds and asset-backed securities. This index is often used to measure the general performance of investment-grade bonds.

- Barclays also has indexes that measure the performance of long-term, mid-term and short term bonds.
- Lipper (a division of Thompson Reuters) has various bond indexes that measure by asset class, credit quality and duration.
- Examples of Lipper asset classes are:
  - U.S. government bonds,
  - Short-term investment grade bonds,
  - Corporate A rated bonds &
  - High-yield bond funds.

Retirement plan investors often choose bond funds that try to mirror certain indexes, such as:

- The Barclays U.S. Aggregate Index,
- The Lipper U.S. Government Index,
- The Lipper Corporate A Rated Bonds Index.

BOND MATURITIES:

The maturities of bonds are normally classified as:

- Short-term (less than 5 years),
- Intermediate-term (5-10 years), and
- Long-term (more than 10 years).

$&₵

Chapter Twenty-Three

_____R_____

Inflation Adjusted Returns

Inflation Adjusted Annual Returns

When planning for retirement, getting a positive return on your investments is important. Earning a return that *outpaces inflation* is critical.

If your retirement investments do not outpace inflation, there is little chance, if any, that you will have enough money for retirement.

What sort of return might you expect from various types of investments?

The following chart illustrates the long-term returns that were achieved, from 1926 through the end of the 20th century, by different classes of investments. These returns are compared to the inflation rate over that same time period.

The ***net return over inflation*** can be considered the "real" investment return. This is the return that increases the purchasing power of your money. This is what you need to make your money grow.

Real returns lead to an increase in purchasing power.

Not surprisingly, the investments with the *lowest risk* have provided the *lowest returns* over long periods of time.

LOWER RISK

Short-term T-bills are 91-day debt issued by the Federal government. The risk is low. The long-term returns have been slightly above inflation. T-bills serve as the "risk-free" investment, against which all other investments are measured.

HIGHER RISK

The S&P 500 has more short-term risk than "safe" T-bills. Stocks returned an average of 11.5% over the 73 year period. This is more than 8.4% *above inflation,* and about 8% above T-bills, the risk-free return.

Note: This illustration highlights investment returns from 1926-2000. If you are wondering if investing has changed dramatically since that time, don't.

From 1928-2014, the S&P 500 had an (arithmetic) average return of 11.53%, right in line with the 11.5% illustrated. T-bills averaged 3.53%. This gives stocks the same 8% real return over T-bills. (Source: St. Louis Federal Reserve, NYU Stern)

The second chart shows the growth of one single dollar invested over that same time frame (from 1926 through the end of the 20th century).

Inflation Adjusted Annual Returns
How Various Asset Classes Have Performed
Relative To Inflation. From 1926 To The
End Of The Last Century

Asset Class:	1926-1999 Average Annual Total Return	1926-1999 Inflation Average	Total Return Net of Inflation	Annual Volatility
Short-Term T-Bills	3.8%	3.1%	0.7%	Low
Int. Term Gov't Bonds	5.2%	3.1%	2.1%	Low
Long Term Gov't Bonds	5.5%	3.1%	2.4%	Medium
Long Term. Corp Bonds	5.6%	3.1%	2.5%	Medium
Stocks (S&P 500)	11.5%	3.1%	8.4%	High
Small Company Stocks	12.8%	3.1%	9.7%	Highest

Sources: Ibbotson, DFA, S&P 500 Index, Lehman Brothers (Barclays) Indexes, CPI (US Treasury)

Note: From 1928-2014, the arithmetic average annual return of the S&P 500 Index was 11.53%. The average T-Bill rate was 3.53%. The average yield for ten-year T-Bonds was 5.28%. These averages align closely with this more detailed illustration. Source: St. Louis Fed, NYU Stern.

Compounded Returns For Various Asset Classes From 1926 to 2000. What Did They Grow To?

Asset Class:	Average 1926 – 1999	Ann. Total Return 1926 – 1999		Average Volatility
Inflation	$1.00	$9.39	3.1%	Low
Short-Term T Bills	$1.00	$15.72	3.85%	Low
Int. Term Gov't Bonds	$1.00	$40.47	5.2%	Low
Long Term Gov't Bonds	$1.00	$50.65	5.5%	Medium
Long Term Corporate Bonds	$1.00	$52.65	5.6%	Medium
Common Stocks (S&P 500)	$1.00	$2845.49	11.5%	High
Small Company Stocks	$1.00	$6639.94	12.8%	Highest

Notice the long-term reward for taking short-term risk?

Sources: Ibbotson, DFA, S&P 500 Index, Lehman Brothers (Barclays) Indexes, CPI (US Treasury)

Stocks can be volatile. Returns are not guaranteed or insured. Past performance is no guarantee of future performance.

As you can see, by assuming greater risk, a long-term investor in small company stocks would have seen her dollar grow to $6,639.94. A low-risk investor who invested in investments with the lowest risk, T-bills, would have seen $1 grow to $15.72.

This is the power of compounding. This is power of taking risk. Would you rather have one dollar grow to $15.72 or $6,639?

As you decide how to invest your money, you must assess your investment time frame. You must then determine the short-term risk you are willing to take to achieve the long-term returns you need.

If you have 20 years until retirement, are married and in decent health, you have a long-term investment horizon (including retirement) of 50 years or more. If you are single, your investment time frame is only a few years shorter.

You will need to take risk to earn the returns you need to complete your retirement plan successfully.

If you are saving for retirement, low risk investments actually increase the risk that you won't have enough money for retirement. Higher risk investments *lower* the risk of you outliving your money.

Make more sense? More on this soon.

$&₵

Chapter Twenty-Four

R

Market Capitalization

MARKET CAPITALIZATION

In order to grow, young companies obtain money from investors. This usually comes in the form of stocks and bonds.

Note: Many companies, especially those in high technology and medicine, find private investors for their early capitalization. These investors may be venture capital firms, universities, or individual "angel investors" with very deep pockets.

Initial investors usually own shares with attributes (strings) such as extra voting, conversion privileges or preference upon liquidation or sale.

When a company goes public, through an Initial Public Offering, these strings eventually get cut away, as equity shares or bonds are converted and/or sold.

The following chart illustrates a hypothetical *initial market capitalization* of a public company.

This sample company issued $100 million in bonds, $100 million in preferred stock (perhaps from early investors), and $100 million in common stock.

Initial Corporate Capitalization

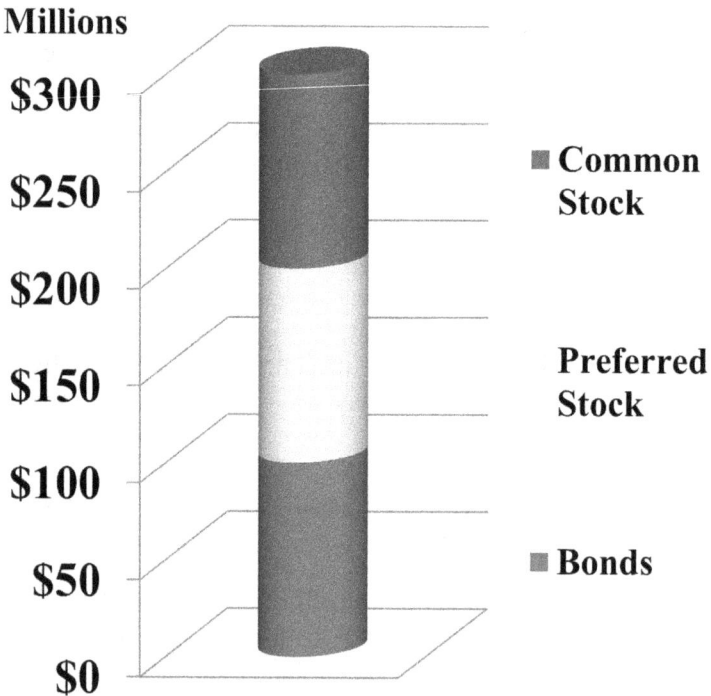

Millions

$300

$250

$200

$150

$100

$50

$0

Common Stock

Preferred Stock

Bonds

Successful companies use their initial capital to grow. When start-ups transition to a viable company, they usually go "public" with an IPO, an initial public offering of shares to the investing public.

The following chart shows the market capitalization after our sample company has used its initial capital to grow and go public.

In this example, the company's common stock now has a market capitalization of $20 billion. This dwarfs the initial capitalization amount. The company's early investors have made money on their stock. Investment share prices have grown many times in value.

This company may grow to become the next Amazon or Google. If so, the $20 billion value of its stock will look like a bargain.

Think back to this book's discussion about large, small, and mid-cap stocks. This example illustrates the capitalization of a company as it transitioned from a small-cap stock to a large-cap stock.

Most initial public offerings involve stocks of small cap companies. Some companies, like Facebook and Google, were never small-cap public stocks. During their IPOs, they became instant large-cap stocks.

Most companies start small, and grow from there. Historically, they reward investors well over the long run.

Corporate Capitalization
After Growth

Billions

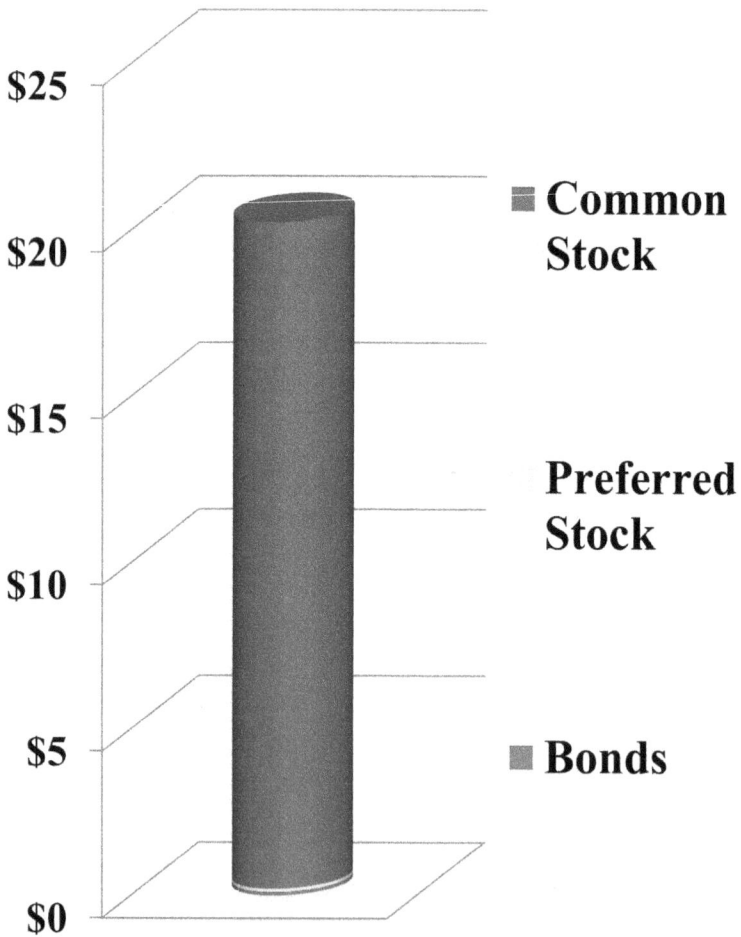

Chapter Twenty-Five

R

Mutual Funds

MUTUAL FUND SUMMARY

In 1924, a group of small investors in Boston pooled their money and placed it with a private manager. The manager treated the investors' pool as one account. This created the first mutual fund. Today, there are more mutual funds than there are stocks.

Each mutual fund has a manager, or a team of managers. These managers determine the fund's *investment objectives*.

Some funds might invest for aggressive growth. Others may invest for growth and income. Still others invest to preserve principal, while achieving some growth of capital and income over time. Managers might choose to hedge their investments with derivatives. Some simply choose a mix of stocks to mirror an index.

There are many objectives and styles that managers can employ.

Most investors who are accumulating for retirement put their money (and trust) in mutual funds. You should understand what they are and how they work. Below, you will find the most important characteristics of mutual funds:

- Mutual Funds were created to give small investors access to professional management and economies of scale.

- Every mutual fund has an investment manager. This person, or group of persons, takes your money and invests it according to specific parameters set up by the fund.

- Each mutual fund has specific investment objectives.

- Growth funds invest for capital growth. This means they try to increase the overall value of the fund.

- Growth and income funds invest with (somewhat) equal objectives of growth and current income.

- Balanced funds invest with two primary objectives—growth & income. One fund might invest for income, with a secondary objective of conservative capital growth. Another might invest for growth, with a secondary objective of income.

- Some funds invest in foreign stocks only. These are usually called foreign funds.

- Other funds invest in a combination of U.S. and foreign shares. These are often called world funds.

- The net capital gains inside a mutual fund account, and the income earned, are passed through to the shareholders, you.

- Funds can invest in many different vehicles, such as cash and cash equivalents, bonds, convertible bonds, preferred stocks, domestic common stocks, options, warrants, international, or emerging market stocks. Each manager has a set of investment parameters that he is supposed to follow.

- There are two basic types of mutual funds—open-ended and closed-ended. Retirement plans usually offer open-ended funds.

- With open-ended funds, investors can buy and sell shares at any time from the fund sponsor. Shares are redeemed at Net Asset Value (NAV), the underlying value of the total portfolio.

- Being open-ended creates a constant inflow and/or outflow of investment funds, over various periods of time, to the fund sponsor. When things are going well, there is often an inflow of cash to be invested. When the markets, or the fund, fare poorly, money can flow out. Large outflows may force the managers to sell stock shares or bonds they might prefer to keep.

- The value of mutual fund shares is adjusted each evening. The NAV is priced to reflect the underlying net value of the fund assets at the end of each trading day (usually after the New York markets have closed).

- There are no guaranteed returns in mutual funds. They do provide diversification. In the long run, diversification is a sound investment strategy.

- Mutual fund trustees normally conduct the shareholder voting for all individual securities owned by the fund. Such voting might include choosing a company's board of directors. The board of directors determine such things as executive compensation, stock options and company dividends.

Wall Street

Company
Management
Buys & Sells
Stocks & Bonds

Shares or $
To Fund

**Investor Buys
& Sells Mutual
Fund Shares**

$

Investor Receives Net
Capital Gains/Losses,
Capital Appreciation/Loss,
Dividends & Interest

**Mutual Fund
Management**

**Owner
Wealth
Grows
To
Create
Nest Egg**

MUTUAL FUNDS IN RETIREMENT PLANS

In retirement plans, mutual fund choices are generally limited to the most common investment objectives.

OBJECTIVES: Examples of the typical investment objectives of retirement plan funds might be as follows:

- Aggressive growth
- Growth
- Growth & income
- Income and growth
- Income
- Corporate bond
- Government bond
- Money market

Investment objectives in stock funds can have a more targeted approach, such as:

- Large, small, and mid-cap value, or
- Large, small and mid-cap growth.

MODELS

Many retirement plans offer asset allocation models, which are managed toward specific objectives. This book will review models shortly.

MUTUAL FUND PASS-THROUGH

Interest earned on bonds and cash, dividends from stocks, and net capital gains (and losses) are passed through to the individual shareholders of mutual funds. Capital gains and losses are passed through only after a fund manager sells the underlying shares. This allows for some mutual fund appreciation without current taxation. Taxes must be paid by shareholders on net gains, or income earned by the fund, unless the fund is owned inside a tax-sheltered vehicle. Pass-throughs are based upon the shares (units) of ownership. Most mutual funds allow the pass-throughs to automatically purchase new mutual fund shares. Tax-sheltered investors ultimately pay taxes when monies are distributed from the tax-sheltered vehicle (such as a retirement plan, IRA or annuity).

OPEN-ENDED VERSUS CLOSED-ENDED

There are two major types of mutual funds: Closed-ended and Open-ended. They operate differently.

CLOSED-ENDED FUNDS

Closed-ended funds raise an initial capital amount and then close the fund to new investors. Closed-end shares trade like a stock. The value is determined by what someone will pay for the shares. The value is usually based upon the "net asset value" of the fund. The fund share price may be higher or lower than NAV, depending upon demand for the shares.

OPEN-ENDED FUNDS

Open-ended funds are always open to new investors. They accept new shareholders any trading day. As previously stated, most retirement plans offer open-ended fund shares.

At the end of each trading day, the "net asset value" of an open-ended fund is calculated. The net asset value is the total underlying value of all assets owned by the fund, minus liabilities.

The net asset value, plus front-end loads or acquisition expenses, determines a *price per unit* that investors must pay for new shares. This value changes daily, based upon the performance of the fund. Fund units are purchased and sold from the fund at the end of each trading day. Some open-ended funds charge a fee, or front-end load, to join. Others do not. Some charge a fee when sold. Most do not. Shares in retirement plans are generally offered without front-end or back-end charges. They are bought and sold at NAV.

Chapter Twenty-Six

_____R_____

Derivatives

Derivatives

Derivatives have become an important, yet little understood, part of the investment landscape.

A derivative does not represent ownership of an underlying asset, but a promise to do something related to the asset, if certain events occur. A derivative can be the *promise to perform* certain contracted obligations relating to that asset. A derivative can be a *promise to convey ownership* of an asset.

The asset upon which the derivative is created is known as the *underlying asset* or *instrument*.

Sound confusing? Derivatives are very complex, but important to understand.

According to the World Federation of Exchanges, in 2014, the total trading value of all global equities (stocks) was about *$70 trillion*. At the same time, the notional value of all outstanding derivative contracts was nearly *$700 trillion*. Derivatives are a large, shadowy part of the investment world, yet few of us know they exist.

This is worth repeating: In 2014, the total value of derivative contracts was *nearly ten times* the value of the assets backing them.

WHAT ASSETS?

About 89% of derivative contracts are tied to the bond markets and to interest rates. There are approximately 22 billion exchange-traded contracts outstanding. Derivative trading is massive.

WHAT IS THE PURPOSE OF A DERIVATIVE?

Common stock derivatives were first offered through the Chicago Board Options Exchange. The CBOE grew from the concept of commodity futures trading. Its first chairman was Edward C. Wilson, a Harvard graduate and commodities trader. Prior to founding the CBOE, Wilson's job was buying and selling futures contracts in commodities like gold and silver, corn and pork bellies—usually for his own account. Wilson teamed with the O'Connor family to do the same with stocks.

COMMODITIES FUTURES

Commodity prices are volatile. Commodity values change wildly because of unpredictable forces like the weather, business conditions or geopolitics. Too much or too little of an essential commodity can change prices immensely. Commodity *futures* contracts were created as a *hedge* against the potential rise or fall in commodity prices.

For example: A corn farmer could "pre-sell" all or a portion of his crop, months before his harvest was due. If the farmer knew what his expenses would be, the farmer could "lock in" a profit by *pre-selling* all (or a portion) of his crop in the commodities market. That way, if prices were low (because of oversupply or low demand) when the crop was harvested, the farmer didn't "lose the farm." He had already sold at a higher, guaranteed price.

The commodity *pre-buyer* might be a cereal producer who needs to guarantee a corn supply and is budgeting months in advance. Or, a beef or pig producer (think bacon pork bellies & T-bones).

The daily trade value of derivatives is approximately $7 trillion.

http://www2.isda.org/

The daily dollar trade volume of the New York Stock Exchange is approximately $40 billion.

http://www.nyxdata.com/

SPECULATION

Speculators can buy or sell futures contracts without owning any commodities at all. If a speculator feels that the price of corn might fall, she might "sell" futures contracts to a corn buyer (such as our cereal maker), or to another speculator. At some point, our corn speculator must deliver the corn. She must "close out" the contract by buying the actual corn (or a corn delivery contract) to deliver before the contract's expiration.

If the price is lower when the contract is closed out, our speculator has made money. If the price is higher than the original sales price, she must make up the difference between the initial contract sales price and the contract purchase price, with new cash.

STOCK OPTIONS

The first stock derivative contracts were "call" and "put" options. These options were (and still are) sold in 100 share increments. Stock options typically expire after nine months or less.

CALLS

A call option can be sold by any stock owner or speculator. For example, if an investor has a big gain on a stock, she might wish to protect her profits against a loss in value. If the current price is $40 per share, the investor might sell someone the "option" to buy the stock at $45 per share. This option might sell for $2. If our stock owner sells an option on 100 shares, this will put $2/share ($200) in her pocket. In nine months, the option will expire.

If, after nine months, the share price has never approached $45, the stock will not be purchased by the option buyer. The option seller still owns her stock, but she has hedged her downside risk by getting an annualized return of 6.67% ($2 on the $40 share price over nine months) for the option. If the current price is now $38/share, our stock owner technically hasn't lost anything, except for taxes on her option sale.

The option *buyer* has lost his speculation investment of $2 per share.

If desired, the stock owner can now sell a new option on her stock. The price will be higher or lower, based upon market conditions at the time. Let's say she sells a second option, just as before.

If the price of the hedged stock goes up to $50 (from $40), the option purchaser can buy the stock for $45, the original option price. The seller of the option must deliver the stock at $45, even though the shares now trade at $50. Our option buyer has paid a total of $47 ($2 for the option and the $45 strike price) for shares that are now worth $50. The call investor was rewarded for purchasing the option.

The second time the seller sold the option, she guessed wrong. She has to sell her stock for $45, even though the current price is $50. But she still made out well, by receiving $45 for her stock and $4 for the two option contracts.

PUTS

With a "put" option, the option buyer purchases the right, but not the obligation, to *sell* 100 shares of a stock for a specific price. In this case, the option *buyer* is betting that the share *price* will go *down*.

Let's say that our original investor thinks that the $40 price of her stock might lose value, and she wants to protect her gains. Another strategy might be to buy a $40 put option on her stock. For example's sake, let's say she pays $2 for the option.

If the price of the stock falls to $35, our investor can "put" her option and still sell the stock for $40. This gives our investor a net price of $38 per share ($40 less the $2 paid per share for the option). The hedge has worked, because without the option, our investor would have only received $35 per share. Our investor could also sell her put option for a profit and keep her stock. Options are quite flexible, and have many uses.

ENDLESS DERIVATIVES

The list of derivatives is virtually endless. Bonds are broken into pieces known as "tranches," or slices. There can be more than a hundred tranches for a single bond issue.

WIN-WIN

Why would someone buy a derivative? Let's explore. A pension plan does not pay taxes on interest. Interest is "worth" more to a pension manager than to someone who must pay taxes on the interest.

A pension manager does *not* get favorable capital gains treatment. But an individual *investor* does. Capital gains can be worth more to individuals.

If a bond can be split into two pieces, an interest piece and a capital gains piece, each investor can get more of what they want from the bond.

The individual might pay a discounted amount for principal that is due years from now. When the bond is redeemed or sold, this gain will be taxed at capital gains rates, which are lower than income tax rates.

The pension manager buys the income stream only, which is not subject to tax inside the retirement plan.

Everybody wins here. Each investor gets more of what they want, including the investment banker who earns a nice fee or commission for brokering the deal.

There are hundreds and hundreds and hundreds of bond tranches. They can be created for any investment need. For example: One might buy the income in years 2023-2025 of a thirty-year note, while other investors purchase the rest. The options for derivatives are virtually endless.

DERIVATIVES AS INSURANCE IN THE BOND MARKET

Derivatives play a crucial role in the bond and currency markets. Derivative investors often deal with very large sums of money. Such investors might face significant currency or political risks. They may have fiduciary obligations to investment beneficiaries. To reduce potential risk, many large, institutional investments are "insured" with derivatives.

ROUND AND ROUND

Unstable nations must pay high interest rates to investors of their bonds. There is a significant risk of default to investors who buy them. The bond payments can be insured. Sometimes they are insured by companies that own the same bonds themselves. This is causing concern among insurers and investors. What if the Euro fails? What if a large economy, like Brazil or Italy, defaults on their bonds? Market ripples could become a tsunami. Or not.

INSURANCE EXAMPLE

Here is an example of how derivative insurance might work.

An investment manager decides to pay an insurer 1% per year to guarantee an entire bond income stream. If a pension manager has purchased high-yield, high-risk corporate bonds with 8% interest, a 1% fee to insure the income might seem worth it. The manager still earns a net interest of 7%.

If the issuing government or company defaults on payments, the *insurer* pays the anticipated interest income, until the end of the agreement, typically the date when the bond was scheduled to be repaid. The pension still earns a current rate of return, and keeps receiving the insurance income even if the bond issuer fully defaults.

In the event of default, a bond issuer will often go into bankruptcy. Debt terms might be re-negotiated. Assets might be sold. Bondholders will be paid in order of seniority. Investors may or may not be made whole.

But an investor with insurance will still get the insured income stream, as long as the insurer remains solvent. They may lose all or part of their investment (principal) but they don't lose the income.

AIG

Insuring bonds is what allowed the company, AIG, to earn very large profits. AIG was paid lots of money to insure bonds. As long as there were few defaults, AIG's insurance premium income was mostly profit.

Investments can be volatile, especially during periods of economic contraction. When the mortgage crisis began (2008-2009), AIG was insuring the payments for hundreds of billions in mortgages. When the crisis started, there was a knee-jerk reaction in the bond markets. This caused a sudden drop in bond prices. The media hyped the problem into a global crisis. Perhaps it was.

As events unfolded, and panic spread quickly, AIG's interest (derivative) guarantees forced it into a rapid insolvency, despite the underlying strength of its assets. The U.S. government provided AIG with *$182 billion* in emergency capital. This allowed AIG to make good on their insurance claims, and avoid its own demise.

The bailout of AIG may have helped avoid a global financial crisis. The ripple effect from its default may have been enormous. Maybe not. No one knows for sure, at least publicly.

By 2013, AIG had repaid the full government bailout, plus a profit of $22.7 billion. (Source: CNBC, March 1, 2013). This led some to wonder whether the global crisis was as acute as everyone thought.

Few of us ever glimpse beneath the investment surface. Maybe the world's financial bedrock was sound, unsettled by the short-term liquidity crunch of a few entities, all precipitated and exacerbated by media hype.

The AIG example does show the magnitude of how the default of a single company could shake the global marketplace. It took a crisis for the government to part with close to $1 trillion. What will the next crisis look like?

Financial institutions take massive positions in derivative contracts. The scale of these investments, plus the insurance, is far larger than that of AIG. You should be aware. Not scared. Just aware.

BANK PONZI

Banks are big bond investors.

Banks borrow money from their depositors or from central banks, like the Federal Reserve. Some of this money is lent to borrowers. The banks also use this money to buy bonds. The positive "spread," between borrowing costs and bond returns, creates profit for the banks. Banks might insure the bond interest payments, and even the default risk, with derivatives.

Many investment banks have 20-30 times more in "assets" than they have real "equity." Most of the bond assets are purchased with borrowed money. These assets are offset by the liabilities of the borrowing.

A dramatic upward change in interest rates, or even a return to historical interest rate norms, would significantly impact the *equity positions* of financial institutions around the world. When interest rates rise, the value of existing bonds falls. Because of this, many banks buy insurance against loss with derivatives. In theory, this reduces their risk.

Some governments even mandate *insurance of the insurance,* where banks purchase insurance against the default of the company that insured the original transaction.

I'LL INSURE YOU IF YOU INSURE ME

Many of the same organizations insuring against their own risk, insure others. Nobody truly knows the extent of this hidden, perhaps risky behavior.

Are the global derivatives marketsdoomed to collapse? Some think so. Others think not. Time will tell.

KEEP WATCHING

Most retirement plans (except for larger pensions) steer clear of pure derivatives. Some basic forms, like puts and calls, might be used by mutual fund managers to hedge risk. This is usually not risky behavior, and is appropriate.

You should understand the concept of derivatives, though. Some derivative and investment strategies fall into the "too good to be true" category. Watch out. They may be in the news someday.

A derivative crisis could cause a large market correction in the future. This would give long-term investors, such as participants in retirement plans, an historic buying opportunity, provided the markets recover, as they always have.

$&¢

Chapter Twenty-Seven

R

Emotions & Investing

On the first trading day of 2016, the Chinese stock market lost 7% of its total value in just seven minutes. Trading was halted, so that investors would have a day to overcome their panic.

Why are humans so emotional about investing? What can change in a few minutes that can cause hundreds of billions of dollars in market value to evaporate? Emotions.

Our emotions are ruled by neurotransmitters we cannot see, and find difficult to control. Emotions are a big part of investing. Human nature can, and does, influence how we save and invest.

THE MEDIA

Weather, politics, sports and the economy are the big subjects covered by the national media. Add celebrities and royalty in the tabloids, and you've got the big stuff. Everything else is filler.

The media love a good story. They can usually find one occurring in the world of finance, whether significant or not. Minor things can be exaggerated until they seem like, or get turned into a crisis.

INVEST THROUGH THE STORM

It is emotionally difficult to hold onto investments when news anchors are predicting the end of civilization (and investing) as we know it. But you must.

This book is devoted to giving you the proper information, so that you are **not** ruled by fear, but by *facts* and **history**.

Good investing demands perspective. Let's continue.

Emotions & Investing

**Tuesday morning
September 1, 1998**

**Tuesday evening
September 1, 1998**

This illustration shows two newspaper headlines that occurred on the same day in 1998. The morning paper ran a headline on how *panic* was hammering the stock market. The afternoon paper focused on how stocks had *bounced back*.

News organizations shape how we perceive the news, particularly in the world of finance.

The media's job is to sell newspapers, secure advertising spots, and capture more views, clicks and likes. The media will sensationalize market woes, especially when it can be tied to politics. That's what sells.

Pay attention. But don't get fooled into thinking that the world will end. If it does, you may have greater things to worry about than your retirement.

STOCK MARKET EMOTIONS

Morningstar Study

219 Growth Funds
1993 through 1997

Fund Performance   12.5%

Investor Performance   −2.2%

Morningstar is a company that compiles statistical data on investments, and then sells it to individuals and members of the securities industry. If you invest in a retirement plan, you may hear how Morningstar rates your fund choices.

From 1993-1997, Morningstar tracked the performance of 219 growth mutual funds. Morningstar also tracked the returns earned by investors in growth funds. Over the five years, the funds earned a respectable 12.5% average annual return. The average individual *investor* in such growth funds actually *lost* 2.2% per year.

DALBAR, INC.

Dalbar, Inc. is the nation's leading financial services market research firm. Each year, Dalbar conducts a detailed study of investment behavior. This report is known as The Quantitative Analysis of Investor Behavior (QAIB).

The 2009 QAIB analyzed the prior 20-year period from January 1989 to December 2008. During this time, the S&P 500 had an average annual return of 8.4%. The average stock investor earned only 1.9%. This represents a return **"gap"** between the S&P and actual investor returns of **6.5%**.

The 2013 report showed a 20 year return of 9.23% for the S&P 500, compared to an average investor return of 5.02%.

By 2014, the gap between the S&P Index, and those investing in the stock market had narrowed to **4.20%**. The narrowing of the return gap may be due to 401(k) education. 401(k) education is the only training that many investors receive.

If your equity investments perform this poorly against the averages, there is little chance that you will achieve your retirement goals.

S&P Versus Average Investor Performance

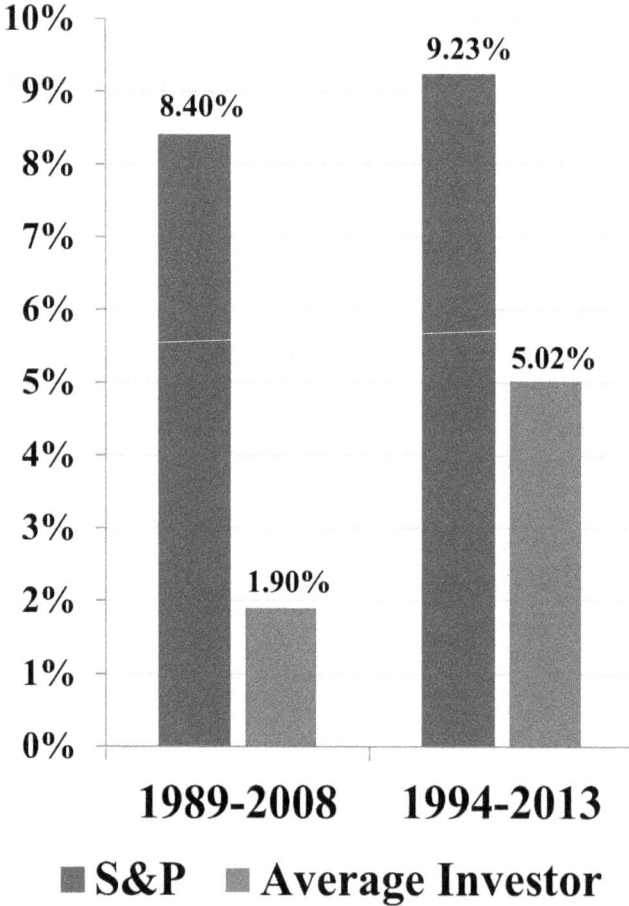

Source: Dalbar, Inc.

Why do investors still earn 45% *less* than the funds they invest in?

We have reviewed the power of compounding. Over thirty years, a 4.2% lower average investment return **would cut your lifetime savings in half.**

Why would investors take the same risk and earn half the money? Why do stock investors fare so poorly? **Emotions!**

Morningstar and DALBAR illustrate what many of us know to be true. Individuals often invest in stocks (or mutual funds) when the markets are moving upward. They often sell after stocks have gone down.

The *emotional fear of losing out on gains* causes us to buy, especially when we see other people making money. The *fear of loss* causes us to sell when the economic news gets bad. When the news gets bad, stocks have already fallen.

Some professional investors, known as contrarians, invest in the opposite direction as the small investor, the general public. How sad is that? When small investors are selling, contrarians buy. When small investors buy, contrarians look to sell. And they often win.

The goal of this book is to educate, so that you remove emotions from the investment equation. This will allow you to achieve average investment returns — which could more than double your ultimate assets in retirement.

This book will help you develop a winning, long-term investment strategy, and reduce your fears of investing.

Successful investment behavior requires holding the course, even steering into the storm, going forward when others are running away. It isn't easy, just profitable. Embrace the opportunity.

$&¢

Chapter Twenty-Eight

R

Stocks During Recessions

The following chart tracks the performance of the S&P 500 Index relative to U.S. economic recessions since 1960. The shaded years represent the months of recession, as determined by the Bureau of Economic Research.

The following lists the beginning and end dates of the eight recessions since 1960.

Recession Begins	Months Before End
April 1960	10 Months
December 1969	11 Months
November 1973	16 Months
January 1980	6 Months
July 1981	16 Months
July 1990	8 Months
March 2001.	8 Months
December 2007	18 Months

Notice what happens to the stock market after, and even during recessions. This is the time when economic conditions appear unusually bleak...when the news is the worst...The stock market goes up!

Stock Performance During Recessions

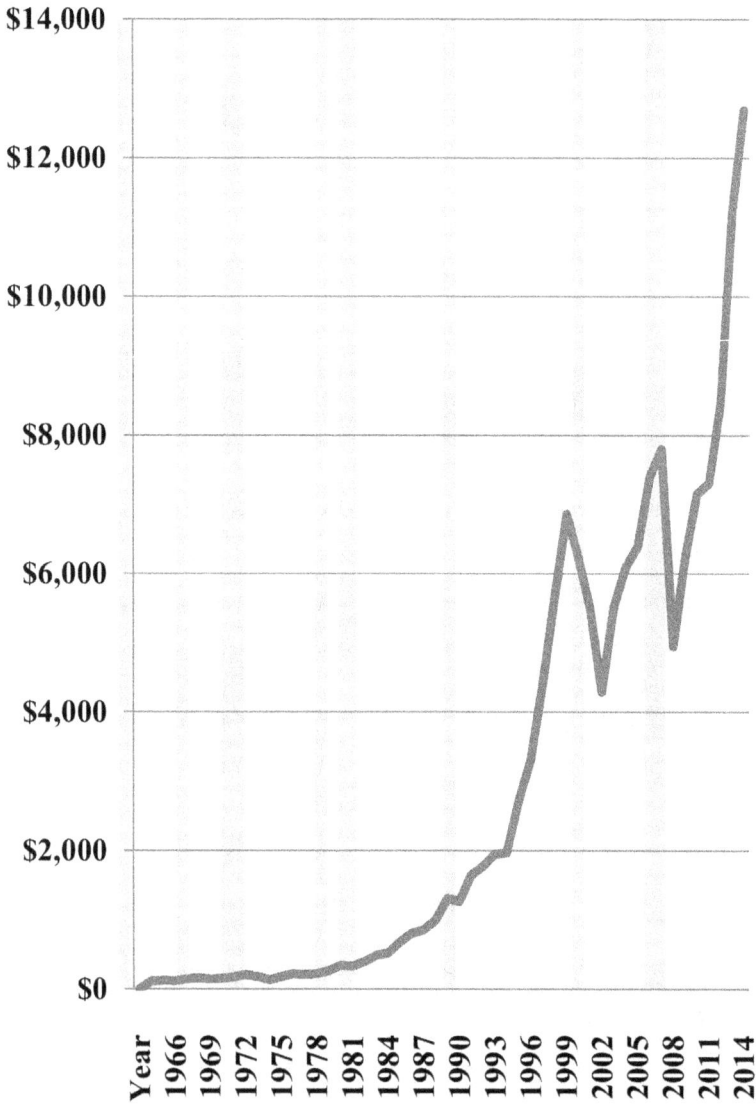

Year: 1966 1969 1972 1975 1978 1981 1984 1987 1990 1993 1996 1999 2002 2005 2008 2011 2014

Recession   **Source: S&P, NBER**

Chapter Twenty-Eight

R

Stocks During Recessions

The following chart tracks the performance of the S&P 500 Index relative to U.S. economic recessions since 1960. The shaded years represent the months of recession, as determined by the Bureau of Economic Research.

The following lists the beginning and end dates of the eight recessions since 1960.

Recession Begins	Months Before End
April 1960	10 Months
December 1969	11 Months
November 1973	16 Months
January 1980	6 Months
July 1981	16 Months
July 1990	8 Months
March 2001.	8 Months
December 2007	18 Months

Notice what happens to the stock market after, and even during recessions. This is the time when economic conditions appear unusually bleak...when the news is the worst...The stock market goes up!

Stock Performance During Recessions

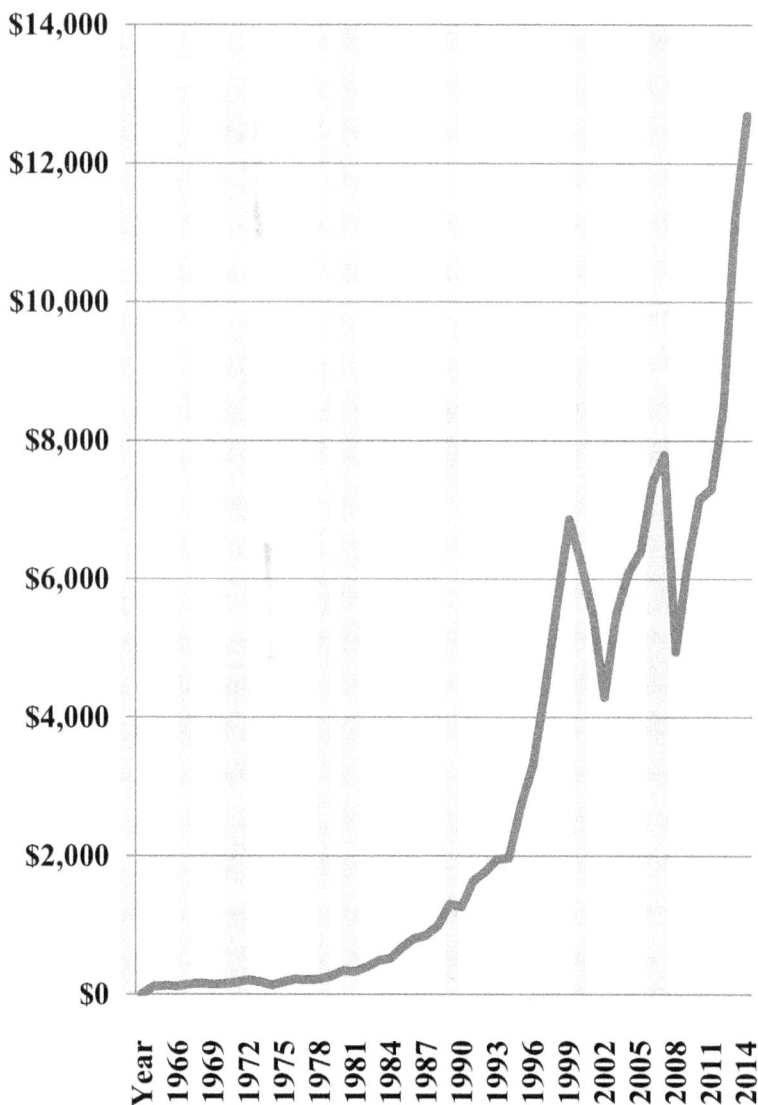

Recession   Source: S&P, NBER

Here is the important concept to understand: **Nobody knows when recessions will end and the stock market will rebound**. Stock market rebounds are unpredictable, and usually quite powerful once they begin.

Here is what you should know: **If you miss the turn (as average investors do) you lose much of your gains, perhaps more than half.** This is why average investors earn so much less than the investments they buy.

Investing is like riding a roller coaster. There are many ups and downs, but you return safely in the end. If you have a long-term investment horizon, you must have faith that the averages will even out in the end. They always have.

$&¢

Chapter Twenty-Nine

R

Modern Portfolio Theory

MODERN PORTFOLIO THEORY

In the early 1950s, Professor Harry Markowitz published a book entitled *Portfolio Selection*. In this book, Professor Markowitz analyzed the relationship between *risk* and *return*. Professor Markowitz's basic premise was that, ***in order to assume greater risk, investors will demand greater returns. Investors want the least risk possible for the returns they need or desire.***

Markowitz said,

"Investors generally want to take the smallest possible risk to secure the greatest possible return."

At the time this was a novel, if not staggering concept—and quite difficult to prove.

Professor Markowitz theorized that "portfolios" of securities could be blended in a manner that reduced long-term risk without sacrificing long-term returns.

Markowitz believed that investments with the least risk would have the lowest returns. Those with the highest risk should return the most.

At the time, the U.S. T-bill represented the least risky investment, with the shortest duration and the highest credit quality.

Markowitz used the T-bill as his base for analysis. The T-bill represented a "risk-free" return. Other investments were then analyzed *relative* to the T-bill. Risk (price volatility) was measured against price changes in the T-bill. Investment returns were compared to the risk-free return of the T-bill. Then they were compared to each other.

A long-term pattern began to emerge. The greater the short-term risk (volatility), the greater the long-term return. The higher the risk, the higher the return. The lower the risk, the lower the return.

During the next 50+ years, Professor Markowitz's theories have provided the basis for what became known as **Modern Portfolio Theory**. Other economists, such as Merton Miller and William Sharpe, have enhanced the theory, adding new analytical algorithms to help investors better predict portfolio outcomes.

In 1990, nearly four decades after his seminal book, Professor Markowitz was awarded the Nobel Prize for Economics. His theories had withstood the test of time.

Modern portfolio theory (MPT) is the basis upon which many successful investment portfolios are built.

You will come across many MPT statistics as you analyze investments, whether inside or outside a retirement plan. The following is a short explanation designed to familiarize you with the big concepts of modern portfolio theory, and how financial advisors employ them with investments.

Theory Basics

Modern portfolio theory analyzes all investments, based upon the laws of probability and statistical analysis. MPT analyzes an investment's growth rate over various time frames, both short and long. MPT studies the volatility characteristics (risk) of each investment—how much an investment goes up and down in value over different time horizons.

Modern portfolio theory analyzes how an investment reacts, *relative to all other investments,* over time. This is critical. Some investments, with certain volatility and return characteristics, move in one direction, while similar investments may move in another.

MPT looks at specific investments. It is also used to analyze different classes of investments, and the indexes that measure them. MPT demonstrates how to *blend* investments together to achieve greater returns, given the *risk* an investor is willing to assume.

Once we've determined the **historical** characteristics of a set of investments (how they have behaved in the past) we can *predict* how they might react in the *future*. We can then assign various *probabilities of outcome* to any investment or mix.

According to MPT, *there is always an efficient blend of assets that will give the highest return for the risk one is willing to assume.*

When charted, these ideal portfolios form what is known as the *Efficient Frontier*.

The efficient frontier creates a theoretical curve, which demonstrates the highest possible return for each level of risk.

The best possible portfolios are created by a process known as asset allocation.

This book helps you look underneath the hood of asset allocation, so that you can learn how to blend and build your own portfolios.

$&¢

Chapter Thirty

R

Asset Allocation

Asset Allocation

You may have heard the saying, "Don't put all your eggs in one basket."

Common sense makes investment sense.

Asset allocation provides diversification and spreads risk among different investments.

When planning for retirement, remember this: The day you retire is the start of a new, but long investment journey. You may still have to invest and plan for 30 years or more.

Proper Asset Allocation

By Far The Most Important Factor In Determining Risk-Adjusted Investment Return

Proper Asset Allocation is the Most Important Factor in Determining Your Risk-Adjusted Investment Return. Over the long run, studies show that you can often achieve higher overall returns (for the risk you are willing to take) with the proper asset allocation.

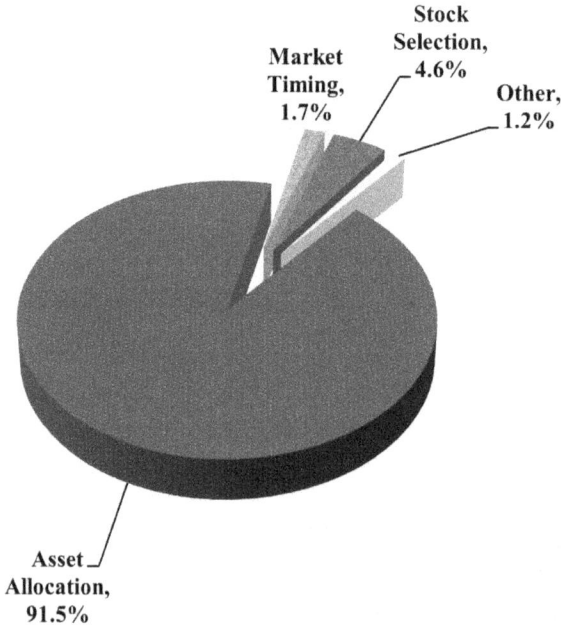

Stock Selection, 4.6%

Market Timing, 1.7%

Other, 1.2%

Asset Allocation, 91.5%

Source: Financial Analyst Journal, G.P. Brinson, B.D. Singer and G.L. Beebower, May-June 1991.

In 1986, a landmark study was conducted by Gary Brinson, L. Randolph Hood, and Gilbert Beebower. The researchers analyzed the managed investments in 91 large pension plans from 1974 to 1983. The researchers created *theoretical* portfolios by substituting the funds' major investment classes with their corresponding *indexes*. The researchers then compared the passively managed accounts to the actively managed accounts.

The researchers found something startling. When adjusted for risk, the indexed portfolios had higher returns than the managed portfolios.

The investment pros were less effective than someone who bought passive indexes and did no investment research at all.

In 1991, Brinson, Beebower and B.D. Singer conducted and published a follow-up study. Brinson, et al. determined that **91.5% of risk-adjusted investment returns** could be attributed to *asset allocation*, rather than the active management of securities.

Both Brinson studies were conducted with just three asset classes—stocks, bonds and cash.

In 2000, Ibbotson and Kaplan conducted a study using five asset classes. Ibbotson found a similar "shared variance" of 81.4%. While not as spectacular as 91.5%, this supported the "proof" that asset allocation is more important for risk-adjusted investment returns than having a pro that chooses the right stocks. Buying passive indexes, and maintaining them, can be more effective than hiring investment professionals to choose the best stocks to own.

In this pie chart, you will find Brinson's conclusions, and the relative factors that impacted investment returns. Note that market timing provides just a tiny fraction of total return. Market timing is when emotions cloud your thinking. Don't try to time the market. It is a bad bet. Your emotions will betray you. Put the odds in your favor and stick to a long-term asset allocation.

The Efficient Frontier
What It Might Look Like For US and Foreign Equities*

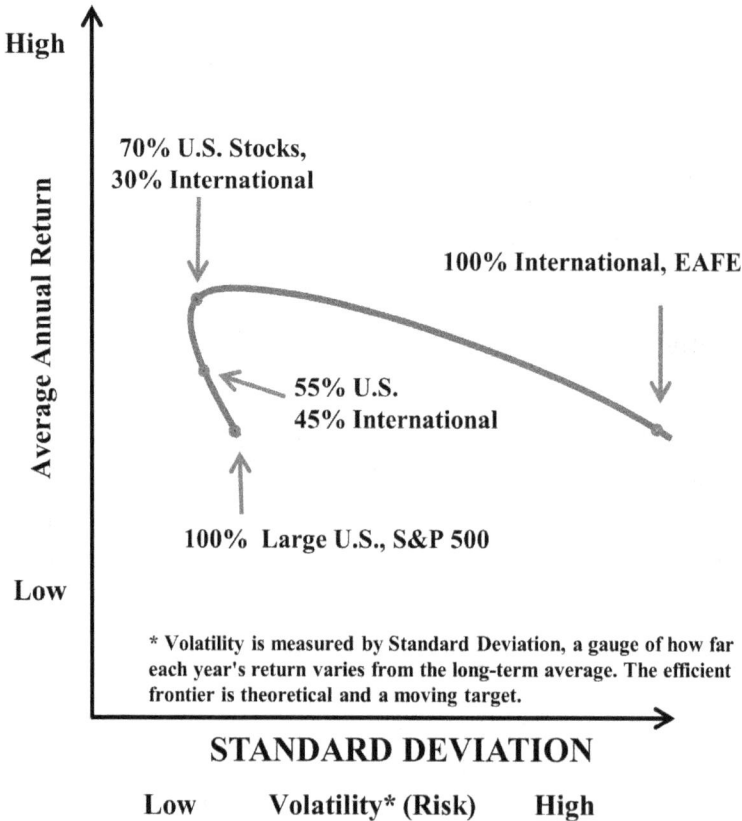

High

Average Annual Return

70% U.S. Stocks,
30% International

100% International, EAFE

55% U.S.
45% International

100% Large U.S., S&P 500

Low

* Volatility is measured by Standard Deviation, a gauge of how far
each year's return varies from the long-term average. The efficient
frontier is theoretical and a moving target.

STANDARD DEVIATION

Low   Volatility* (Risk)   High

The preceding graph illustrates the Efficient Frontier as you might find it for U.S. and foreign large stocks. Risk is measured by the horizontal axis. The farther one moves to the right, the greater the risk. Return is measured vertically. Greater returns are higher on the vertical axis.

On the bottom of the graph, you will find a portfolio of 100% large U.S. stocks. If we change the mix to 70% U.S. stocks and 30% foreign stocks we might *lower volatility (risk) and increase return*. We would still own 100% stocks, but we achieve greater returns with the same risk by blending U.S. and foreign securities. This is because U.S. and foreign stocks rise and fall at different times. This is an example of how asset allocation works.

The efficient frontier is a moving target, changing with the performance of individual securities and asset classes, as well as time frames. The general shape remains somewhat constant. Returns rise with risk. Asset allocation can lower risk. Return increases become smaller as risk becomes great.

In this graph, the return for U.S. stocks (S&P 500) and foreign stocks (EAFE) is essentially the same. However, the risk of foreign stocks is greater. Depending upon the time frame, this graph will change. If the frontier graph is for a relatively short time frame, it will change more rapidly. If long-term risk and return characteristics are utilized, the graph will change less from year to year.

Notice how the frontier curve *flattens* as we reach our *higher potential returns*. As *returns increase* the *risks grow even faster*. In order to achieve higher returns, we must take greater and greater risks. At some point, added risk can even bring lower returns.

Portfolios of U.S. stocks and bonds 1970–2000

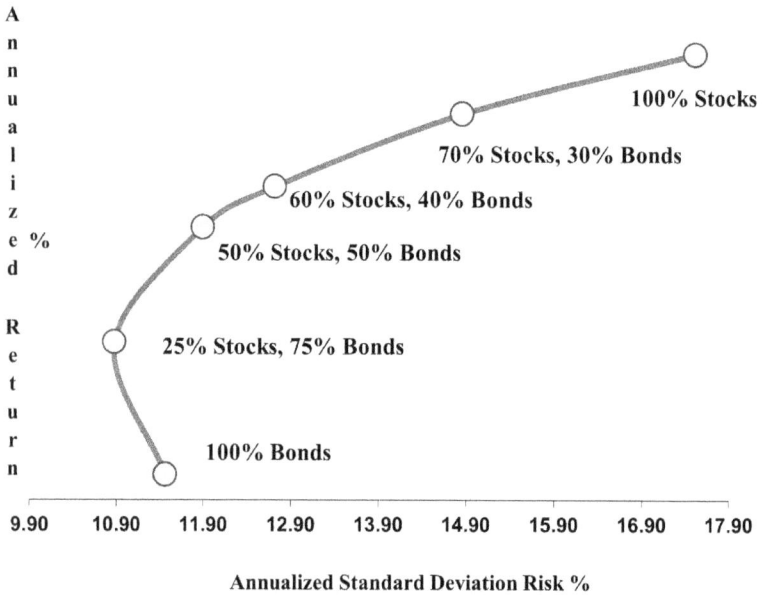

A
n
n
u
a
l
i
z
e %
d

R
e
t
u
r
n

100% Stocks

70% Stocks, 30% Bonds

60% Stocks, 40% Bonds

50% Stocks, 50% Bonds

25% Stocks, 75% Bonds

100% Bonds

9.90   10.90   11.90   12.90   13.90   14.90   15.90   16.90   17.90

Annualized Standard Deviation Risk %

Source: Ibbotson Associates Inc. Bonds are represented by long-term government bonds. Stocks are represented by the unmanaged S&P 500 Index.

This chart illustrates six 30-year indexed portfolios of stocks and bonds from 1970-2000. (Source: Ibbotson Associates, Inc.) Notice how adding stocks to a bond portfolio can decrease risk, even though stocks are more risky than bonds. This is because stock and bond prices move at different times. When bonds are moving down, stocks could be rising, or falling less. This leads to lower risk overall.

Don't forget: The longer the time horizon, the less "risky" stocks become.

ALPHA

If asset allocation is the greatest determinant of long-term performance, why are there so many mutual funds? Why not buy indexes funds and sit tight?

Since there are more mutual funds than stocks, there must be something to this management stuff.

Some investment managers (or groups of managers) are better than others. There is a term used in Modern Portfolio Theory that measures the effectiveness of managers. It is called alpha.

Alpha measures of the difference between a fund's actual returns, versus its expected performance, given its risk.

A *positive* alpha means that the fund manager has a positive influence on investment returns. A negative alpha means that the manager is underperforming the fund's target return.

This is a simplified explanation. However, when you choose investments for your retirement, choosing ones that have positive long-term alphas may help your portfolio perform better over time.

The Efficient Frontier
What It Might Look Like For
Asset Allocation Models*

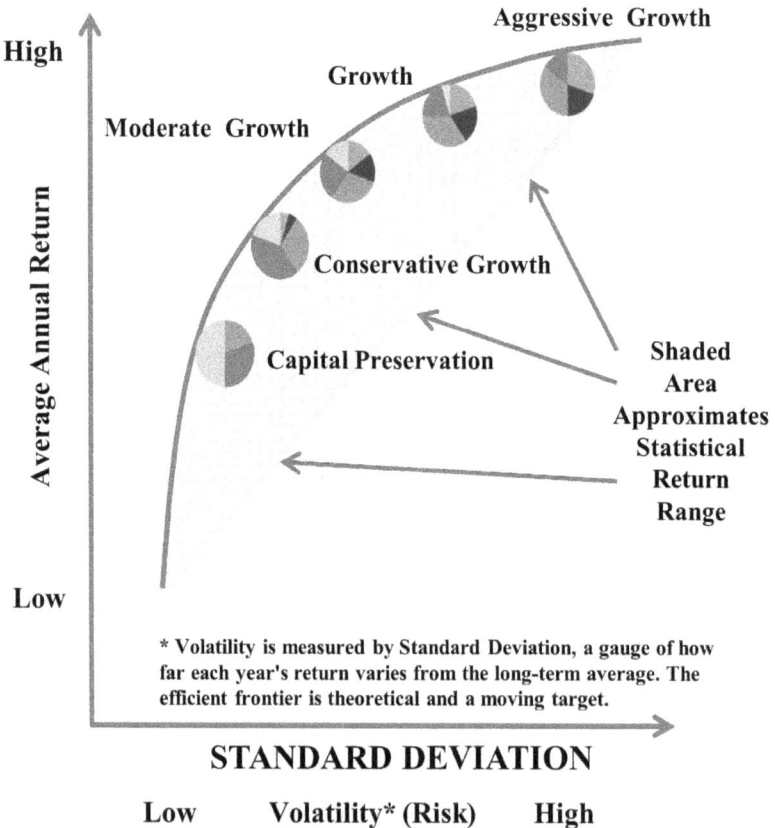

Efficient frontier curve plotted with Average Annual Return (Low to High) on the vertical axis and Standard Deviation on the horizontal axis, showing asset allocation models: Capital Preservation, Conservative Growth, Moderate Growth, Growth, and Aggressive Growth. Labels indicate "Shaded Area Approximates Statistical Return Range" and axis markings "STANDARD DEVIATION — Low Volatility (Risk) High".*

* Volatility is measured by Standard Deviation, a gauge of how far each year's return varies from the long-term average. The efficient frontier is theoretical and a moving target.

This graphic shows how the Efficient Frontier might look for asset allocation models in a retirement plan. Note how growth relates to risk. As returns reach their maximum, risk grows more rapidly.

Remember: Over the long run, efficient portfolios with higher risk have a greater chance of outpacing inflation.

Over time, the risk curve reverses itself. Low risk investments have a poor chance of outpacing inflation. Higher risk investments have a greater risk of outpacing inflation.

BETA

Asset allocation reduces volatility (risk). Risk is the sensitivity of an investment to movements of the market. Risk is measured by beta.

By definition, beta is equal to 1. If an investment is being compared to the S&P 500 Index, a beta of 1.1 means that the investment performs 10% better than the S&P in up markets, and 10% worse in down markets. A beta of .9 means that the investment performs 10% better in down markets and 10% worse in up markets.

This is a simple explanation of beta. However, beta can be highly useful when analyzing a mix of mutual funds. Beta can help you understand how volatile your mix will be when compared to a market index.

For example, a mix with 60% stocks and 40% bonds should have a beta closer to .6 than 1, when compared to the S&P 500 Index. Can you see why? If your portfolio has only 60% stocks, you would expect lower risk. Why have the risk of the S&P without the same potential return?

A positive alpha with a beta below 1 is ideal.

Long-Term Inflation-Adjusted Risk
What It Might Look Like For
Asset Allocation Models*

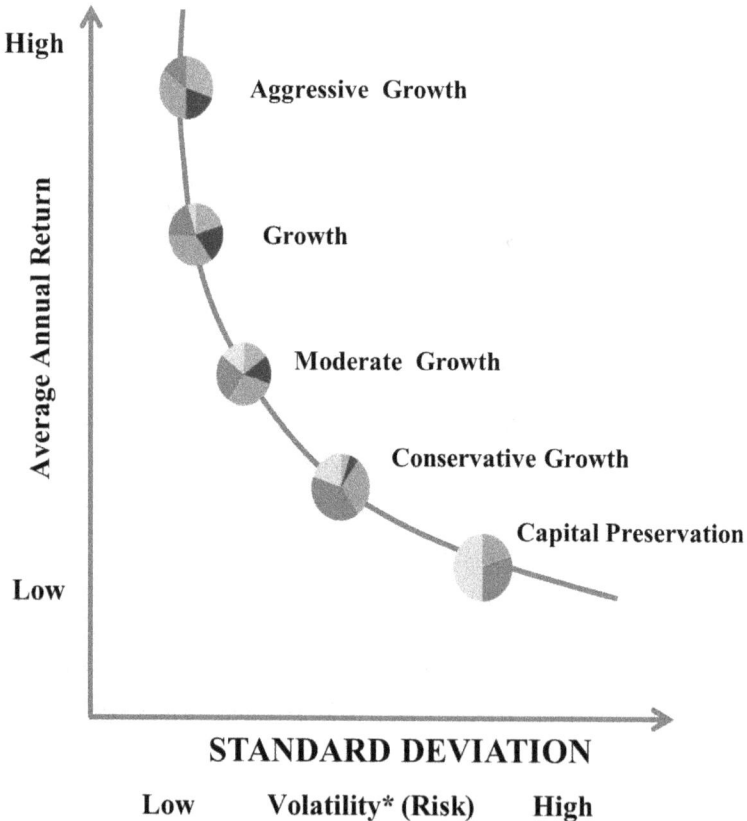

Average Annual Return

High

Low

Aggressive Growth

Growth

Moderate Growth

Conservative Growth

Capital Preservation

STANDARD DEVIATION

Low   Volatility* (Risk)   High

* Volatility is measured by Standard Deviation, a gauge of how
far each year's return varies from the long-term average. The

LONG-TERM INFLATION ADJUSTED RISK

The preceding chart illustrates how inflation-adjusted risk and returns might appear for asset allocation models.

Using a time-frame of more than twenty years, stocks have demonstrated lower purchasing power risk than bonds.

When investing for retirement, stocks have a greater chance of outpacing inflation than bonds. The higher the risk (within reason), the better the chance of achieving positive growth.

Risk gets reversed.

Of course, there are no guarantees that the future will behave like the past. It is just our best guess.

Diversification Continued
Notice How The Best Performers Rotate Year By Year.

Small Growth Stocks	Large Growth Stocks	Small Value Stocks	Large Value Stocks	Small Stocks	Large Stocks	Foreign Stocks	Bonds

2001	2002	2003	2004	2005	2006	2007	2008	2009	2010
Small Value 14.03%	Bonds 10.26%	Small Growth 48.54%	Small Value 22.25%	Foreign Stocks 14.02%	Foreign Stocks 26.86%	Foreign Stocks 11.63%	Bonds 5.24%	Small Growth 34.47%	Small Growth 29.09%
Bonds 8.44%	Small Value -11.43%	Small Stocks 47.25%	Foreign Stocks 20.70%	Large Value 5.82%	Small Value 23.48%	Large Growth 9.13%	Small Value -28.92%	Foreign Stocks 32.46%	Small Stocks 26.85%
Small Stocks 2.49%	Foreign Stocks -15.66%	Small Value 46.03%	Small Stocks 18.33%	Large Stocks 4.91%	Large Value 20.80%	Small Growth 7.05%	Small Stocks -33.79%	Large Growth 31.57%	Small Value 24.50%
Small Growth -9.23%	Small Stocks -20.48%	Foreign Stocks 39.17%	Large Value 14.31%	Small Value 4.71%	Small Stocks 18.37%	Bonds 6.97%	Large Growth -34.92%	Small Stocks 27.17%	Large Value 15.10%
Large Value -11.71%	Large Value -20.85%	Large Value 31.79%	Small Growth 14.31%	Small Stocks 4.55%	Large Stocks 15.79%	Large Stocks 5.49%	Large Stocks -37.00%	Large Stocks 26.46%	Large Stocks 15.06%
Large Stocks -11.89%	Large Stocks -22.10%	Large Stocks 28.68%	Large Stocks 10.88%	Small Growth 4.15%	Small Growth 13.35%	Large Value 1.99%	Small Growth -38.54%	Large Value 21.18%	Large Growth 15.05%
Large Growth -12.73%	Large Growth -23.59%	Large Growth 25.66%	Large Growth 6.13%	Large Growth 4.00%	Large Growth 11.01%	Small Stocks -1.57%	Large Value -39.22%	Small Value 20.58%	Foreign Stocks 8.21%
Foreign Stocks -21.21%	Small Growth -30.26%	Bonds 4.10%	Bonds 4.34%	Bonds 2.43%	Bonds 4.33%	Small Value -9.78%	Foreign Stocks -43.06%	Bonds 5.93%	Bonds 6.54%

The preceding table illustrates the *year-by-year returns* for eight major *asset classes* from 2001-2010. Each year, the best performing asset class is listed on top. The worst performing index is entered on the bottom.

Note that bonds spend a lot of time near the bottom. Yet, in years when stocks suffer large losses, even a small bond return (5.24% in 2008) can make it the top performing asset class.

Note the volatility of small growth stocks, and the more consistent, middle-of-the-road performance of large-cap stocks. During the decade illustrated, foreign stocks and small value stocks spent the most time near the top. This does not mean that the same will happen in the next decade. While small value and mid-cap value stocks have achieved historically strong risk-adjusted performance, investment markets are highly unpredictable. Over longer periods of time, returns become more reliable. During a decade (or even two), anything can happen.

By maintaining a balanced portfolio, investors have the best chance to grow their investments without subjecting them to the extreme volatility of any one asset class.

Chart Source: © 2011 Morningstar. Large stocks are represented by the S&P 500. Large growth stocks are represented by the S&P 500/Barra Growth Index until 1995 and the S&P 500 Growth Index thereafter. Large value stocks are represented by the S&P 500/Barra Value Index until 1995 and The S&P 500 Value Index thereafter. Small stocks are represented by the Russell 2000® Index. Small growth stocks are represented by the Russell 2000 Growth Index. Small value stocks are represented by the Russell 2000 Value Index. Foreign stocks are represented by the MSCI EAFE Index. Bonds are represented by the Barclays Capital U.S. Aggregate Index. Indexes are unmanaged, and one cannot invest directly in an index.

$&¢

Chapter Thirty-One

R

The Markets Are Unpredictable

Financial markets are highly unpredictable, especially in the short run. Returns change randomly from year-to-year. The following graph shows an example of how eight different asset classes performed in two consecutive years.

In 2008, every asset class, except bonds, lost money. The media were giving daily reports about the imminent and ongoing collapse of the global financial markets. Companies like Bank of America, General Motors and AIG were being bailed out by the U.S. government. Hundreds of billions of dollars were pumped into the capital markets. The investment world seemed bleak. The mortgage shell game was cracking at its core. The United States was in the middle of the greatest recession since the 1930s. Were breadlines next?

With all of this uncertainty, how did the capital markets react in 2009? They soared. In the midst of the "great recession," the stock market exploded.

Capital markets look beyond current news into the future. Markets care less about today than they do about tomorrow. Where individual investors feel that the sky is falling and start running for shelter, investment professionals see buying opportunities and run toward the carnage, not away.

What do you see when the news goes negative? Do you see a time to sell and sit on the sidelines? Or, do you see an opportunity to go bargain shopping, a great time to add risk assets to your portfolio?

Markets Are
Unpredictable

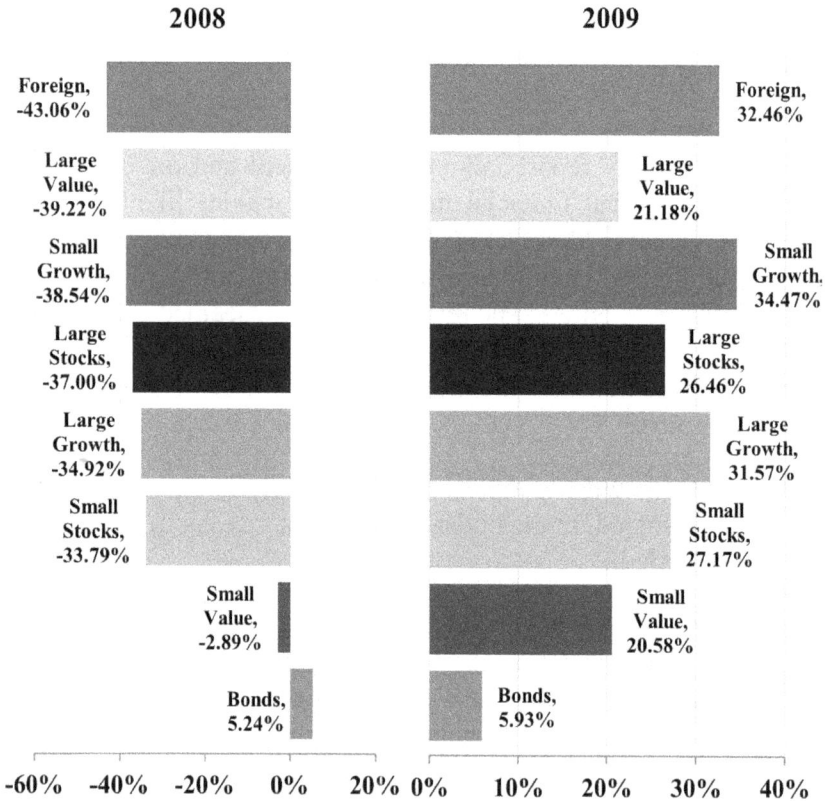

2008   **2009**

Foreign, -43.06%

Foreign, 32.46%

Large Value, -39.22%

Large Value, 21.18%

Small Growth, -38.54%

Small Growth, 34.47%

Large Stocks, -37.00%

Large Stocks, 26.46%

Large Growth, -34.92%

Large Growth, 31.57%

Small Stocks, -33.79%

Small Stocks, 27.17%

Small Value, -2.89%

Small Value, 20.58%

Bonds, 5.24%

Bonds, 5.93%

-60% -40% -20% 0% 20%   0% 10% 20% 30% 40%

Markets Are Unpredictable

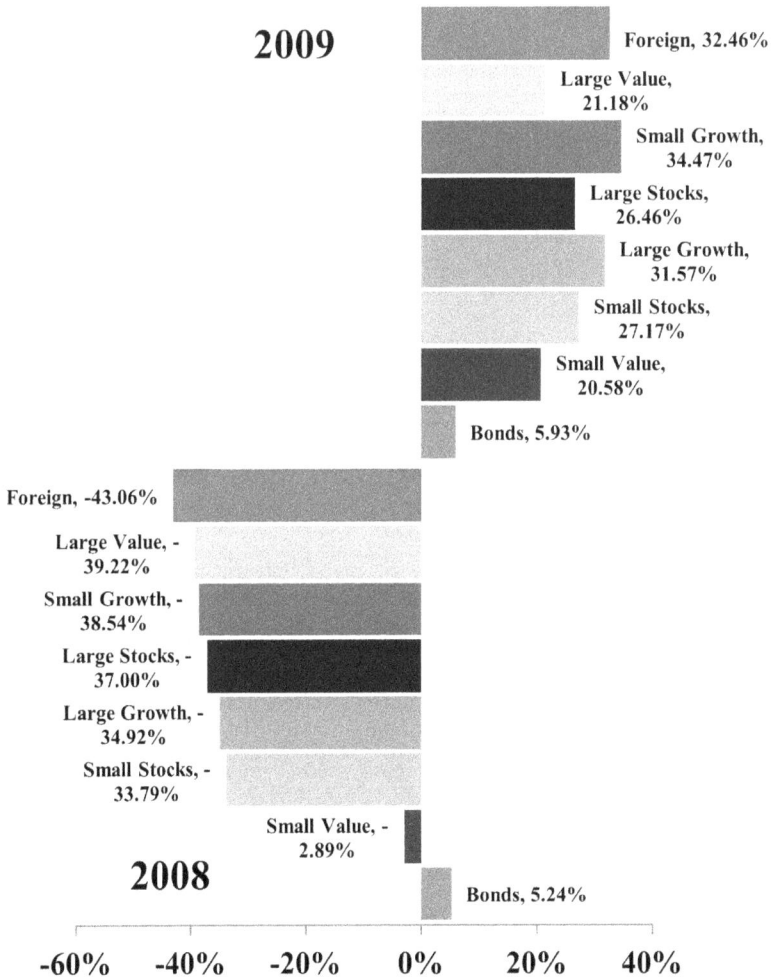

2009

Foreign, 32.46%

Large Value, 21.18%

Small Growth, 34.47%

Large Stocks, 26.46%

Large Growth, 31.57%

Small Stocks, 27.17%

Small Value, 20.58%

Bonds, 5.93%

Foreign, -43.06%

Large Value, -39.22%

Small Growth, -38.54%

Large Stocks, -37.00%

Large Growth, -34.92%

Small Stocks, -33.79%

Small Value, -2.89%

2008

Bonds, 5.24%

-60%   -40%   -20%   0%   20%   40%

The preceding charts illustrate the same data in slightly different styles. Notice how the "safer" bonds never lost money. They didn't have big gains either. Over the long run, Modern Portfolio Theory predicts that owning a blend of investments is the best way to manage risk, and to have the best chance to outpace inflation over time. Adding stocks to a "safer" bond portfolio can lower risk, and increase expected long-term performance.

This page is intentionally blank, so that you can view the following chart beside its explanation. Learning about the stock market is confusing enough, without making you turn pages while you try to remember what you just saw.

Diversification
**Different Types of Investments Gain and
Lose Value At Different Times. That Is
Why Diversification Is Critical To Long-
Term Retirement Investing**

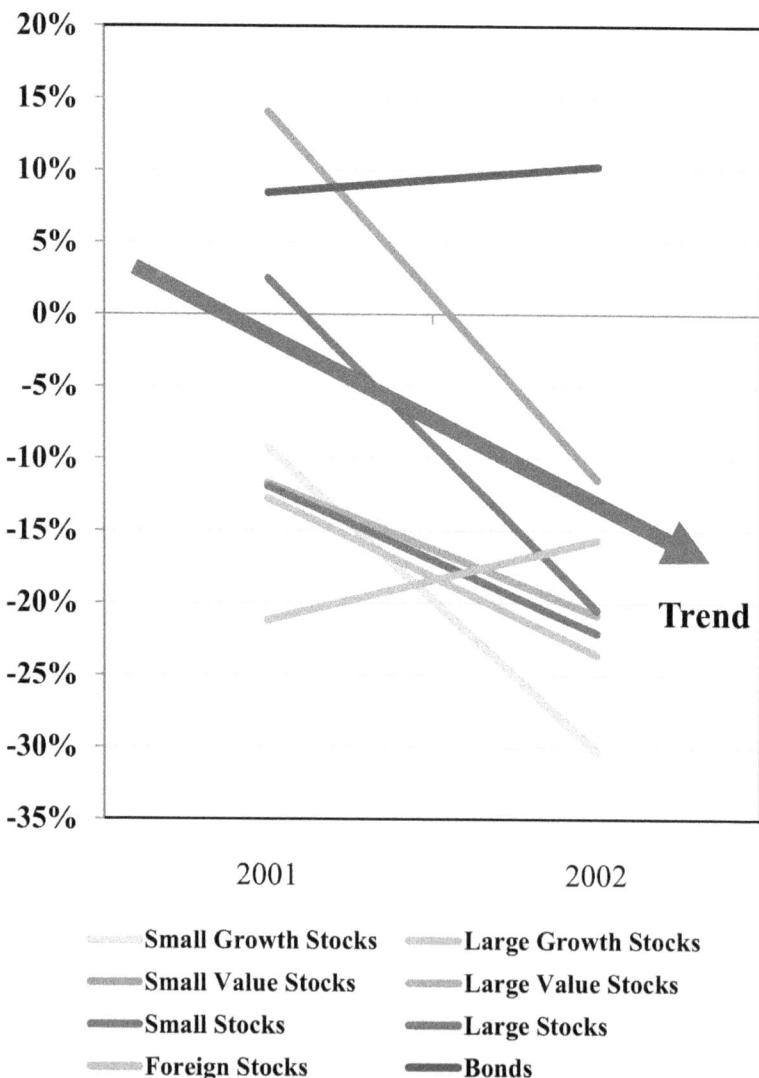

Legend:
- Small Growth Stocks
- Large Growth Stocks
- Small Value Stocks
- Large Value Stocks
- Small Stocks
- Large Stocks
- Foreign Stocks
- Bonds

The preceding chart illustrates eight different asset classes, and how they performed in 2001 and 2002.

In the short run, there appears to be very little correlation between investment returns. Given such short-term data, you would predict that market returns were trending downward, and that there was little correlation between returns.

Short-term data is deceiving.

Diversification
Different Types of Investments Gain and Lose Value At Different Times. That Is Why Diversification Is Critical To Long-Term Retirement Investing

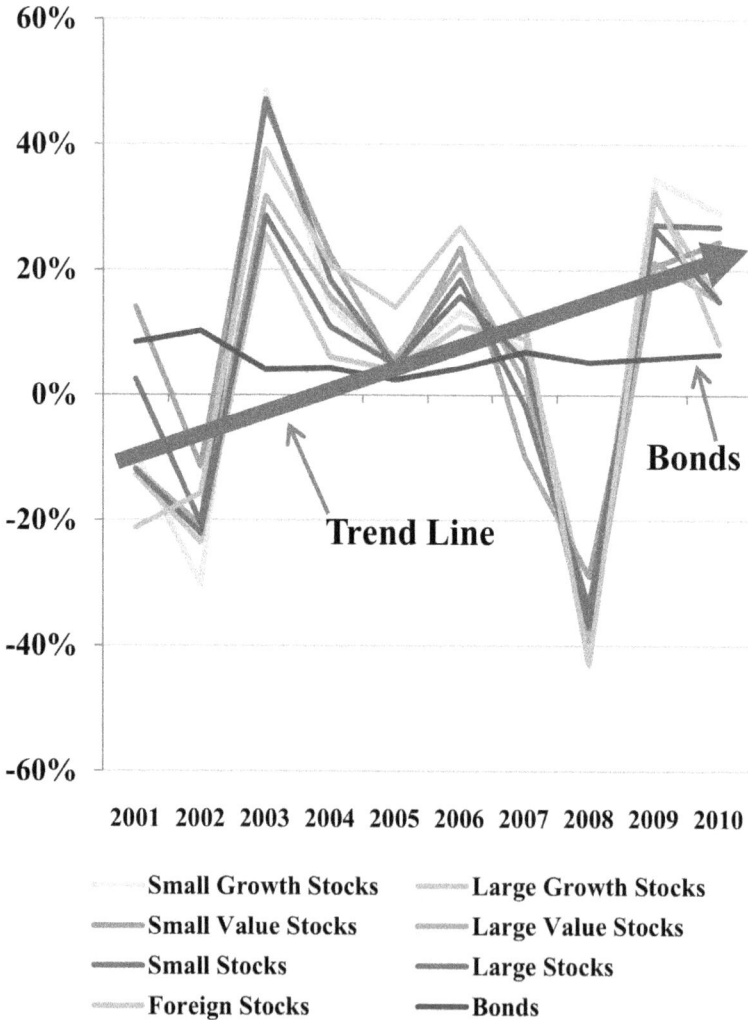

Small Growth Stocks					Large Growth Stocks				
Small Value Stocks					Large Value Stocks				
Small Stocks					Large Stocks				
Foreign Stocks					Bonds				

This chart shows the same asset classes over a longer, ten-year investment horizon.

Notice how equity asset classes move in the same general direction, but not together.

In the middle of the graph, you can see the more stable and consistent performance of bonds.

Mixing bonds with stocks will lower the volatility of a portfolio.

By blending asset classes together, investors can lower risk, as they seek to achieve the investment amount they need for retirement—the Number.

Stocks Over Time

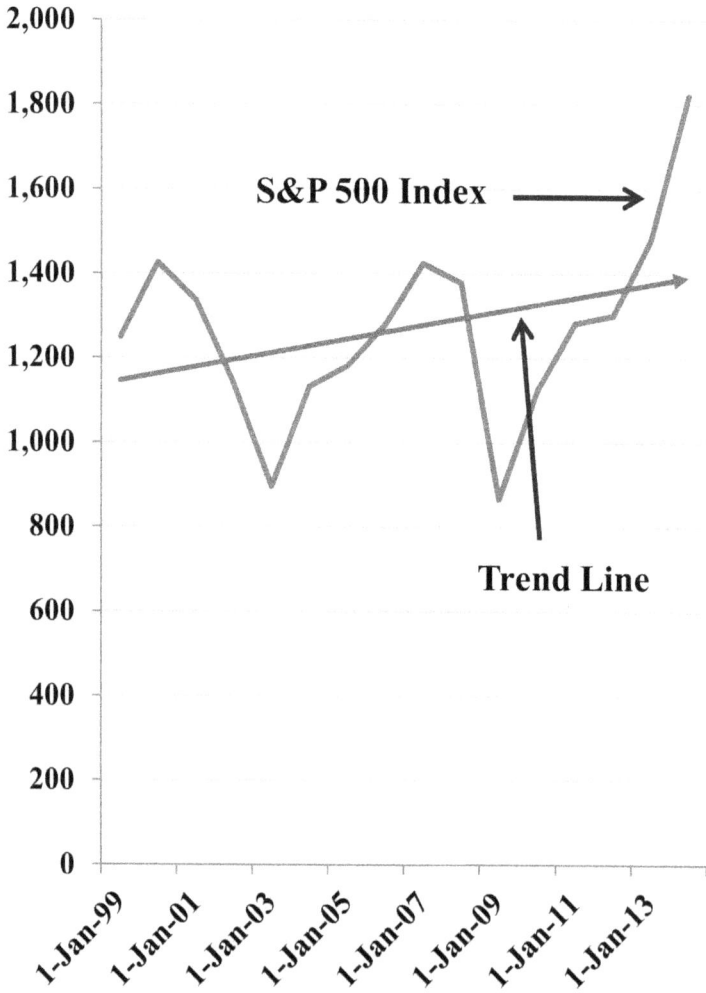

The preceding chart illustrates the S&P 500 Index over a 15-year horizon. During that time, the United States experienced two sizable recessions, two significant market "crashes," and subsequent stock rebounds.

There was the "technology bubble" of 2000. This is when investors realized that the Internet increased business efficiency, but also increased global competition. Investors pulled out of the market. It fell more than 40% during a three-year period. This was bad timing for those who sold, because the market corrected strongly over the next five years.

In 2008, the world faced the "global mortgage crisis." Many in the media termed it the "Great Recession." The market (S&P) fell more than 35% in 2008 alone.

If you sold stocks after the market fell, you would have missed one of the longest bull markets in history — with consecutive gains of 25.9%, 14.8%, 2.1%, 15.9%, 32.1% and 13.5%.

Despite two major market corrections, stocks continued their long-term advance — for those who remained fully invested.

When you view market performance over an expected lifetime, you will find a far more predictable upward trend than any short-term performance of today.

Shouldn't you invest for the long-run? Stand back and keep some perspective.

$&₵

Chapter Thirty-Two

R

Stocks — Styles Of Buying

Stocks — Different Styles of Buying Them

Common stocks come in many shapes and sizes. They are often classified by a specific style. Some investment managers specialize in owning just one style of stock.

Equity styles can be broken into major categories, such as:

- Value
- Growth
- Yield
- Small
- Medium
- Large

This book has demonstrated how the stock market moves in cycles. It goes up and down. Sometimes the market favors one type of stock or investment style. The next year, it might favor another.

If you mix these styles together you can lower your risk and increase returns. Let's discuss some major investment styles in greater detail.

Value:

- A value manager adds up the value of a company's underlying assets and compares it to the liabilities and share price.

- Value stocks are inexpensive relative to earnings, book value, dividends and other fundamentals. Value stocks usually pay above average dividends (regular payments to shareholders), but have below average dividend growth.

- Value stocks are attractive when the price per share is undervalued, relative to book value, or other value measurements like cash on hand.

- Value investing is a conservative equity strategy that tends to do well in down markets. This style delivers consistent long-term returns. Conservative growth funds often purchase value stocks. This style can also become aggressive, when a manager sees value in distressed companies that are on the brink of financial collapse.

A traditional value manager analyzes the underlying value of a company's assets and compares them to its liabilities and stock price. If the manager feels that the company's value/share is undervalued by the marketplace, the stock might make the manager's "buy" list. If the assets, less liabilities, are low relative to stock price, the stock might become a "sell."

The value manager looks for certain company characteristics. A value company may be undergoing structural changes that increase future earnings expectations. Its pieces may be worth far more than the current whole. Value stocks could be merger candidates when other companies prize the underlying assets. They may pay high current dividends that make them attractive. A company's earnings might be "turning around," after a period of slowed growth or decline. There are many attributes that may influence an investment manager's decisions.

At the time of this writing, Yahoo's ownership shares in the publicly traded search engines Alibaba and Yahoo Japan are worth more than the total market capitalization of Yahoo itself. This makes owning Yahoo stock a classic value play.

Yahoo is attempting to turn its core, search engine business around. If it can't, don't be surprised to see Yahoo's shareholders force it to divest itself of its stakes in Alibaba and Yahoo Japan, or even liquidate and cease to exist.

An important characteristic to know about value stocks is that they are usually *less volatile* than growth stocks. Over time, value stocks can perform as well, or better, than growth stocks. For every successful growth company like Apple, Google and Facebook, there might be a Napster, Myspace, or Lotus that failed to match its early potential.

The dividends paid by most value stocks can make them act a bit like bonds during market downturns. Higher dividends can keep value shares from falling as rapidly as growth shares. This makes them less volatile, especially when the market falls rapidly.

Growth:

- Some companies are growing faster than others. When a public company is growing quickly, it is usually considered a growth stock.

- Growth managers always analyze a company's growth potential. Growth stocks are expected to achieve above average earnings growth.

- Growth stocks usually pay *below average* dividends, but have *above average* dividend growth.

- The price per share will be much higher than the company's liquidation or book value.

- A growth stock can be a good buy, if future company growth is strong.

- Aggressive growth funds often buy growth stocks.

Growth managers are concerned with a company's **expected growth** and earnings **potential**.

EARNINGS POTENTIAL

One portion of a stock's value is the future earnings it might deliver for shareholders. This is especially true for growth stocks. If a company is growing rapidly, the stock's price will be high, relative to current earnings. Earnings may be small, or even negative with a young, rapidly growing company. This gives growth stocks high Price/Earnings Ratios (P/E). Facebook is an excellent example of a growth stock.

P/E RATIO

The Price/Earnings Ratio is a representation of a stock's price, relative to its earnings. P/E is determined by dividing a stock's price by the stock's earnings per share.

Stocks have P/E ratios that are based upon *current* and *future* earnings. For example, if a company is currently earning $1 per share and is selling for $20 per share, it has a current price/earnings ratio of 20. A P/E of 20 means that the company is earning a 5% return on the stock price (1/20=5%).

Compared to a savings account today, a 5% underlying return might seem like a pretty good return on investment. If savings accounts pay 10%, as they did in the late 1970s, a 5% underlying return won't be so attractive.

Remember our discussion of interest rates? Stocks become less attractive as interest rates rise.

Remember the twenty ounces of water? There is only so much money going around. It tries to find the best place to be at all times. If a CD suddenly yields 10%, stocks will become less attractive to investors.

HIGH GROWTH = HIGH P/E

If the earnings of a growth stock are expected to increase substantially, the P/E ratio can be high. A P/E ratio can be 40/1, 100/1, 200/1 or higher.

The higher the P/E, the more rapidly earnings are expected to grow. If the earnings of a high P/E stock begin to fall, watch out. The price of a growth stock can plummet when earnings expectations are not met. The price can soar if earnings expectations are surprisingly exceeded.

Yield:

A yield manager looks for stocks that are paying above average dividends. Yield stocks tend to be well-established, mature companies. Balanced mutual funds often utilize this equity style. Yield stocks have lower than average volatility relative to the total stock market, with decent long-term returns. Exxon-Mobil is a good example of a yield stock. It can also be a value stock, depending upon the price of oil and gas. When oil and natural gas prices are high, Exxon-Mobil has more value.

SMALL & MID-CAP STOCKS:

Small and mid-cap stocks have historically performed well, relative to larger stocks. While they have more volatility than large stocks, they tend to have more potential for long-term growth.

Small and mid-cap value shares can be an appropriate holding in any investment portfolio. You might avoid small growth stocks if your retirement horizon is less than ten years away.

Sector Investing:
- Some managers specialize in buying stocks within a specific investment sector. Sector examples would be technology, biotechnology, oil & gas and medical stocks.
- Other investment managers rotate between sectors, or seek specific styles within certain sectors.
- "Sector rotation" naturally occurs within the stock market, as different sectors fall in and out of favor. The goal of a sector investor is to invest in a sector before it comes into

favor, and sell before those stocks fall out of favor. Good luck if you choose this strategy. It is difficult to predict.

- Sector investing can be unusually volatile. For example: Technology stocks come and go. Now and then, one breaks through the pack and becomes a Microsoft, Google, Apple or Facebook. Many technological innovations have a short window, such as the flip phone or the Atari computer.

- Sector investing can be used to round out or target the asset allocation within model portfolios. This can lessen risk, and be quite appropriate. It can also increase risk and potential return—only if you know what you are doing. You should probably leave sector investing to the professionals.

Examples of Large Growth & Value Stocks

Growth Stocks	Value Stocks
Apple	Exxon-Mobil
GoPro	Ford
Facebook	Citigroup
Netflix	E.I. Dupont
Google	Capital One
Amazon	Phillip Morris

These two lists illustrate some well-known companies, and how they might be categorized as growth or value securities.

Apple and Exxon Mobil are two of the two largest companies in the world when viewed by market capitalization. At the time of this writing, Apple stock is selling at a P/E of 19.13 times current earnings. Conversely, Exxon's P/E is 11.17. Apple's share price is 71% higher relative to earnings versus than that of Exxon. This is because the outlook for oil isn't trending, while Apple was on a roll with iPhones, watches and its upcoming car.

Even so, Apple is becoming a more mature company, with the challenging task of maintaining its extraordinary profitability and earnings growth. Apple's P/E ratio is falling.

A better example of a growth stock would be Facebook. At the time of this writing Facebook's P/E ratio is 61.88. The P/E based upon expected next-year earnings is 64.78. This means that Facebook's profits represent a mere 1.6% return on one's investment. Compare this to Exxon's 8.5% underlying earnings return (on its share price) and you can see how growth stock investors depend upon rapid earnings and revenue growth.

The hope with Facebook is that it can turn two billion social eyeballs into hundreds of billions in profits from advertising dollars and fees.

Time will tell if Facebook is successful in meeting investor expectations. If it meets earnings expectations, Facebook could become another Apple, Google, or Microsoft—large, profitable and still growing. If Facebook doesn't meet today's high investor expectations, the share price could fall dramatically, and take its place beside Wang, Polaroid and Lycos.

Of the companies we've discussed, Exxon Mobil is the best example of a yield stock. Its current dividend is 3.22%. (Exxon Mobil is also a traditional value stock.) General Electric is another yield stock at 3.3%. Apple's dividend is half that of GE, at 1.51%. Facebook doesn't pay a dividend that you can spend today. It is a pure growth stock.

Combining Growth & Value

- Value and growth styles come into favor at different times during an investment cycle.

- By combining investment styles you can reduce the volatility of your portfolio without sacrificing overall long-term performance.

- Blending the two styles together can reduce investment risk.

repetitio est mater studiorum

Over the long run, both growth and value stocks have produced substantial long-term investment returns.

But these categories of stock appreciate, or depreciate, at different times in an investment cycle.

By combining the two styles together, an investor can reduce the short-term volatility of a portfolio, without sacrificing long-term investment returns.

Combining growth and value stocks is a good way for investors to reduce risk and increase risk adjusted returns.

Remember our twenty ounces of water? The same concept holds true in the security marketplace. When money leaves one asset class it is flowing to another. Diversification among investment styles helps smooth the ride of a portfolio.

BENEFITS OF INVESTMENT STYLE DIVERSIFICATION

S&P Index Relative to Growth & Value Stocks
The S&P is a combination of growth & value stocks.

Percent

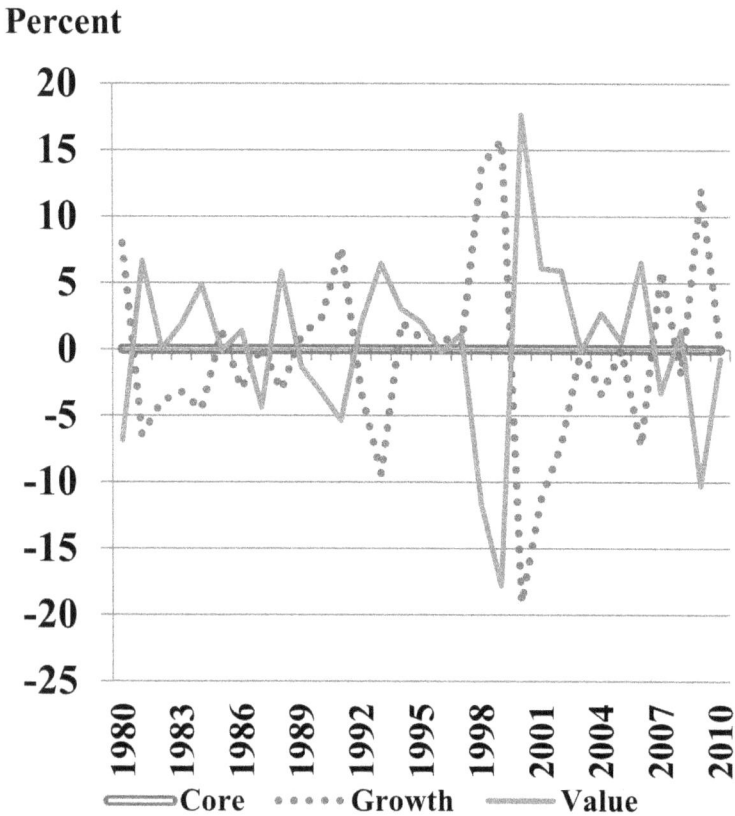

Source: Dow Jones Large Growth & Large
Value Index, S&P Index

This chart illustrates large growth and large value securities relative to the S&P 500 Index, which is composed of both.

The S&P is leveled to zero, in order to show the *relative performance* of its growth and value components. As you can see, growth and value move differently. When combined, volatility and risk can be reduced. Now, let's examine other types of stocks.

Combining Large & Small Stocks

- Large company stocks and small company stocks come in and out of favor at different times as well.

- By combining large and small company stocks, you can potentially reduce the volatility of your portfolio and still achieve competitive long-term returns.

- Blending various styles together is a good way to reduce long-term investment risk.

Small growth companies are usually growing more rapidly than large growth companies. Their high P/E ratios result in higher volatility (risk). Large companies have better capitalization, and can withstand turbulent economic conditions more easily. When the markets fall, larger stocks can help manage your losses. When the markets take off, smaller stocks can lift your total returns.

Blending Styles

Refer back to Chapter 29, to the chart showing the eight different investment styles, and how they performed year by year. This shows how styles come in and out of favor.

Blending different styles helps investment portfolios approach the optimum return for the risk we choose to take. Remember the Efficient Frontier? The efficient frontier is composed of the perfect *blend* for each measure of risk.

$&ℂ

Chapter Thirty-Three

R

Global Investing

For many years, the ownership of American stocks (only) could deliver near-optimum risk adjusted returns. This has changed.

The following charts show how foreign stocks and U.S. securities outperform each other at different times. In the years from 1994 to 2014, foreign stocks outgained U.S. Securities more than half the time.

Combining the shares of foreign companies with those from the U.S. will increase portfolio diversification.

Over time, diversification can lead to lower portfolio volatility, often without sacrificing long-term investment performance.

In the efficient frontier graphs, we saw that a portfolio consisting of U.S. and foreign stocks can have lower risk and higher returns than either asset class alone. Let's take a closer look.

Global Investing

Foreign Stocks Often Outperform U.S. Stocks. A Balanced U.S./Global Portfolio Can Reduce Overall Volatility And Manage Risk

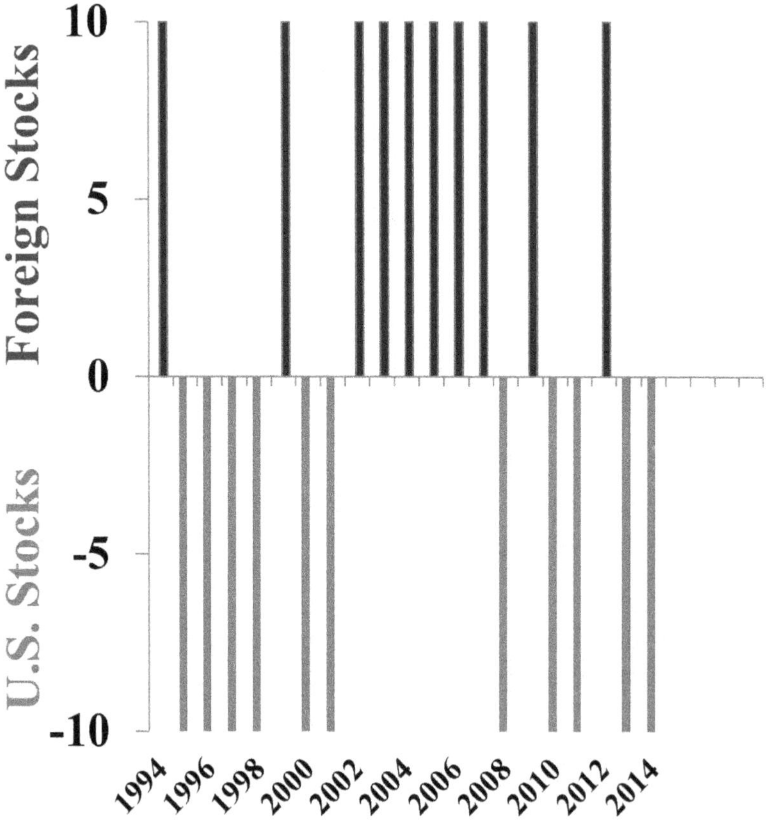

Foreign Stocks
U.S. Stocks
10
5
0
-5
-10
1994
1996
1998
2000
2002
2004
2006
2008
2010
2012
2014

Each bar represents the <u>top performing index</u> for the year indicated. This is not a return illustration, but "winner take all" illustration to show the unpredictability of the markets.

Source: U.S. = S&P 500. International = Morgan Stanley EAFE Index

U.S. Versus The World
Major Market Capitalization

Source: Dow Jones, Bloomberg

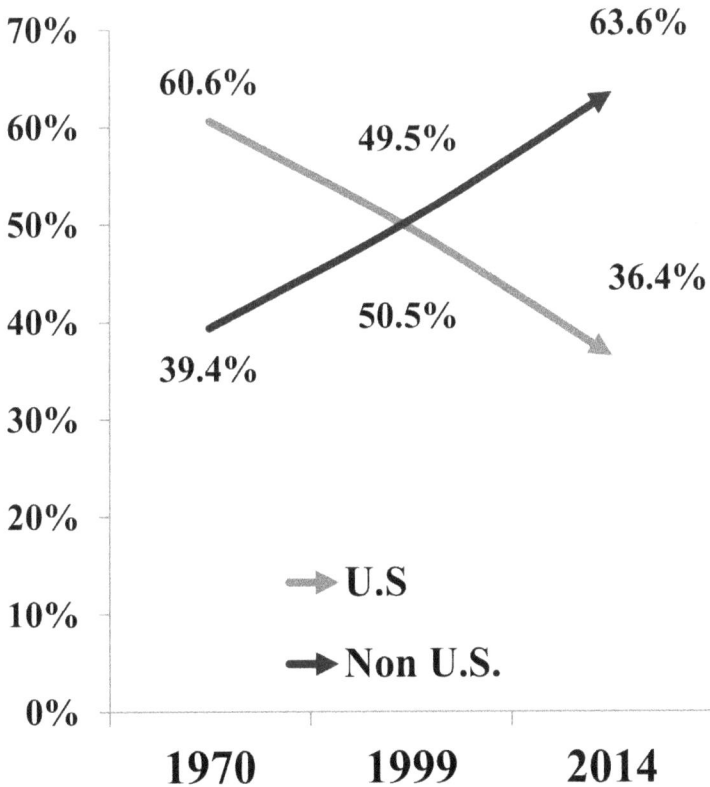

**World markets are growing faster than the United States.
U.S. stocks represent far less than half of total market
capitalization. Remember this when choosing your
investment portfolio.**

NO MORE GLOBAL DOMINANCE

In 1970, the United States represented more than 60% of the world's stock market capitalization. Since that time, many things have changed. Undeveloped countries without telephone lines now have sophisticated cell phone networks. Countries without the Internet have become connected to the Web. The U.S. (and other developed countries) have outsourced their manufacturing (and pollution) to countries like China, and technology support services to India. This has helped these economies grow. By the end of 2014, the percentage of U.S. market capitalization had fallen to 36.4%.

The world is growing faster than the United States. Therefore, most long-term portfolios should include both foreign and U.S. stocks.

repetitio est mater studiorum (Repetition is the mother of studies)

Some people think better with lines. Others learn better with bars. The next chart shows the same world market capitalization a bit differently.

If you are going to invest for many years, doesn't it make sense to include foreign securities in your portfolio?

U.S. Versus The World
Major Market Capitalization

Source: Dow Jones, Bloomberg

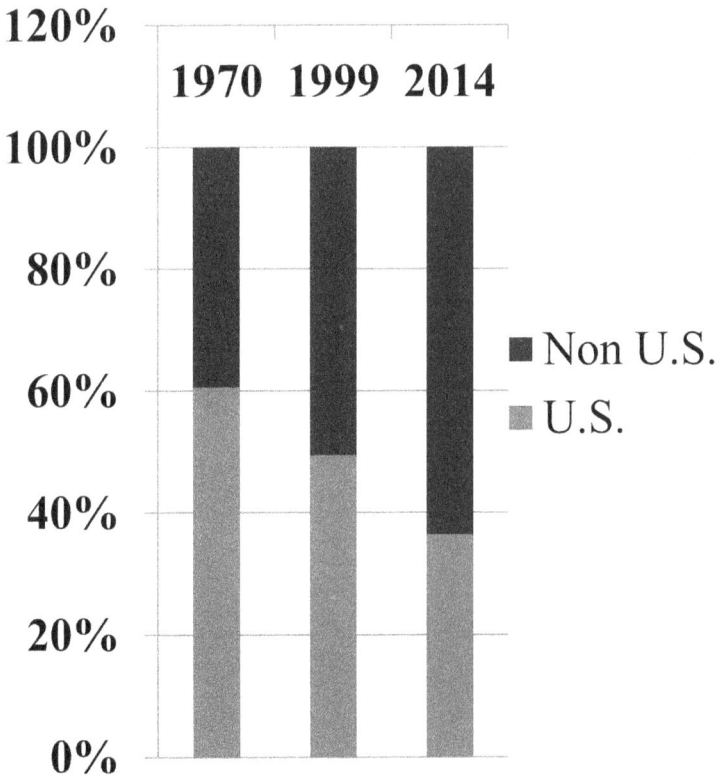

World markets are growing faster than the United States.
U.S. stocks represent far less than half of total market
capitalization. Remember this when choosing your
investment portfolio.

$&¢

Chapter Thirty-Four

_____R_____

Risk – Part Two

Risk

This book has reviewed many aspects of investment risk. Risk is complicated. Good investors don't need to understand every small nuance of risk. Understanding the basic concepts is usually enough to help you invest like a pro.

Risk is the chance of losing money.

TWO TYPES OF RISK

Investors face two great risks when saving toward retirement. There is the risk of losing money. There is also the risk of losing *purchasing power*—of not having enough for retirement.

In the short run, the risk of losing money in stocks is greater than in the long run. But, if we don't take enough short-term risk with our investments, there is a greater chance that our investments will lose purchasing power, when compared to the inflating cost of retirement. Remember inflation?

If you are investing for retirement, you must take a long-term view with your investments. If you have a 20, 30 or 40-year investment time horizon, take some risk. You should be rewarded with greater asset growth.

Look back to the charts in chapter twenty-two. Notice the relation between investment risk and inflation-adjusted returns. In order to retire comfortably, ***your investments must outpace inflation***.

Inflation Protection
How Often Various Asset Classes
Have Outpaced Inflation

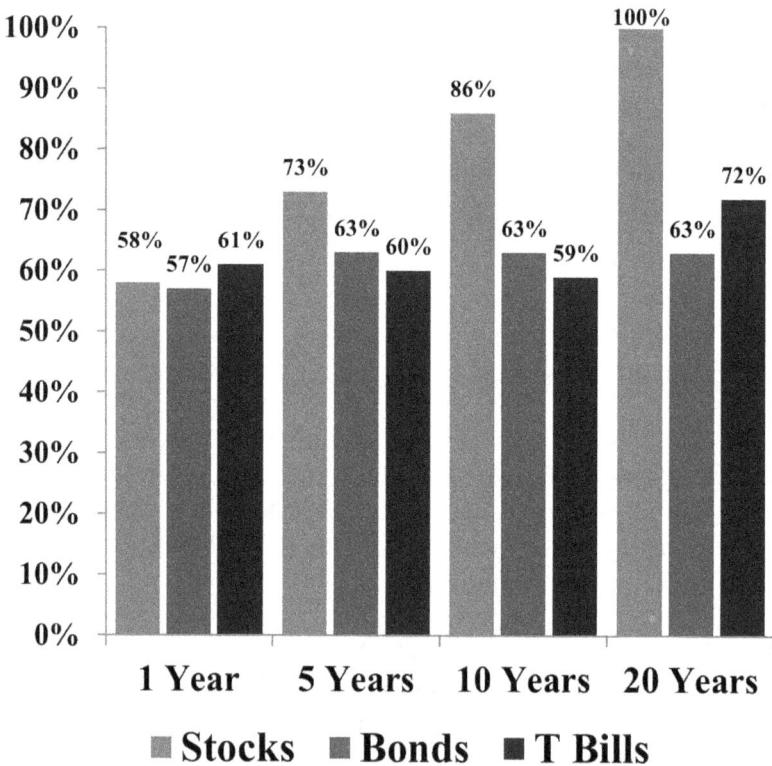

Inflation Protection chart showing how often Stocks, Bonds, and T Bills have outpaced inflation over 1, 5, 10, and 20 year periods.

	1 Year	5 Years	10 Years	20 Years
Stocks	58%	73%	86%	100%
Bonds	57%	63%	63%	63%
T Bills	61%	60%	59%	72%

Chapter twenty-two illustrates the long-term inflation-adjusted re-turns of different asset classes.

The preceding chart shows how different asset classes perform relative to inflation. Notice how stocks have the greatest chance of outpacing inflation in any **average** time frame of **five years or longer**.

Stocks are not infallible. There have been decades where stock performance has been comparatively poor. Does this mean you should avoid them? How can you avoid them and still retire? The numbers won't work.

Don't touch the water with your toes. Jump into the pool with some of your money. There has never been a twenty-year time frame where stocks have not out-performed inflation.

Growth of $100
S&P 500 From 1927-2014
The Stock Market Is Volatile. But
Over The Long Run It Has Grown

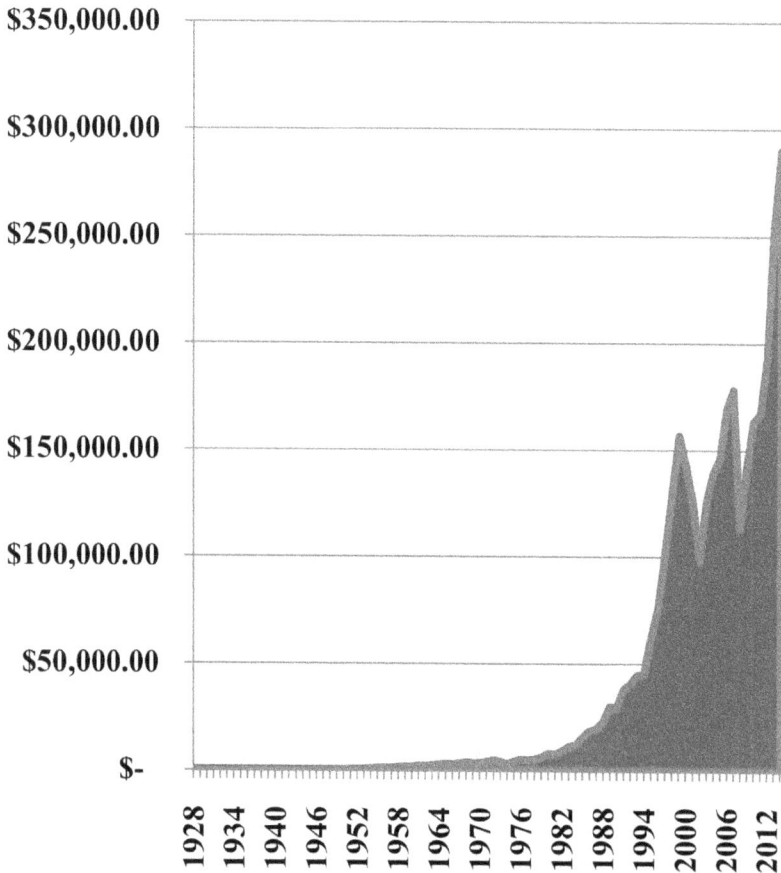

Source: NYU Stern, S&P Index

The preceding chart illustrates $100 invested in stocks (S&P 500) from 1927 through 2014. This illustrates two important concepts.

First, it demonstrates how compounding growth can increase the value of investments over time. A single investment of $100 grew to nearly $300,000 during an expected lifetime.

Second, notice the volatility of stocks.

It is difficult to see volatility in the early years of this illustration because of scale. The market has always been as jagged as you see in the later years.

While the long-term trend is definitely up, there are major bumps along the way.

The next chart shortens the time frame. Notice the volatility. The market always goes down. Then it rises. Can you see the long-term trend of stocks?

Growth of $100
S&P 500 From 1964-2014

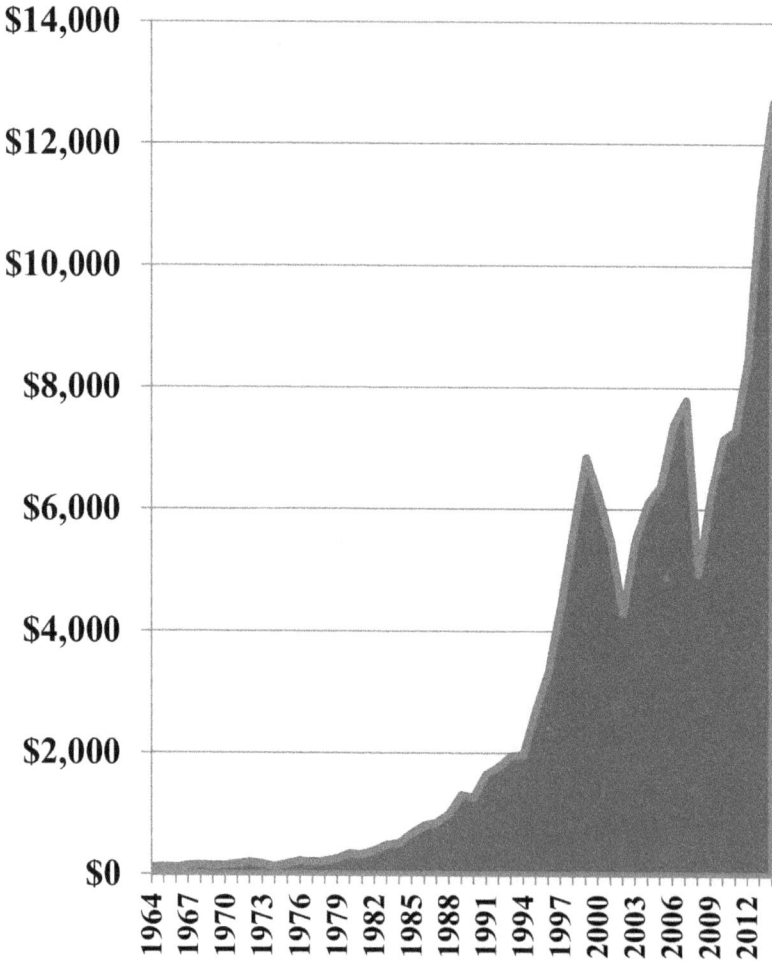

The preceding chart shows stock performance over the last fifty years. This chart shows volatility in greater detail. The stock market goes up and it goes down. Then up. There might be times when the S&P will fall 20%, 30%, even 40% or more. This has happened before and it will probably happen again. You must be prepared. You will have to ride it out—even if it looks like the world might end. This is the emotional price of long-term investment accumulation.

You must be prepared to fight your instinct to sell stocks when the economy is in crisis. Crisis is normal.

After Napoleon lost the battle of Waterloo, Baron Nathan Rothschild is credited with saying that you must, "buy when there's blood in the streets." He saw economic uncertainty as a chance to increase risk and have faith in history. He was right. The world recovered and prospered.

In order to achieve historical investment returns, you must learn to view market corrections as normal. You might even see corrections as a chance to increase your growth-oriented assets. (Sound like a common theme?) This may seem like running towards a fire. With investing, burning embers hold tomorrow's biggest market gains.

Remember dollar cost averaging? Stocks have recovered from every low they have encountered. Are there guarantees? No. That's why there is opportunity. Remember Harry Markowitz and Modern Portfolio Theory? If an investment has greater risk, the market *demands* greater return.

Don't be afraid to get your returns. Put your money to work. Don't worry if it gets roughed up now and then. And it will. Your money is resilient and can bounce back stronger than before.

S&C

Chapter Thirty-Five

_____R_____

Style Boxes

If you invest in a retirement plan, or buy mutual funds, there is a good chance that you will see Morningstar ratings or reports.

Morningstar was built upon the concepts of Modern Portfolio Theory. Morningstar analyzes and measures the MPT statistics of stocks, bonds and mutual funds. Then it presents the information in a manner that is (relatively) easy to understand.

Morningstar crunches a lot of numbers. Morningstar's data is sold to financial advisors throughout the world. Some of this information is for advisor use only, and not legally shared with clients. Other data is formatted for investor consumption.

Let's simplify two of Morningstar's visual devices. They can be extremely helpful in conceptualizing a diversified portfolio.

STYLE BOXES

While Morningstar didn't create the concept of investment styles, they did popularize a simple way to illustrate them. Morningstar created a nine box grid for equities and bonds. Each stock, bond, or mutual fund gets placed into one or more of these boxes. This illustration shows how it is done with mutual funds.

http://www.morningstar.com/invglossary/morningstar_style_box.aspx

Investment Style

The following illustrates the quadrants of style boxes for equity and debt investments.

Stock
Investment Style

Value	Blend	Growth	
			Large Size Companies
			Medium Size Companies
			Small Size Companies

Bond
Maturity

Short	Medium	Long	
			High Quality Debt
			Medium Quality Debt
			Low Quality Debt

Stocks

Morningstar breaks stocks down by size—small, medium and large. Morningstar also illustrates by style—growth, value or a blend of the two (such as the S&P 500).

Morningstar looks to the underlying assets of a mutual fund and categorizes them in terms of size and style. If a mutual fund's management states that they will invest in large value stocks, and they actually do, their fund's equity portion will be placed in the upper left hand quadrant of the style box.

The S&P would be placed in the upper middle box. This is because the S&P is a blend of large-cap growth and large-cap value stocks. A fund that invests in mid-cap value stocks would land in the middle left quadrant. Small growth would be in the bottom right hand corner.

Risk moves from left to right and top to bottom. Large value stocks tend to have the lowest equity risk. Small growth stocks tend to have the highest equity risk. Get the picture? The box system is an easy way to illustrate a mutual fund's predominant investment style. Read this section until you understand how to use the boxes.

Bonds

Bonds are illustrated according to quality—high, medium and low. They are also categorized by duration, their sensitivity to interest rates. This is measured as short, medium and long.

Risk moves in the same direction as the equities boxes. T-bills would be represented in the upper left quadrant. They have the lowest risk and shortest duration. Long-duration junk bonds and foreign junk debt (especially emerging markets and failing governments) would be represented in the bottom right quadrant.

Morningstar prepares a lot of good information. Morningstar reports are available through most retirement plans, financial advisors, and many mutual funds. Use their information if you can.

Risk Continuum

Emerging Markets
Small Cap Growth
Mid-Cap Growth
Large Cap International
Large Cap Growth
Small Cap Value
Mid-Cap Value
Large Cap Value
Growth & Income
Balanced

Low Risk

← **RISK**

High Risk

Convertible Bonds
Long-term Corporate
Long-term Gov't
Med-Term Corporate
Med-Term Gov't
Money Market, GIC, Short-Term Gov't

Chapter Thirty-Six

R
_____

Risk Charts

The preceding chart shows a risk/return continuum that places the major asset classes in order of their relative risk. Remember, more risk usually means greater potential for long-term gain.

This is not an absolute ranking. It is a general guide to let you see where asset classes might fall as they relate to the risk and return potential for your portfolio. Every stock, or fund, is unique.

Bonds have lower investment risk than equities. Notice how T-bills (short-term government) represent the lowest risk. As bonds grow longer in duration, and lower in quality, bond risk increases.

The debt of stable governments will be less risky and more highly rated than most corporate debt. Governments have taxing power. Companies don't. But some companies have more cash on hand than many governments.

Bond risk increases as duration increases and quality decreases.

The debt with the greatest risk is (normally) convertible bonds. If a company goes into bankruptcy, convertible bonds are normally paid after other bond holders. There are usually fewer assets backing convertible bonds.

Notice the different equity asset classes. Large value securities have the lowest equity risk. Growth stocks have more risk than value stocks. Small stocks have more risk than big stocks. Foreign stocks from developed countries have less risk than emerging market shares, which have the greatest risk. Making more sense?

Risk Continuum

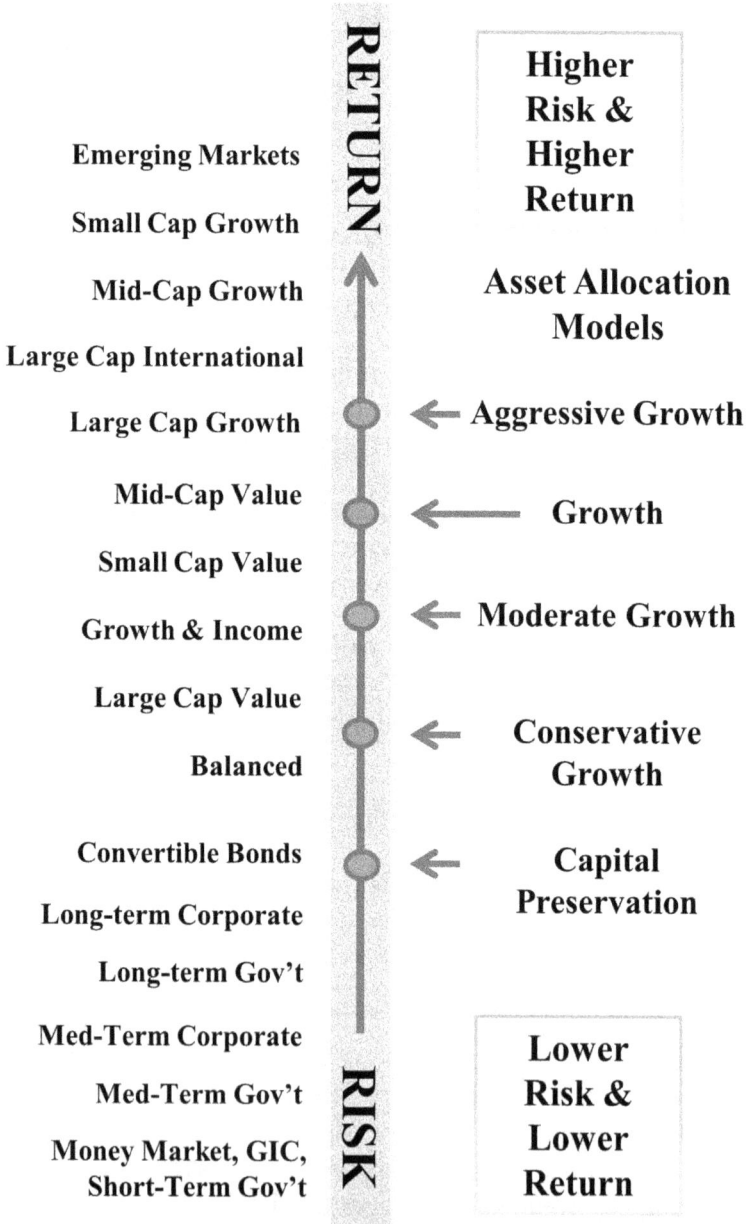

	RETURN	**Higher Risk & Higher Return**
Emerging Markets		
Small Cap Growth		**Asset Allocation Models**
Mid-Cap Growth	↑	
Large Cap International		
Large Cap Growth	● ←	**Aggressive Growth**
Mid-Cap Value	● ←	**Growth**
Small Cap Value		
Growth & Income	● ←	**Moderate Growth**
Large Cap Value		
Balanced	● ←	**Conservative Growth**
Convertible Bonds	● ←	**Capital Preservation**
Long-term Corporate		
Long-term Gov't		
Med-Term Corporate		**Lower Risk & Lower Return**
Med-Term Gov't	**RISK**	
Money Market, GIC, Short-Term Gov't		

Some people think horizontally. Others think vertically. Here is the same information presented vertically.

This chart includes asset allocation models, and where they might fall along the risk/return continuum.

All models are different. Models will move along the continuum based upon the ongoing performance of the managers, as well as the underlying securities. This should help you visualize where different models might reside.

Asset allocation models should lie closer to the Efficient Frontier than individual asset classes. A model will normally have greater long-term performance than most single asset classes of similar risk.

THE NEXT CHARTS

Some people understand better with pyramids. The following illustration shows where different types of debt instruments fall on the risk continuum by using a pyramid. The higher the investment risk, the higher it lies on the pyramid.

The second pyramid shows equity investment classes. This includes indexes.

The third pyramid compares the risk characteristics of stocks and bonds. Bonds have less risk than stocks, so they sit at the base of the pyramid. Stocks have higher risk, so they reside on top. Along the outer edge, you will see the priority of income, as it comes from a company to investors. Income gets paid from the bottom up.

The fourth and final chart shows how the underlying assets of different portfolios (or models) might be mixed.

Pyramid of Risk - Debt

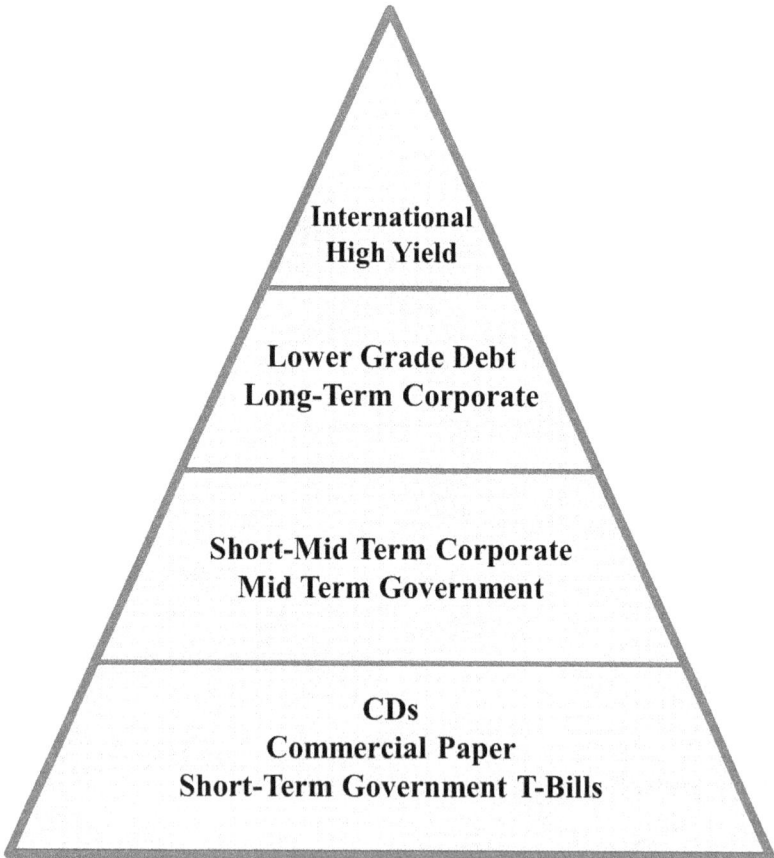

International
High Yield

Lower Grade Debt
Long-Term Corporate

Short-Mid Term Corporate
Mid Term Government

CDs
Commercial Paper
Short-Term Government T-Bills

Pyramid of Risk - Equity

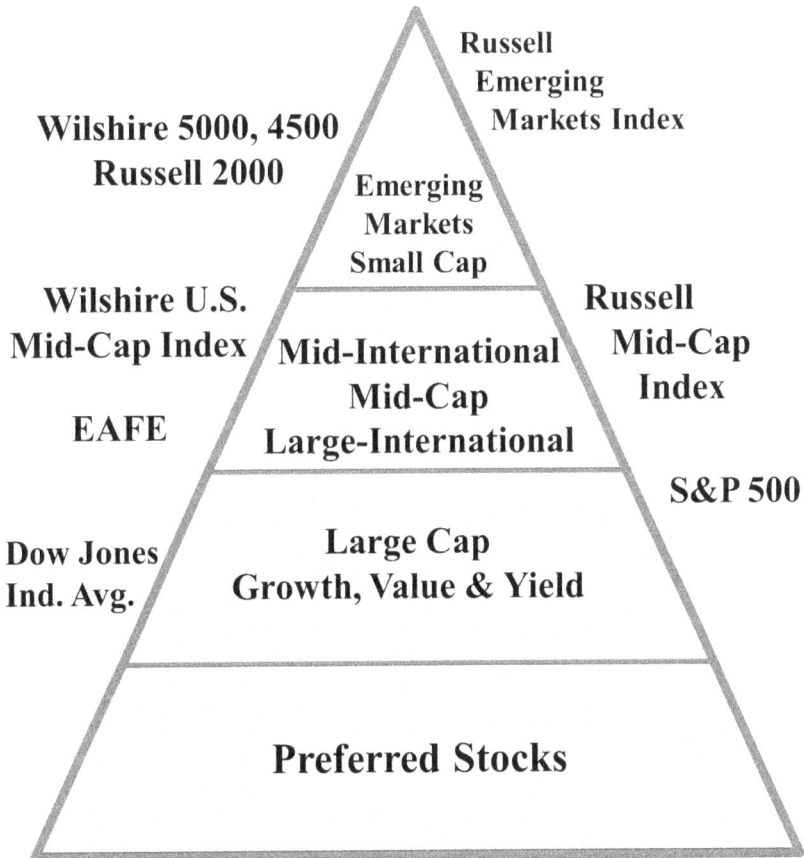

Russell
Emerging
Markets Index

Wilshire 5000, 4500
Russell 2000

Emerging
Markets
Small Cap

Wilshire U.S.
Mid-Cap Index

Russell
Mid-Cap
Index

Mid-International
Mid-Cap
Large-International

EAFE

S&P 500

Dow Jones
Ind. Avg.

Large Cap
Growth, Value & Yield

Preferred Stocks

Stocks & Bonds Relative Risk & Reward

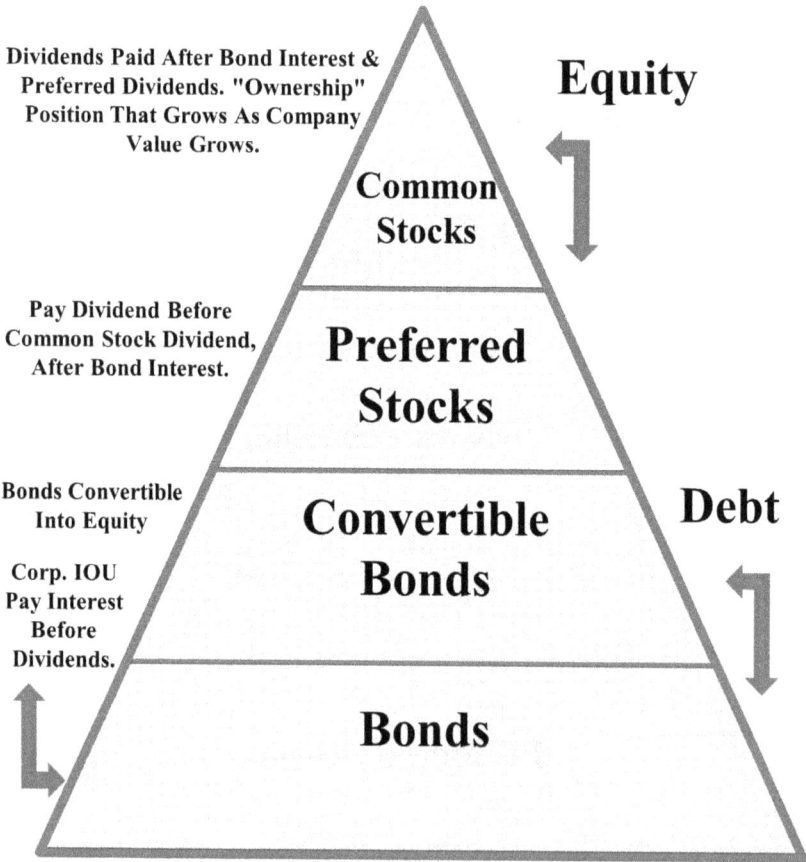

Dividends Paid After Bond Interest & Preferred Dividends. "Ownership" Position That Grows As Company Value Grows.

Equity

Common Stocks

Pay Dividend Before Common Stock Dividend, After Bond Interest.

Preferred Stocks

Bonds Convertible Into Equity

Convertible Bonds

Debt

Corp. IOU Pay Interest Before Dividends.

Bonds

Models: Risk & Return

General Investment Characteristics:

85-100% stocks. International & emerging market. Small, mid-cap & large-cap U.S. stocks. Long-term & mid-term bond mix.

Aggressive Growth

70-85% stocks. Blended portfolio with domestic and large international. Small, mid, & large-cap U.S. stocks. Less small & mid-cap. Diversified moderate bond mix.

Growth

50-70% large U.S & foreign, plus mid-cap stocks. More conservative bonds. Some T-bills.

Moderate Growth

30-50% large-cap stocks. Mostly large-cap. Some large foreign. Mix of bonds & cash. More short-term corporate & government bonds. More T-bills.

Conservative Growth

Less than 30% stocks. Mix of bonds. More than 50% mid & short-term corporate & government bonds. Even more cash & T-bills.

Capital Preservation

GICs, T-bills & Money Market Instruments (Cash).

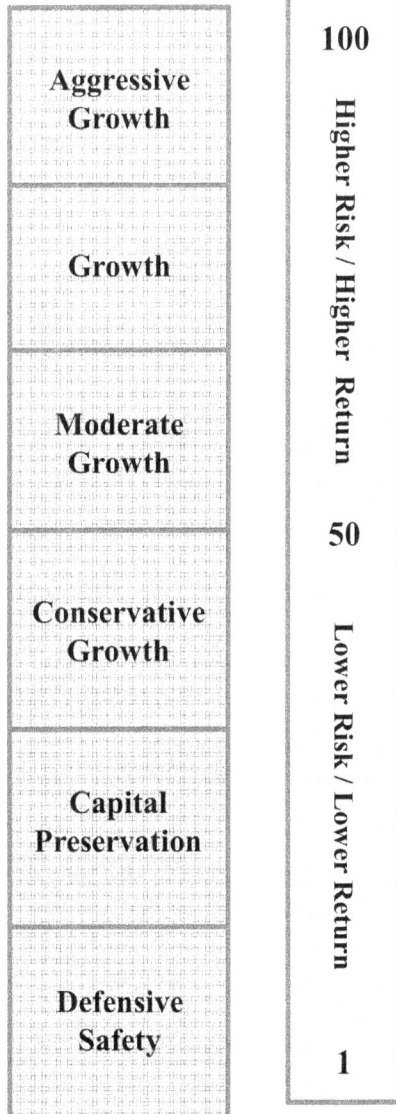

Defensive Safety

100

Higher Risk / Higher Return

50

Lower Risk / Lower Return

1

The previous pages have illustrated the risk and return characteristics of various asset classes. Now we let's start putting investments together.

The mix with the highest risk and return potential is illustrated at the top. Higher risk mixtures contain mostly stocks. They might include large, medium and small, growth and value, domestic and international stocks.

As we move downward in risk, we own fewer stocks and more bonds.

Lower risk portfolios contain high quality and short duration debt. In theory, they should also include some large stocks. Adding stocks to a safe bond portfolio can actually reduce investment risk and boost returns.

This explanation may seem repetitious. That is the intention of this book. Eventually, the material will sink in and make sense for everyone—enough to impact investment behavior and affect long-term returns. It will become natural.

Some people have a knack for finance and learn quickly. Others have a different skill set. Some people require more time to understand these challenging concepts. This does not mean that quick learners will be more successful investors. Think of the turtle and the hare. Sometimes, those who learn easily veer off course because they think they can outsmart the market. They can't. Highly educated professionals often make very poor investors.

The material in this book has been repeated in different ways. It must be. Repetition is the mother of all learning. When the same information is presented differently, it takes a different pathway through the brain. Make sure you understand the important concepts of this book. They are the key to your financial survival.

If you need more clarification on something, go back and read again. It will come. For you pros, new and old, this book will now move on to the implementation phase of investing.

Chapter Thirty-Seven

R

Asset Allocation Models

Asset Allocation Models

- Most 401(k) plans offer asset allocation models as part of their investment choices.
- Asset allocation models are designed to approach the highest return, given the short-term risk that an investor is willing to assume.
- Models may be given designations such as:
– Capital Preservation
– Conservative Growth
– Moderate Growth
– Growth
– Aggressive Growth
- Models may be presented as Target Date Funds, such as:
– 2020
– 2030
– 2040
– 2050
– 2060

The nearer the target date, the more conservative the fund. The farther the target date, the more aggressive the fund.

Models

Asset Allocation Models are created for specific investment objectives.

A model will own a mix of investments designed to fit a particular risk/return profile, or a specific investment objective. Models attempt to achieve the highest return, given the level of risk one is willing to assume.

Asset allocation models can be constructed from "scratch," where managers choose individual securities for the model portfolio.

Asset allocation models can also combine existing mutual funds (or accounts), by percentage, to create their target mix of assets.

If you are investing in asset allocation mutual funds, there is a good chance that you will own a "fund of funds." This is a fund that is built by combining other existing funds. The percentage ownership of each underlying fund will determine the ultimate asset allocation and risk/return profile.

Age-Based Models

Many asset allocation funds are created, and managed, for a specific *target date*. Age-based models choose a hypothetical target or retirement date. This determines the underlying mix of the fund. When the date is far away, such as thirty years or more, the model will own a high percentage of equities, usually 85-90%. As the fund draws closer to the target date, the model allocation will be adjusted. The fund will become progressively more conservative as the target date draws near. This takes the thinking out of investing.

Target funds allow retirement plan participants to choose one fund and let it do the asset allocation planning for them.

Models Terms

Traditional asset allocation models state their intended objective.

- Aggressive growth funds are for the young and the fearless.

- Growth funds are for those with more than twenty years until retirement.

- Moderate growth investors typically have a 10-30 year retirement horizon.

- Conservative growth investors have 1-15 years until they retire. Many investors maintain a moderate growth portfolio, even in retirement.

- Capital preservation investors are either huge savers or uneasy sleepers.

The overlap between time frames is a result of funding ability and individual risk preferences. Someone who is able to save aggressively may be able to "afford" less risk. Someone who is on a tighter budget may have to assume more risk to achieve their Number.

Customization

An individual investor can choose a model, or a target date fund, and then tweak the risk profile by combining it with a mutual fund or two. For example, if someone is young and wants to seek higher returns than the most aggressive model available, he can tweak it by combining a mid-cap, small-cap, and/or emerging market fund with the model account. This way, most of the asset allocation work is done by professionals, with a touch of personalization for greater long-term growth potential.

Customization might also be appropriate after a significant market correction (think fire sale). Models weather downturns better than most individual stocks. Don't sell and go to bonds or cash as markets are falling hard. But when the markets are in flames, when there is blood in the streets, it might be appropriate to sell a small portion of your less aggressive investments and take advantage of growth bargains. Think Black Friday sales.

Do not try to time the market, though. It doesn't work. Exceptional buying opportunities don't happen much more than once a decade. They are difficult to recognize. After reading this book you might notice some of the signs. The stock market will need emergency medical attention. The media will be talking about the end of life as we know it. Your friends will be selling all they own. The world will be in one of the worst crises in modern history. The president will be speaking on national television assuring us all.

Investment life is never as bad or as good as it seems. Perhaps you will have the fortitude of Baron Rothschild and move toward the red on Wall Street—or at least keep from running away.

Age-Based Beware

A problem with some age-based models is that they are designed for accumulation toward retirement. They are not normally built to produce and maintain income *in* retirement.

Investors should not stay in an age-based model when they retire, unless it is a "to and through" fund that is designed to readjust its portfolio once a participant reaches retirement age.

Investors should always *re-allocate* their investments once they *switch* from *accumulating* and begin *distributing* their assets.

Asset Allocation Model Review

Asset allocation models have names like aggressive growth, growth, or moderate growth. They might also have target dates, like 2025, 2040 or 2050.

A 2050 fund will be more aggressive than a 2025 fund. A later retirement date gives fund managers a longer time horizon to invest shareholder money. The fund can buy more stocks. If stocks go down in value, there is time to regain lost values and outpace inflation.

There have been poor investment decades. Since 1928, there has never been a twenty-year time frame where stocks have not outpaced inflation.

As a target date approaches, a target fund will grow progressively more conservative. This is because the fund can't afford to lose a sizable portion of principal, as its investors are nearing retirement. Fund managers normally choose an ultimate asset allocation goal, which will be achieved by the actual target date.

HANDS ON TEACHING

Nothing teaches investors better than hands-on experience. This book will now illustrate the performance of five customized asset allocation models—using actual historical returns. This should help you see how the risk and return differences might affect your own portfolio choices.

MODELS

The following models are constructed with five major asset classes. The asset classes are as follows: T-bills, T-bonds (10-year U.S. government), S&P 500 Index (large U.S. blend), EAFE Index (foreign), and the Russell 2000 Index(small-mid cap blend). These asset classes represent a broad swath of the available investment pool, and should help you understand the effects of risk and return.

CHARTS

The following charts show the amount of each asset class owned within each model. The aggressive growth model has no T-bills. The capital preservation model has no small, mid-cap, or international stocks.

Asset Allocation Models Structure

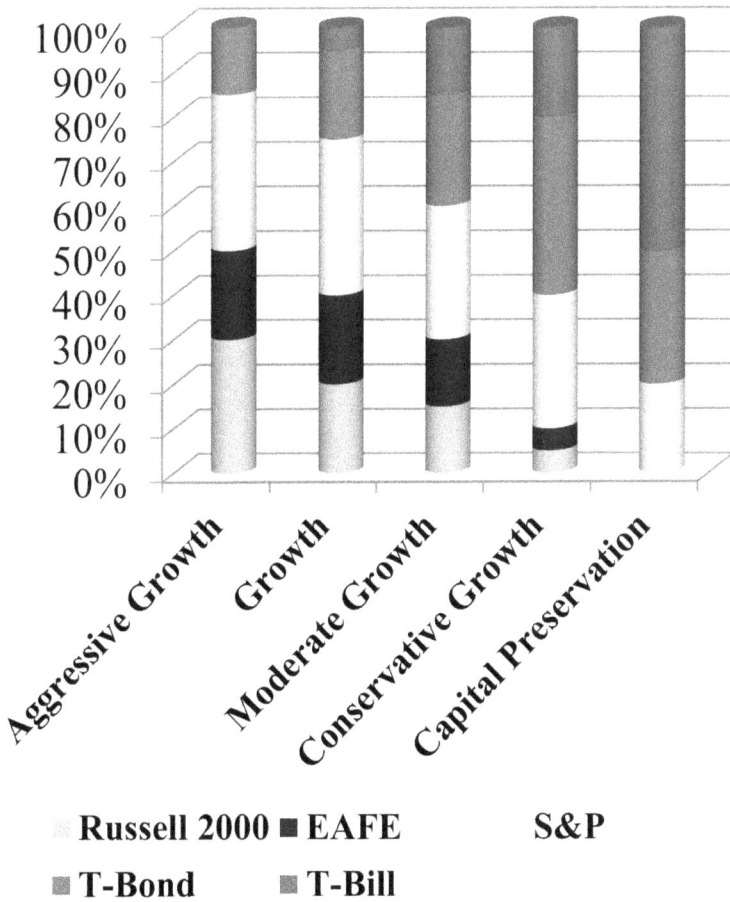

Russell 2000   ■ EAFE   S&P
■ T-Bond   ■ T-Bill

Asset Allocation Model –
Aggressive Growth

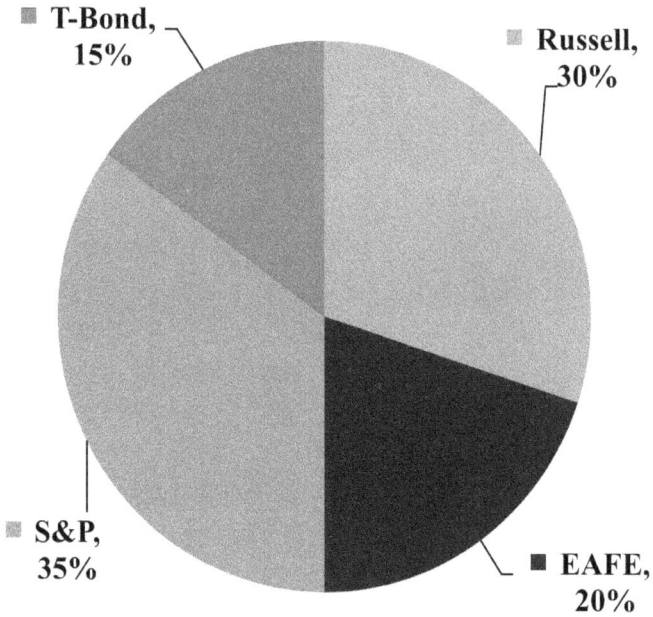

Russell 2000 ■ EAFE
S&P ■ T-Bond

ASSET ALLOCATION — Aggressive Growth Model

The aggressive growth model consists of 85% stocks and 15% bonds.

The bonds are mid-term, high quality.

The equities are divided as follows: S&P 500—35%, Russell 2000—30%, EAFE—20%.

This portfolio holds a relatively heavy concentration of small and mid-sized companies, with about 30%.

Over the long-term, small and mid-cap stocks have produced greater returns than large cap stocks. The aggressive model wants to take advantage of this trend, but still have diversification to manage risk and optimize returns.

Foreign stocks represent 20% of the portfolio. This percentage might be a little low for an aggressive model, especially since emerging markets are not included. This would be a manager's decision.

The intent of this exercise is to deepen your understanding of investment risks and returns, so that you can become more comfortable with choosing your own portfolio. This is a good mix for that purpose. Large cap, U.S. securities represent 35% of this portfolio.

Asset Allocation Model – Growth

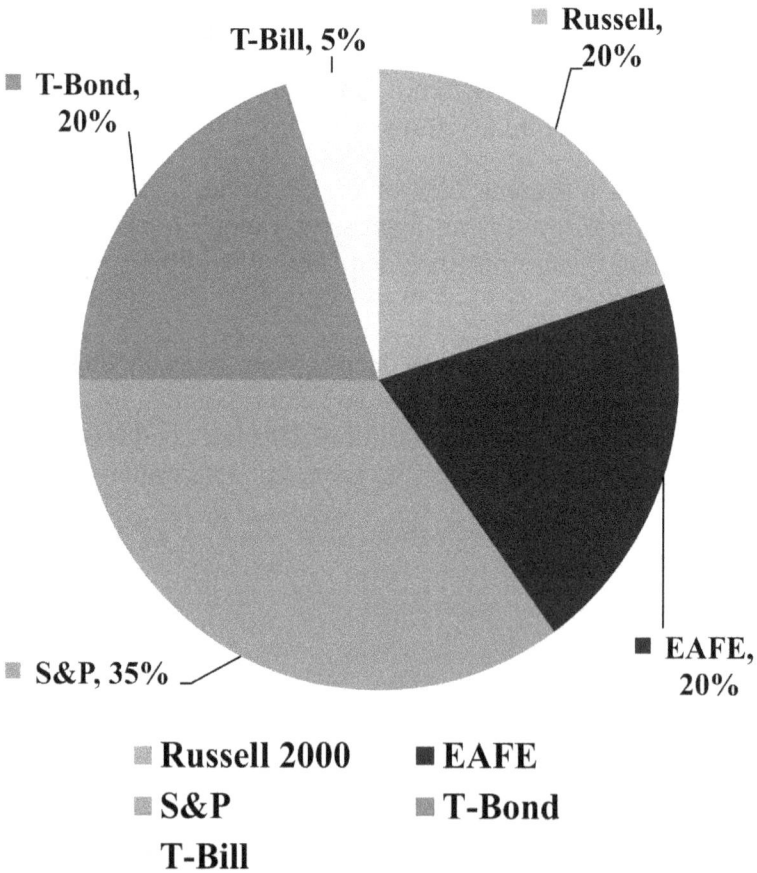

ASSET ALLOCATION — Growth Model

The growth model is a little less risky than the aggressive growth model. It consists of 75% stocks and 25% bonds.

The bonds are 20% mid-term, high quality and 5% short-term, high quality.

Equities are divided as follows: S&P 500—35%, Russell 2000—20%, EAFE—20%.

There is less of a concentration toward small and mid-sized companies. The S&P 500 remains the same, as does the EAFE.

The bond holdings have increased by 10%, with half of that increase composed of safer T-bills.

More bonds and fewer small and mid-cap securities should lower volatility, relative to the aggressive growth model. In theory, this should also reduce long-term growth.

Asset Allocation Model –
Moderate Growth

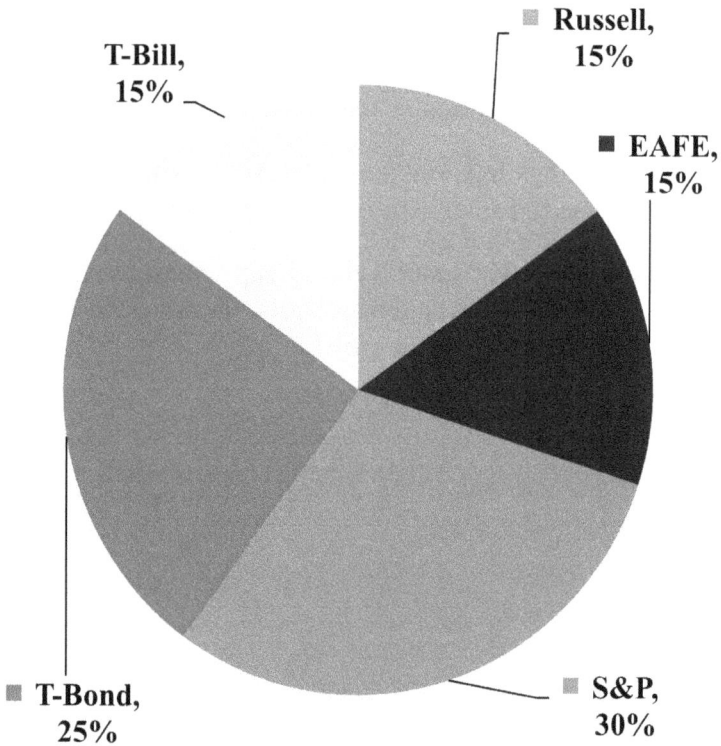

Russell, 15%

EAFE, 15%

T-Bill, 15%

T-Bond, 25%

S&P, 30%

Russell 2000   EAFE
S&P   T-Bond
T-Bill

ASSET ALLOCATION — Moderate Growth Model

The moderate growth model is much like a traditional balanced mutual fund. This is the old "investment stand-by." It consists of 60% stocks and 40% bonds.

T-bonds represent 25% of the portfolio. These are 10-year treasuries issued by the U.S. Government. Corporate bonds might normally be in this type of model. They would have higher yields, and a bit more risk.

This portfolio has 15% low-risk T-bills. T-bills historically match inflation (more or less), and move little when external market forces are stressing securities. This helps manage volatility.

On the stock side, the model maintains 30% in the S&P, and holds 15% in the EAFE (foreign) and 15% Russell (small and mid-cap companies).

Asset Allocation Model –
Conservative Growth

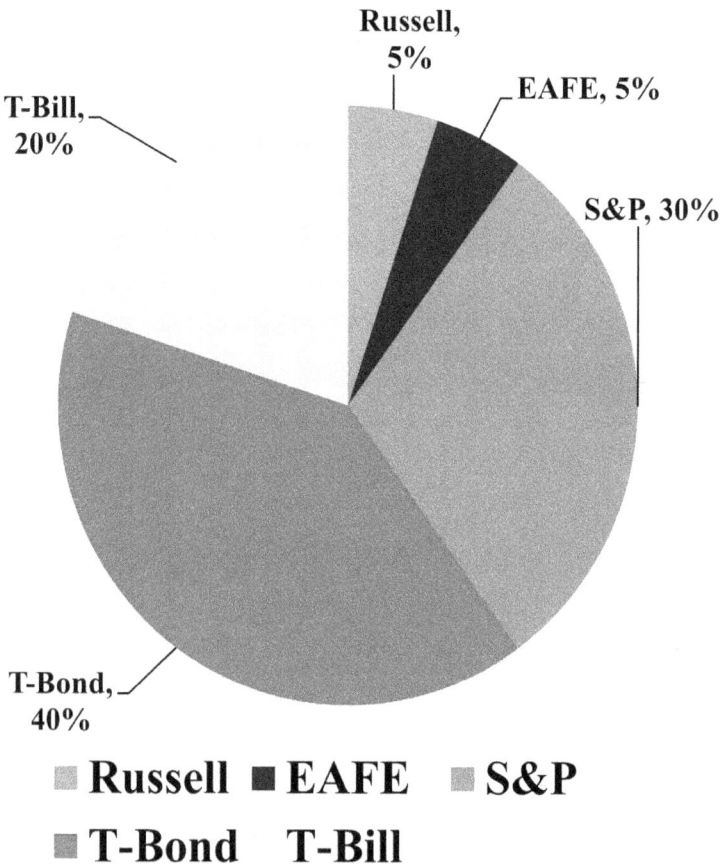

Russell,
5%

EAFE, 5%

T-Bill,
20%

S&P, 30%

T-Bond,
40%

■ Russell ■ EAFE ■ S&P
■ T-Bond   T-Bill

ASSET ALLOCATION — Conservative Growth Model

The conservative growth model owns 40% stocks and 60% bonds.

T-bills represent 20% of the portfolio. 10-year treasuries represent 40%.

Equities are owned as follows: 30% S&P, 5% foreign (EAFE), and 5% small and mid-cap (Russell 2000).

This portfolio should have lower risk than the moderate model. The equity portion will, hopefully, provide enough risk to outpace inflation.

Asset Allocation Model –
Capital Preservation

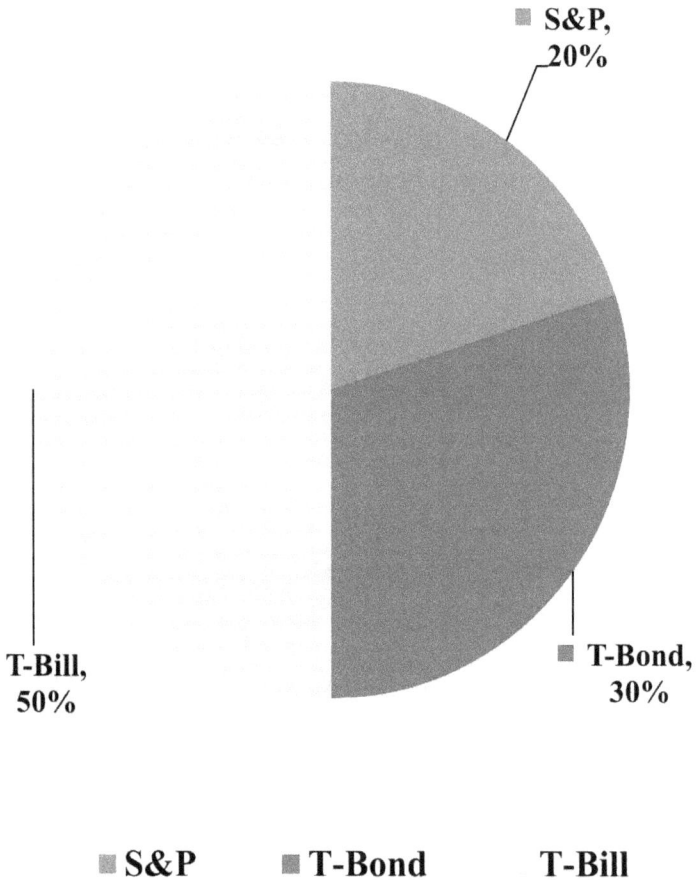

**S&P,
20%**

**T-Bill,
50%**

**T-Bond,
30%**

S&P ■ T-Bond T-Bill

ASSET ALLOCATION — Capital Preservation Model

The capital preservation model has 50% invested in T-bills, the investment with the least risk and return.

30% of the portfolio is composed of T-bonds. T-bonds have slightly more risk, but deliver a higher return over time.

20% of the portfolio is composed of the S&P Index. Stocks should still allow the portfolio to appreciate above inflation. A small portion of stocks should also help lower risk.

This model may have an inherently lower risk than a portfolio composed of bonds only.

Asset Allocation Models:
Savings Growth Over Time
$3,000 Invested First Year
Deposits Grow By 3%/Year (Example: $3,090 in Year 2)
Investment For 35 Years: From 1980-2014

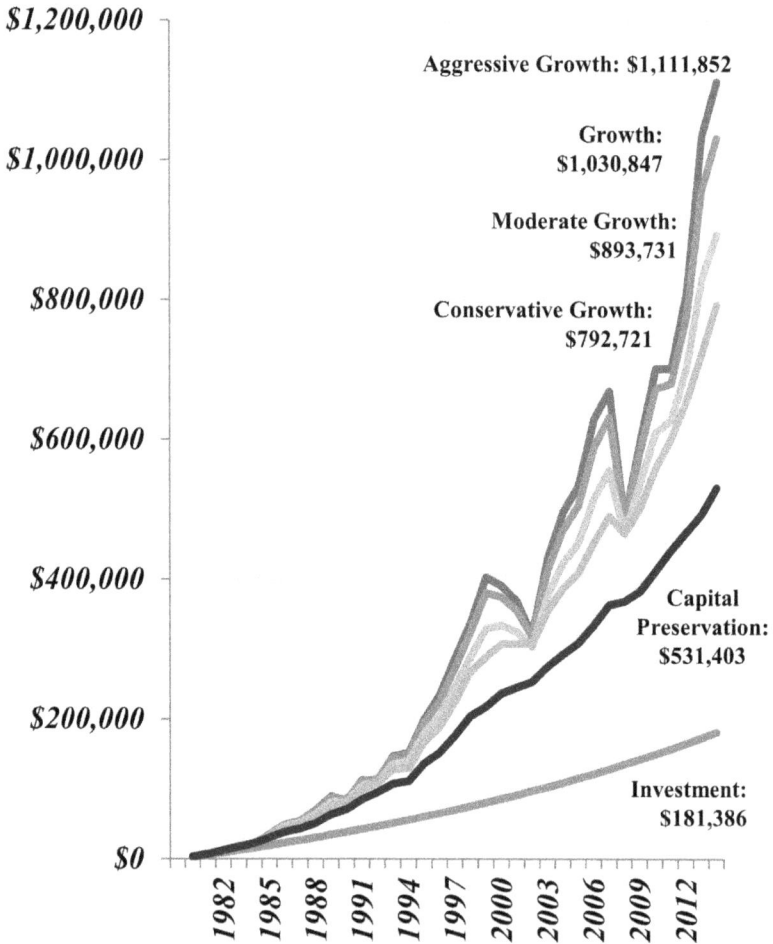

Asset Allocation Models: Savings Growth Over Time. Aggressive Growth: $1,111,852. Growth: $1,030,847. Moderate Growth: $893,731. Conservative Growth: $792,721. Capital Preservation: $531,403. Investment: $181,386.

Legend: Investments, Aggressive Growth, Growth, Moderate Growth, Conservative Growth, Preservation

Chapter Thirty-Eight

R

Asset Allocation Performance

Asset Allocation Models: Investment Growth Over Time

Let's take a look at the actual 35-year investment returns for the five models. The models illustrate annual investments beginning at $3,000 (10% of a $30,000 salary). The investment amount increases by 3% per year, as an employee might do with a 401(k).

3% inflation creates a contribution in year ten of $3,914. By year twenty, the contribution is $5,261. In year 30, the contribution is $7,069.

In this example, total investments over the theoretical thirty-five year work history were $181,386. The asset allocation models grew to the following amounts:

Investment:	**$181,386**
Capital Preservation:	**$531,403**
Conservative Growth:	**$792, 721**
Moderate Growth:	**$893,732**
Growth:	**$1,030,847**
Aggressive Growth:	**$1,111,852**

Let's take a close look at the actual model statistics.

35-Year Actual Model Statistics
$3,000 Initial Annual Investment
Increase Investments by 3% Each Year

Model	Aggressive Growth	Growth	Moderate Growth	Conservative Growth	Capital Preservation
Best Year	35.34%	33.89%	30.00%	25.51%	17.70%
Worst Year	-28.59%	-24.13%	-17.28%	-6.4%	-0.49%
Average Return	11.86%	11.28%	10.33%	9.48%	7.53%
Compound Annual	10.85%	10.51%	9.84%	9.22%	7.41%
% Years Positive	68%	76%	76%	84%	92%
% Years Negative	32%	24%	24%	16%	8%
Sum Invested	$181,386	$181,386	$181,386	$181,386	$181,386
35 Yr. Growth	$1,111,852	$1,030,847	$893,731	$792,721	$531,403

Asset Allocation Models Year By Year Returns

YEAR	Aggressive Growth	Growth	Moderate Growth	Conservative Growth	Preservation
1980	26.75%	23.30%	19.63%	13.63%	11.06%
1981	-0.26%	0.66%	2.75%	4.72%	8.67%
1982	19.18%	18.88%	19.44%	22.61%	19.43%
1983	21.78%	19.44%	16.69%	12.31%	9.65%
1984	3.55%	5.43%	6.76%	9.27%	10.16%
1985	35.34%	33.89%	30.00%	25.51%	17.70%
1986	25.71%	26.66%	23.79%	20.23%	14.00%
1987	3.58%	4.49%	3.74%	1.70%	2.54%
1988	20.18%	18.41%	15.98%	12.21%	9.00%
1989	20.66%	20.32%	19.10%	19.48%	15.66%
1990	-10.67%	-8.03%	-4.67%	0.94%	5.03%
1991	29.07%	25.50%	22.39%	19.10%	13.35%
1992	-4.25%	-1.66%	0.35%	5.09%	6.01%
1993	25.94%	22.20%	18.78%	13.20%	7.75%
1994	0.27%	0.25%	-0.12%	-1.72%	-0.15%
1995	27.32%	25.92%	23.81%	23.64%	17.24%
1996	14.31%	12.98%	11.30%	9.51%	7.48%
1997	20.14%	18.65%	16.79%	16.12%	12.13%
1998	15.39%	16.63%	15.56%	16.29%	12.51%
1999	17.84%	15.53%	12.11%	6.28%	3.96%
2000	-4.40%	-2.98%	-0.26%	4.25%	6.07%
2001	-6.85%	-6.64%	-4.45%	-1.54%	1.14%
2002	-14.75%	-11.87%	-8.03%	-2.03%	0.97%
2003	31.87%	27.22%	21.63%	13.15%	6.30%
2004	13.98%	12.44%	10.32%	7.19%	4.11%
2005	6.20%	6.03%	5.33%	4.10%	3.33%
2006	16.54%	15.03%	12.58%	8.64%	6.05%
2007	5.21%	6.11%	6.33%	7.14%	6.48%
2008	-28.59%	-24.13%	-17.28%	-6.47%	-0.49%
2009	21.92%	18.65%	13.86%	6.31%	1.92%
2010	16.06%	13.81%	11.77%	9.59%	5.57%
2011	-1.08%	0.14%	1.79%	6.10%	5.25%
2012	14.38%	12.89%	10.57%	7.65%	4.09%
2013	26.09%	21.75%	16.62%	9.09%	3.73%
2014	6.82%	6.87%	6.74%	8.35%	5.95%
Average	11.86%	11.28%	10.33%	9.48%	7.53%
% Positive	68.00%	76.00%	76.00%	84.00%	92.00%
% Negative	32.00%	24.00%	24.00%	16.00%	8.00%

Historical analysis of the five models illustrates many of the concepts discussed in this book. The models performed as predicted. The higher the risk, the greater a model returned over time. Investors were rewarded over the long run for taking risk.

The ultimate investment difference between the aggressive model and the growth model was *less* than the difference between the growth model and the moderate growth model.

Look back to The Efficient Frontier models graph in Chapter Twenty-Nine. Notice how the return axis flattens as we move farther to the right? This is the upper right hand portion of the frontier line, where the risk and returns are the greatest. See how flat it becomes as we take more risk? This is because the returns we achieve for assuming greater risk get smaller and smaller. Keep this in mind as you choose your investment strategy. If you have many years until retirement, you can afford to take more risk. If retirement is less than twenty years away, extreme risk may not reward you with better accumulation.

Over the thirty-five years analyzed, there were times when the markets fell severely. There were years when the markets delivered substantial gains.

The models performed as their risk profiles would predict. The less risky models returned the least over time. They were also less volatile. The low-risk models had the *best* "bad years." The more aggressive models had the greatest volatility, and the *worst* "bad years." The higher risk models returned the most, and had progressively better "best years."

Let's examine the numbers more closely.

Best Year: The best return years declined by model, as predicted by risk. The best annual return for the aggressive growth model was 35.34%. The best year for the capital preservation model was 17.7%.

Worst Year: The worst portfolio year occurred with the aggressive growth model, -28.59%. The worst year for the capital preservation model was -0.49%.

In its *worst year*, the capital preservation model lost less than half of 1%. Yet, mainly because of stocks, the portfolio was still able to appreciate $350,000 *more* than deposits.

Historically, investors are rewarded over time for taking risk. Taking even a little risk here paid off, especially when compared to taking no risk at all.

Average Returns: The Aggressive Growth Model and the Growth Model delivered returns that were close to the long-term average for the S&P Index. The *average annual returns* were 11.86% and 11.28%. The most aggressive model averaged only **.58%** more than the growth model. This is because of the flattening yield curve on the efficient frontier. Even though the return increase was minimal, the portfolio still earned nearly $100,000 more over 35 years. This would have made a nice down payment on a Florida vacation home.

The *compound annual return* of the aggressive growth model was only **.34%** more than the growth model. This reduction, versus the .58% difference in average returns, is because of the difference in **volatility**.

Greater volatility produces *lower* compound returns over time, even if the average returns are the same. This distinction is important, particularly in retirement. Compound returns determine how fast your money will grow. Volatility can determine how long you might keep it in retirement.

All of the models performed well, and relative to their risk profiles.

Market pessimists would argue that these returns are higher than the ones you should expect moving forward.

Pessimists point out that unusually high bond yields skewed the early years of this illustration. The high yields were due to high in-flation, brought on by such things as government controls and reg-ulations, increased government spending, loose monetary policy, commodity price squeezes and the formation of OPEC. OPEC's creation led to significantly greater oil prices. This caused a shock of higher prices for just about everything.

Bond yields are historically low at the present time. Commodity prices are down. Inflation is low. Will bond yields go up? History says they will.

Market pessimists would argue that tax cuts and the closing of tax shelter loopholes in the 1980s led to greater productivity and a long bull market. And that tax increases seem more likely today. They would claim that regulations are strangling economic growth, and that budget deficits are ultimately bad for the economy. They see disaster on the horizon.

Market optimists predict that technology will produce new indus-tries and an economic boom that will drive stocks higher. Dis-eases, such as certain cancers, will be cured, so research monies can be devoted to new technologies and economic infrastructure. Optimists see low energy prices as OPEC crumbles, and forward leaps for mankind with quantum computers, genetic therapy and private space exploration.

There are always two sides of the investment story. The reality is this: The stock market is the economic expression of the human condition. We continually strive to improve our lives. As we do, more goods and services are produced with fewer resources. This leads to greater productivity and profitable business earnings. Pro-ductivity and earnings drive the stock market.

World economics are too complicated, even for the experts. Don't let the noise deter you from your long-term plan.

While humans still have two eyes, two ears, and one mouth, you shouldn't need to change your long-term investment strategies. When humans become more machine than mankind, maybe then you will need to rethink the benefits of remaining invested in stocks.

Keep an eye out, but have faith. The past repeats itself, especially with the stock market.

Compound Returns Versus Annual Returns:

Look again at the Model Statistics chart. Notice the difference between the *average rates of return* for the model portfolios and their *compound annual growth rates*.

Average return rates get touted by mutual fund companies. Compound returns are what matter when you are accumulating for retirement. Average returns are higher than compound returns. Here is the reason why: It takes greater returns to recover from a decline. For example, if the stock market falls 50%, it must increase by 100% to return to its former value.

If the price of a stock falls from $10/share to $5, the price drop has been 50%. In order to increase from $5/share back to $10, the stock price must now double. It must increase by 100%, not 50%.

If the stock market falls by 50% in one year, and it takes one year to return to where it started, the "net" stock market gain would be zero. An investor would be right back where he started.

But the *average* annual return for those two years would be 25%. Here's why:

- We lose 50% in the first year.
- We gain 100% in the second year.
- -50% plus 100% equals 50%.
- 50%/2 years = 25% average return.

Our *compound annual* growth rate is zero. We made no money. Our portfolio had an *average rate* of return of 25%. Get it?

The difference between the *average return* and the *compounded return* will narrow as risk decreases and time increases.

% Years Positive:

The capital preservation model had positive gains 92% of the time. In its worst year it was barely negative.

The aggressive growth fund was positive 68% of the time. About once in every three years, this model lost money. Short-term losses are normal. You must accept risk if you need long-term growth. Don't let market fluctuations cause you stress. When the market falls, it is behaving as it should.

If an investor moved to cash after the worst year, and returned to the portfolio after the market corrected, her compound returns would be much lower. Timing the market doesn't work. Time *in* the market does work. New purchases are bargains when stocks are down.

If you are going to invest for gains, you MUST be determined to **remain invested** during and after every down year.

FEES

Beware of paying excessive investment management and advisory fees. Fees have an impact on the net amount that you earn and save. Make sure you get what you pay for.

This book will show you how expenses affect the value of your portfolio. Expenses are necessary. Reasonable expenses provide value.

You should not look at stock market averages without including expenses in your planning. While it is possible to earn above-average returns, you should not count on matching or beating the averages because expenses are involved with your portfolio.

Chapter Thirty-Nine

R

Volatility In Retirement

Volatility In Retirement

Investment returns come with risk. Risk presents itself as volatility.

Volatility is important while you accumulate money for retirement. It is more important when you withdraw funds in retirement.

If you draw income from funds after they have declined substantially, this reduces your investment principal.

After Retirement

If investments have similar average returns, and one has substantially less volatility, the fund with lower volatility is usually more appropriate.

In Modern Portfolio Theory, volatility is measured with an investment term known as beta. The lower the beta, the lower the risk. If two funds, or models, have equal long-term average returns, but one has lower beta, the fund with the lower beta will usually be more appropriate in retirement.

For Example: Let's say you are drawing $50,000 per year from a portfolio of $1,000,000 (5% withdrawal).

In a perfect world, your portfolio might gain 8% to $1,080,000. You would withdraw $50,000 and still have $1,030,000 invested for retirement. The portfolio growth will help you keep pace with inflation.

If your portfolio dropped by 30%, rather than gaining 8%, your portfolio value would fall to $700,000. A $50,000 year-end income now represents a withdrawal of 7.14%. This drops your portfolio value to $650,000. If your portfolio stays level in the next year, a $50,000 withdrawal drops the portfolio to $600,000.

Now, your portfolio must grow by 70% to bring it back to your initial $1,000,000. Even worse, your portfolio will need to earn higher than normal stock market averages for the remainder of your retirement. If income had come from the bond or cash portion of your portfolio, you could have avoided this crisis.

The stock market is volatile. You don't want your entire portfolio behaving poorly, especially in the early years of retirement.

This is why you should consider lowering your investment risk (volatility) as you approach and enter retirement. You will still need risk with your portfolio. But it must be managed.

RISK/RETURN TRADEOFF:

Over time, risk can help an investor accumulate a substantial sum toward retirement.

Risk is usually needed in retirement as well. But, too much portfolio risk in retirement can be dangerous, particularly if you don't have surplus funds. This book will review this in greater detail shortly.

INVESTING IN RETIREMENT

We have examined how risk and return are interconnected. Historically, the more risk one takes (within reason), the higher the long-term returns.

When you have many years until retirement, temporary bear markets (down 20% or more) will not prevent you from achieving your long-term goals. But what happens if there is a bear market just as you retire?

MODEL PORTFOLIOS

This book has illustrated five asset allocation portfolios, and how they accumulated funds over 35-years. Long-term returns were tied to short-term risk. The greater the risk, the greater the chance of short-term losses. The greater the risk, the better the long-term gains.

TIMING IN RETIREMENT

There is a common saying that, "timing is everything." This can be especially true with retirement investing. If you suffer large portfolio losses shortly before you retire, you may not have the amount that you planned on. If you achieve unusually large gains before retirement, you may have more than you need. At least when you begin.

The same holds true in retirement. Timing is critical.

The returns that you earn in the early years of retirement will impact how much you will have at the end. The prior page gave an example of what large portfolio losses can do to a lifetime of planning. How much risk should you take?

Let's look at our models and see how they would have performed in thirty-five years of retirement, from 1980-2014.

RETIREMENT COMPARISON

In the previous chapter, we analyzed the growth performance of our model portfolios.

These portfolios were constructed with five indexes. Be advised that investors cannot own an actual index. Investors can only buy funds (or accounts) that consist of the securities in those indexes. According to Morningstar, there are 49 separate S&P Index funds, with 145 different share classes.

http://www.morningstar.com/advisor/t/103471396/the-only-s-p-500-index-funds-you-will-ever-need.htm

Index funds come with expenses. Most index funds, such as an S&P Index fund, have reasonable expenses. If you are paying fees to an advisor using index funds, make sure your advisor uses funds with low expenses. That advisor should have access to indexes with very low expenses. If not, something is wrong.

Advisors can be extremely helpful in coordinating your investment strategy. But don't pay an advisor or broker to put you into indexes and just let them sit. They must still be managed. Make sure your advisor earns her money.

Some financial advisors utilize mutual funds that pay commissions. Sometimes it makes sense to pay commissions in lieu of paying advisory fees, especially if accounts are small. When held for the long-term, such an arrangement can be cost-beneficial. Again, make sure your advisor earns her money with long-term service.

Think of an advisor as a gardener. Your advisor(s) should help you tend to your portfolio as if it were a garden. If they don't, your money will grow a lot of weeds. Weeds suck energy from portfolio growth.

If you choose indexes on your own, you must do some research. No-load companies like Fidelity and Vanguard offer low-cost index funds to choose from. Some require a certain account size to receive the lowest fees. If you choose this path, don't let your emotions destroy a long-term plan. One emotional mistake can erase a lifetime of investing. This is where many advisors earn their fees. They can help you keep your financial ship on course during stormy investment times.

The next few pages compare how two models would have performed if you had retired in 1980, and maintained these models until 2014. This time frame represents a typical retirement horizon.

We will compare these models with and without an expense of 1%. This will demonstrate the impact of portfolio expenses.

We will then compare these same portfolios as if you had retired at the end of 1999. Why?

1980 represented the beginning of a bull market for stocks. This is an example of retiring at the right time. Bond interest rates were high, as was inflation. Together, stocks and bonds delivered greater than average returns at the beginning of this retirement example.

1999 represents the beginning of a market downturn. The stock market fell sharply in 2000. Bonds began a slow decline in interest rates, with low yields for close to a decade. The stock market rose again, only to plummet for a second time later in the decade. Then it rose once more. This period represents a more challenging retirement scenario. You should be prepared for such volatile returns when you retire.

CAPITAL PRESERVATION VS. GROWTH

Let's now illustrate and compare the retirement history of two retirees.

Retiree A chose to retire with the safer Capital Preservation Model. This portfolio was detailed in the previous chapter. It consists of 20% large stocks, 50% T-bills and 30% Treasury bonds. This is a low-risk portfolio, with some equity exposure to capture long-term appreciation to outpace inflation. This portfolio achieved an average long-term return of nearly 7.5%. The average returns were higher in the early years of retirement. Returns declined in the later years.

Retiree B chose to retire with the Growth Model. This model consists of 75% stocks and 25% bonds. The stocks are a mixture of large-cap, mid-cap, small-cap and international. The portfolio achieved an average return of about 11.25% over the 35 year retirement horizon.

Note: There is about a 3.75% difference in the average portfolio returns between the growth and conservative growth models. This difference is *less* than the long-term disparity between growth investors and growth index returns. Remember our chapter on emotions, and the DALBAR studies? Emotions cause many investors to deviate from equity positions at precisely the wrong time. Do not fall prey to a *hold and sell when the news gets bad* investment strategy. It does not work. This is where good advisors earn their money. While some advisors may help you earn better than average returns, their highest value can come as an experienced sounding board when difficult market conditions might cause your emotions to ruin your long-term plans.

Good advisors use their access to investment resources to help you succeed. Bad ones will try to systematically move money from your pocket to theirs. Especially with seniors. You must learn to recognize the difference. This book shows you how to analyze investments. It shows you what to expect, and what is possible. Let's continue the education.

Expenses Matter: All portfolios are affected by fees and expenses—especially over time. Expenses in a low-risk portfolio can be a high percentage of total return. If you have a low-risk portfolio, make sure your advisors bring something valuable to the planning table.

CAPITAL PRESERVATION PORTFOLIO IN RETIREMENT

The following table shows the income and asset growth of the capital preservation model. It assumes an annual 4% year-end withdrawal from 1980-2014. This table uses index returns with no fees or expenses. Our sample retiree began with a retirement portfolio of $1,000,000. Over 35 years, income has increased from $44,424 to $121,980 per year. Assets have grown from $1,000,000 to $3,049,504. This portfolio managed to mirror our projected 3% inflation. Total income received during retirement was nearly $3.5 million.

Cap Preservation W/4% Withdrawal
35 Years With No Fee

YEAR	Cap Pres No Fee	Initial Amount	Year-End Value	4% Withdrawal	Cumulative Income
1980	11.06%	1,000,000	$1,110,601	44,424	44,424
1981	8.67%	1,066,177	$1,158,607	46,344	90,768
1982	19.43%	1,112,263	$1,328,411	53,136	143,905
1983	9.65%	1,275,274	$1,398,354	55,934	199,839
1984	10.16%	1,342,420	$1,478,749	59,150	258,989
1985	17.70%	1,419,599	$1,670,933	66,837	325,826
1986	14.00%	1,604,096	$1,828,696	73,148	398,974
1987	2.54%	1,755,548	$1,800,062	72,002	470,977
1988	9.00%	1,728,060	$1,883,577	75,343	546,320
1989	15.66%	1,808,234	$2,091,370	83,655	629,974
1990	5.03%	2,007,715	$2,108,757	84,350	714,325
1991	13.35%	2,024,407	$2,294,733	91,789	806,114
1992	6.01%	2,202,943	$2,335,335	93,413	899,527
1993	7.75%	2,241,921	$2,415,624	96,625	996,152
1994	-0.15%	2,318,999	$2,315,444	92,618	1,088,770
1995	17.24%	2,222,826	$2,606,058	104,242	1,193,012
1996	7.48%	2,501,816	$2,688,852	107,554	1,300,567
1997	12.13%	2,581,298	$2,894,377	115,775	1,416,342
1998	12.51%	2,778,602	$3,126,143	125,046	1,541,387
1999	3.96%	3,001,097	$3,119,815	124,793	1,666,180
2000	6.07%	2,995,022	$3,176,864	127,075	1,793,254
2001	1.14%	3,049,789	$3,084,494	123,380	1,916,634
2002	0.97%	2,961,115	$2,989,851	119,594	2,036,228
2003	6.30%	2,870,257	$3,051,048	122,042	2,158,270
2004	4.11%	2,929,006	$3,049,373	121,975	2,280,245
2005	3.33%	2,927,399	$3,024,944	120,998	2,401,243
2006	6.05%	2,903,946	$3,079,622	123,185	2,524,428
2007	6.48%	2,956,437	$3,148,049	125,922	2,650,350
2008	-0.49%	3,022,127	$3,007,392	120,296	2,770,645
2009	1.92%	2,887,096	$2,942,515	117,701	2,888,346
2010	5.57%	2,824,814	$2,982,103	119,284	3,007,630
2011	5.25%	2,862,819	$3,012,982	120,519	3,128,149
2012	4.09%	2,892,462	$3,010,897	120,436	3,248,585
2013	3.73%	2,890,461	$2,998,294	119,932	3,368,517
2014	5.95%	2,878,362	$3,049,504	121,980	3,490,497

Investment portfolios incur expenses, between mutual funds, ETFs (exchange-traded, low-expense mutual funds that often approximate indexes), advisory fees and commissions. Let's look at the same portfolio mix with 1% annual expenses.

Can you see the final portfolio value after thirty-five years? 1% of annual expense has caused the final value total to shrink from $3,049,504 to $2,197,335. Think expenses don't matter?

All investment portfolios will incur expenses. Expenses are normal and necessary. Many mutual funds charge reasonable expenses. Index fund charges can be even lower.

Good financial advice isn't free. Many investment advisors are worth every penny they are paid. They may even help you achieve above-average returns. They may steer you through adverse markets, or help you with other aspects of financial planning.

But you must pay attention to the fees and expenses of your portfolio. Ask your advisor to explain how they get paid. Make sure that your fees and expenses are reasonable.

Net Returns: Don't look at "gross returns." Look at "**net returns**," which occur after all expenses and fees. Gross returns mean far less than your net returns. Net returns affect the money growth of your portfolio. They are what matters. Reduce your expectations by your expenses.

If you look to the table on the previous page, in 1980 you will see a gross portfolio return of 11.06%. This is one percent more than the 10.06% illustrated in the following table. We have added a 1% expense to our portfolio. Look to the Year-End Value column for 1980. In the previous example, our year-end value in **1980** was $1,110,601. The table on the following page shows a year-end value of $1,100,601. This is because there was a 1% expense on the initial $1,000,000 amount. In this case, expenses are $10,000. An expense of 1% on $2 million in assets is $20,000. (Note: Portfolios deduct fees and expenses daily, monthly or quarterly.)

Cap Preservation W/4% Withdrawal
35 Years   With 1% Expense

YEAR	Cap Pres 1% Fee	Initial Amount	Year-End Value	4% Withdrawal	Cumulative Income
1980	10.06%	1,000,000	$1,100,601	44,024	44,024
1981	7.67%	1,056,577	$1,137,609	45,504	89,528
1982	18.43%	1,092,105	$1,293,414	51,737	141,265
1983	8.65%	1,241,678	$1,349,098	53,964	195,229
1984	9.16%	1,295,134	$1,413,710	56,548	251,777
1985	16.70%	1,357,162	$1,583,869	63,355	315,132
1986	13.00%	1,520,515	$1,718,207	68,728	383,860
1987	1.54%	1,649,479	$1,674,809	66,992	450,853
1988	8.00%	1,607,816	$1,736,434	69,457	520,310
1989	14.66%	1,666,977	$1,911,324	76,453	596,763
1990	4.03%	1,834,871	$1,908,867	76,355	673,118
1991	12.35%	1,832,512	$2,058,888	82,356	755,473
1992	5.01%	1,976,533	$2,075,552	83,022	838,495
1993	6.75%	1,992,530	$2,126,984	85,079	923,575
1994	-1.15%	2,041,905	$2,018,355	80,734	1,004,309
1995	16.24%	1,937,621	$2,252,306	90,092	1,094,401
1996	6.48%	2,162,214	$2,302,239	92,090	1,186,491
1997	11.13%	2,210,150	$2,456,111	98,244	1,284,735
1998	11.51%	2,357,867	$2,629,204	105,168	1,389,903
1999	2.96%	2,524,036	$2,598,642	103,946	1,493,849
2000	5.07%	2,494,696	$2,621,214	104,849	1,598,698
2001	0.14%	2,516,365	$2,519,837	100,793	1,699,491
2002	-0.03%	2,419,043	$2,418,329	96,733	1,796,224
2003	5.30%	2,321,595	$2,444,611	97,784	1,894,009
2004	3.11%	2,346,827	$2,419,802	96,792	1,990,801
2005	2.33%	2,323,009	$2,377,186	95,087	2,085,888
2006	5.05%	2,282,098	$2,397,334	95,893	2,181,781
2007	5.48%	2,301,441	$2,427,587	97,103	2,278,885
2008	-1.49%	2,330,483	$2,295,815	91,833	2,370,718
2009	0.92%	2,203,983	$2,224,249	88,970	2,459,688
2010	4.57%	2,135,279	$2,232,821	89,313	2,549,000
2011	4.25%	2,143,508	$2,234,506	89,380	2,638,381
2012	3.09%	2,145,126	$2,211,509	88,460	2,726,841
2013	2.73%	2,123,048	$2,181,021	87,241	2,814,082
2014	4.95%	2,093,780	$2,197,335	87,893	2,901,975

5% INCOME VERSUS 4%

Let's see what happens if we take a 5% income from the capital preservation portfolio with a 1% expense.

The first thing to notice is that the income in 1980, the first year of retirement, is $55,530 rather than $44,024. That is a substantial raise in retirement income.

A consistent, five percent income withdrawal subjects the portfolio to a greater risk of steep decline. 1980 began a run of very good investment years. In the first decade, there were only two years where the portfolio earned less than the 8% this portfolio must earn to keep pace with 3% inflation. Of course, during the 1980s, inflation was growing at nearly 6%.

The early positive years helped this portfolio grow to nearly $2.2 million (by 1998). Since then, the portfolio has fallen steadily in value, to its final total of $1,539,136. This is about half the final value with 4% withdrawals and no expense. It is worth $658,000 less than the portfolio with 4% withdrawals and equivalent fees. The 5% portfolio is falling more rapidly in value.

How much more income did the portfolio with 5% withdrawals generate than the one with 4% withdrawals?

5% withdrawals created about $10,000 more income in year one. By the end of retirement, this portfolio is generating $10,000 *less* annual income. The portfolio with 5% withdrawals generated a total combined income of $3 million. The total income for the portfolio with 4% withdrawals was just over $2.9 million.

By taking an income of 4%, rather than 5%, a retiree would have earned about $500,000 *more money* over retirement.

Remember this as you determine how much you plan to spend from your portfolio.

Cap Preservation W/5% Withdrawal
35 Years   With 1% Expense

YEAR	Cap Pres 1% Fee	Initial Amount	Year-End Value	5% Withdrawal	Cumulative Income
1980	10.06%	1,000,000	$1,100,601	55,030	55,030
1981	7.67%	1,045,571	$1,125,759	56,288	111,318
1982	18.43%	1,069,471	$1,266,609	63,330	174,648
1983	8.65%	1,203,278	$1,307,377	65,369	240,017
1984	9.16%	1,242,008	$1,355,720	67,786	307,803
1985	16.70%	1,287,934	$1,503,077	75,154	382,957
1986	13.00%	1,427,923	$1,613,577	80,679	463,636
1987	1.54%	1,532,898	$1,556,438	77,822	541,458
1988	8.00%	1,478,616	$1,596,898	79,845	621,303
1989	14.66%	1,517,053	$1,739,425	86,971	708,274
1990	4.03%	1,652,454	$1,719,093	85,955	794,229
1991	12.35%	1,633,138	$1,834,885	91,744	885,973
1992	5.01%	1,743,141	$1,830,467	91,523	977,496
1993	6.75%	1,738,944	$1,856,287	92,814	1,070,311
1994	-1.15%	1,763,473	$1,743,134	87,157	1,157,467
1995	16.24%	1,655,978	$1,924,921	96,246	1,253,713
1996	6.48%	1,828,675	$1,947,101	97,355	1,351,068
1997	11.13%	1,849,746	$2,055,599	102,780	1,453,848
1998	11.51%	1,952,819	$2,177,545	108,877	1,562,726
1999	2.96%	2,068,667	$2,129,813	106,491	1,669,216
2000	5.07%	2,023,322	$2,125,935	106,297	1,775,513
2001	0.14%	2,019,638	$2,022,424	101,121	1,876,634
2002	-0.03%	1,921,303	$1,920,735	96,037	1,972,671
2003	5.30%	1,824,698	$1,921,385	96,069	2,068,740
2004	3.11%	1,825,316	$1,882,074	94,104	2,162,844
2005	2.33%	1,787,970	$1,829,668	91,483	2,254,327
2006	5.05%	1,738,185	$1,825,956	91,298	2,345,625
2007	5.48%	1,734,658	$1,829,738	91,487	2,437,112
2008	-1.49%	1,738,251	$1,712,393	85,620	2,522,732
2009	0.92%	1,626,773	$1,641,732	82,087	2,604,818
2010	4.57%	1,559,645	$1,630,891	81,545	2,686,363
2011	4.25%	1,549,347	$1,615,121	80,756	2,767,119
2012	3.09%	1,534,365	$1,581,847	79,092	2,846,211
2013	2.73%	1,502,755	$1,543,790	77,189	2,923,401
2014	4.95%	1,466,600	$1,539,136	76,957	3,000,357

TIME VALUE OF INCOME & GROWTH

From 1980-2014, the Capital Preservation Model earned an average return of 7.53%. After 1% expenses, a retiree would have earned a long-term return of 6.5% on this portfolio.

During this time frame, goods and services increased in price. It costs more to live today than it did in 1980. Remember our discussion of inflation? The following chart illustrates the net income and return earned by the portfolio. It then compares the returns to income and growth, inflated at 3% per year, our long-term target. Remember our discussion of time value?

The initial value is $1 million (upper left of the table), as retirement begins in 1980. The next column shows the year-end value after earning the investment return for that year. The table then shows the withdrawal of 4%. Notice how it increases every year at first? Bond yields were high back then. Stocks also did well.

Next is a column entitled, Portfolio at Inflation. This grows $1 million at 3% inflation. This helps us compare our actual portfolio growth to the planned-for inflation. The next column shows what the income would be at an inflation rate of 3%.

The final two columns compare portfolio income and asset growth to what it should be to match 3% inflation. When we divide the inflated figures into the actual portfolio figures we create a ratio. A ratio *greater* than 100% means that our income and/or year-end portfolio total have grown *more* than inflation. A figure *below* 100% means that the portfolio and income are *losing* to inflation.

You can see that the portfolio peaked in value at $2,629,204 in 1998. This represented a discounted present value of 150% of our initial $1 million. Income peaked at 154%. At the end of 35 years, the value is $2,197,335. With 3% inflation, the portfolio would have grown to $2,813,862. This represents a time value *loss* in our portfolio. It is worth just 78% of its initial amount. Adjusted for 3% inflation, our portfolio now has a purchasing power of $780,000 in 1980 dollars. This is the ultimate cost of low risk.

Capital Preservation W/4% Withdrawal
35 Years With 1% Expense Vs. Inflation

Year	Begin Value	Year-End Value	4% Withdraw	Portfolio At Inflation	Income Needed 3% Inflation	Pres Value Of Inc	Pres Value Of Port
1980	$1,000,000	$1,100,601	$44,024	$1,030,000	$40,000	110%	107%
1981	$1,056,577	$1,137,609	$45,504	$1,060,900	$41,200	110%	107%
1982	$1,092,105	$1,293,414	$51,737	$1,092,727	$42,436	122%	118%
1983	$1,241,678	$1,349,098	$53,964	$1,125,509	$43,709	123%	120%
1984	$1,295,134	$1,413,710	$56,548	$1,159,274	$45,020	126%	122%
1985	$1,357,162	$1,583,869	$63,355	$1,194,052	$46,371	137%	133%
1986	$1,520,515	$1,718,207	$68,728	$1,229,874	$47,762	144%	140%
1987	$1,649,479	$1,674,809	$66,992	$1,266,770	$49,195	136%	132%
1988	$1,607,816	$1,736,434	$69,457	$1,304,773	$50,671	137%	133%
1989	$1,666,977	$1,911,324	$76,453	$1,343,916	$52,191	146%	142%
1990	$1,834,871	$1,908,867	$76,355	$1,384,234	$53,757	142%	138%
1991	$1,832,512	$2,058,888	$82,356	$1,425,761	$55,369	149%	144%
1992	$1,976,533	$2,075,552	$83,022	$1,468,534	$57,030	146%	141%
1993	$1,992,530	$2,126,984	$85,079	$1,512,590	$58,741	145%	141%
1994	$2,041,905	$2,018,355	$80,734	$1,557,967	$60,504	133%	130%
1995	$1,937,621	$2,252,306	$90,092	$1,604,706	$62,319	145%	140%
1996	$2,162,214	$2,302,239	$92,090	$1,652,848	$64,188	143%	139%
1997	$2,210,150	$2,456,111	$98,244	$1,702,433	$66,114	149%	144%
1998	$2,357,867	$2,629,204	$105,168	$1,753,506	$68,097	154%	150%
1999	$2,524,036	$2,598,642	$103,946	$1,806,111	$70,140	148%	144%
2000	$2,494,696	$2,621,214	$104,849	$1,860,295	$72,244	145%	141%
2001	$2,516,365	$2,519,837	$100,793	$1,916,103	$74,412	135%	132%
2002	$2,419,043	$2,418,329	$96,733	$1,973,587	$76,644	126%	123%
2003	$2,321,595	$2,444,611	$97,784	$2,032,794	$78,943	124%	120%
2004	$2,346,827	$2,419,802	$96,792	$2,093,778	$81,312	119%	116%
2005	$2,323,009	$2,377,186	$95,087	$2,156,591	$83,751	114%	110%
2006	$2,282,098	$2,397,334	$95,893	$2,221,289	$86,264	111%	108%
2007	$2,301,441	$2,427,587	$97,103	$2,287,928	$88,852	109%	106%
2008	$2,330,483	$2,295,815	$91,833	$2,356,566	$91,517	100%	97%
2009	$2,203,983	$2,224,249	$88,970	$2,427,262	$94,263	94%	92%
2010	$2,135,279	$2,232,821	$89,313	$2,500,080	$97,090	92%	89%
2011	$2,143,508	$2,234,506	$89,380	$2,575,083	$100,003	89%	87%
2012	$2,145,126	$2,211,509	$88,460	$2,652,335	$103,003	86%	83%
2013	$2,123,048	$2,181,021	$87,241	$2,731,905	$106,093	82%	80%
2014	$2,093,780	$2,197,335	$87,893	$2,813,862	$109,276	80%	78%

GROWTH MODEL IN RETIREMENT

Now, let's look at how the Growth Portfolio performed in retirement.

The following table illustrates the same 4% year-end income. No fees and expenses are illustrated here, just the average returns of the underlying asset classes. This is done to show you the power of compounding, and the cost of expenses.

Note that the end value in year 35 has grown to $8,246,593. This is over $5 million more than the Capital Preservation portfolio value in year 35.

See the power of compounding, and of taking risk in a portfolio? The income in 2014 has grown to $329,864. Compare this to $121,980 with the Capitalization Portfolio with no expenses. Cumulative income is about $6.5 million versus $3.5. This is a big difference.

Note: This book does not necessarily recommend that you have a portfolio consisting of 75% stocks in retirement. A mix with 50%-60% stocks is usually more appropriate.

This illustration was created so that you can see how long-term income and asset growth follow risk and reward. Is this making more sense?

Growth Model With 4% Withdrawal
35 Years   With No Expense

YEAR	Growth Portfolio	Begin Value	Year-End Value	4% Withdrawal	Cumulative Income
1980	23.30%	1,000,000	1,233,024	49,321	49,321
1981	0.66%	1,183,703	1,191,504	47,660	96,981
1982	18.88%	1,143,843	1,359,779	54,391	151,372
1983	19.44%	1,305,388	1,559,213	62,369	213,741
1984	5.43%	1,496,845	1,578,100	63,124	276,865
1985	33.89%	1,514,976	2,028,419	81,137	358,002
1986	26.66%	1,947,282	2,466,344	98,654	456,655
1987	4.49%	2,367,690	2,474,106	98,964	555,620
1988	18.41%	2,375,141	2,812,482	112,499	668,119
1989	20.32%	2,699,982	3,248,634	129,945	798,064
1990	-8.03%	3,118,688	2,868,133	114,725	912,789
1991	25.50%	2,753,408	3,455,461	138,218	1,051,008
1992	-1.66%	3,317,242	3,262,023	130,481	1,181,489
1993	22.20%	3,131,542	3,826,738	153,070	1,334,558
1994	0.25%	3,673,668	3,682,779	147,311	1,481,869
1995	25.92%	3,535,467	4,451,939	178,078	1,659,947
1996	12.98%	4,273,862	4,828,745	193,150	1,853,097
1997	18.65%	4,635,595	5,500,075	220,003	2,073,100
1998	16.63%	5,280,072	6,158,092	246,324	2,319,424
1999	15.53%	5,911,769	6,829,779	273,191	2,592,615
2000	-2.98%	6,556,588	6,361,205	254,448	2,847,063
2001	-6.64%	6,106,756	5,701,307	228,052	3,075,115
2002	-11.87%	5,473,255	4,823,801	192,952	3,268,067
2003	27.22%	4,630,848	5,891,323	235,653	3,503,720
2004	12.44%	5,655,671	6,358,981	254,359	3,758,079
2005	6.03%	6,104,621	6,472,979	258,919	4,016,999
2006	15.03%	6,214,060	7,148,186	285,927	4,302,926
2007	6.11%	6,862,259	7,281,801	291,272	4,594,198
2008	-24.13%	6,990,529	5,303,867	212,155	4,806,353
2009	18.65%	5,091,713	6,041,355	241,654	5,048,007
2010	13.81%	5,799,701	6,600,550	264,022	5,312,029
2011	0.14%	6,336,528	6,345,590	253,824	5,565,853
2012	12.89%	6,091,766	6,877,148	275,086	5,840,938
2013	21.75%	6,602,062	8,038,220	321,529	6,162,467
2014	6.87%	7,716,691	8,246,593	329,864	6,492,331

GROWTH MODEL WITH 1% EXPENSES

The following table shows the same Growth Portfolio with 1% in expenses. The final value has fallen by more than $2 million, when compared to the no-fee example. Year-35 income is about $90,000 less. Total income has fallen by more than $1 million.

Do you see the impact that a 1% difference in returns will make?

When 1% is removed from an account each year, it becomes quite significant over time. This is why it is important to be conservative with your return expectations.

Don't expect average returns if your portfolio has expenses, especially if they are significant. Adjust your expectations by total expenses.

You should also plan for lower-than-average returns with your portfolio. Investment returns are never guaranteed and they are extremely unpredictable.

Remember how we used a long-term accumulation rate of return of 7.5% before retirement? Remember how we used long-term rates of 5.5% and 6.5% for our planning in retirement? This is why.

The great philosopher, Forrest Gump, would have said that, "Investing is like eating a box of chocolates. You never know what you are going to get."

Invest to meet or exceed the averages, but plan for less. Anything more is a bonus, like fancy options on a new car.

Growth Model With 4% Withdrawal
35 Years   With 1% Expense

YEAR	Growth Portfolio	Begin Value	Year-End Value	4% Withdrawal	Cumulative Income
1980	22.30%	$1,000,000	$1,223,024	$48,921	$48,921
1981	-0.34%	$1,174,103	$1,170,099	$46,804	$95,725
1982	17.88%	$1,123,295	$1,324,119	$52,965	$148,690
1983	18.44%	$1,271,154	$1,505,611	$60,224	$208,914
1984	4.43%	$1,445,387	$1,509,395	$60,376	$269,290
1985	32.89%	$1,449,019	$1,925,619	$77,025	$346,315
1986	25.66%	$1,848,594	$2,322,863	$92,915	$439,229
1987	3.49%	$2,229,949	$2,307,874	$92,315	$531,544
1988	17.41%	$2,215,559	$2,601,360	$104,054	$635,599
1989	19.32%	$2,497,305	$2,979,798	$119,192	$754,790
1990	-9.03%	$2,860,606	$2,602,180	$104,087	$858,878
1991	24.50%	$2,498,092	$3,110,065	$124,403	$983,280
1992	-2.66%	$2,985,662	$2,906,106	$116,244	$1,099,524
1993	21.20%	$2,789,862	$3,381,306	$135,252	$1,234,777
1994	-0.75%	$3,246,054	$3,221,643	$128,866	$1,363,642
1995	24.92%	$3,092,778	$3,863,567	$154,543	$1,518,185
1996	11.98%	$3,709,024	$4,153,483	$166,139	$1,684,324
1997	17.65%	$3,987,344	$4,691,059	$187,642	$1,871,967
1998	15.63%	$4,503,417	$5,207,254	$208,290	$2,080,257
1999	14.53%	$4,998,963	$5,725,239	$229,010	$2,309,267
2000	-3.98%	$5,496,230	$5,277,482	$211,099	$2,520,366
2001	-7.64%	$5,066,383	$4,679,344	$187,174	$2,707,540
2002	-12.87%	$4,492,170	$3,914,209	$156,568	$2,864,108
2003	26.22%	$3,757,641	$4,742,860	$189,714	$3,053,822
2004	11.44%	$4,553,146	$5,073,820	$202,953	$3,256,775
2005	5.03%	$4,870,867	$5,116,070	$204,643	$3,461,418
2006	14.03%	$4,911,428	$5,600,622	$224,025	$3,685,443
2007	5.11%	$5,376,597	$5,651,544	$226,062	$3,911,505
2008	-25.13%	$5,425,482	$4,062,177	$162,487	$4,073,992
2009	17.65%	$3,899,690	$4,588,014	$183,521	$4,257,512
2010	12.81%	$4,404,494	$4,968,642	$198,746	$4,456,258
2011	-0.86%	$4,769,896	$4,729,018	$189,161	$4,645,419
2012	11.89%	$4,539,857	$5,079,761	$203,190	$4,848,609
2013	20.75%	$4,876,570	$5,888,613	$235,545	$5,084,154
2014	5.87%	$5,653,069	$5,984,732	$239,389	$5,323,543

Growth Model With 5%
Withdrawal 35 Years   1% Expense

YEAR	Growth Portfolio	Begin Value	Year-End Value	5% Withdrawal	Cumulative Income
1980	22.30%	$1,000,000	$1,223,024	$61,151	$61,151
1981	-0.34%	$1,161,873	$1,157,911	$57,896	$119,047
1982	17.88%	$1,100,015	$1,296,677	$64,834	$183,881
1983	18.44%	$1,231,843	$1,459,049	$72,952	$256,833
1984	4.43%	$1,386,097	$1,447,479	$72,374	$329,207
1985	32.89%	$1,375,105	$1,827,394	$91,370	$420,577
1986	25.66%	$1,736,024	$2,181,413	$109,071	$529,647
1987	3.49%	$2,072,342	$2,144,760	$107,238	$636,885
1988	17.41%	$2,037,522	$2,392,320	$119,616	$756,501
1989	19.32%	$2,272,704	$2,711,803	$135,590	$892,092
1990	-9.03%	$2,576,213	$2,343,479	$117,174	$1,009,265
1991	24.50%	$2,226,305	$2,771,696	$138,585	$1,147,850
1992	-2.66%	$2,633,111	$2,562,949	$128,147	$1,275,998
1993	21.20%	$2,434,801	$2,950,974	$147,549	$1,423,546
1994	-0.75%	$2,803,425	$2,782,343	$139,117	$1,562,664
1995	24.92%	$2,643,226	$3,301,977	$165,099	$1,727,762
1996	11.98%	$3,136,878	$3,512,776	$175,639	$1,903,401
1997	17.65%	$3,337,137	$3,926,099	$196,305	$2,099,706
1998	15.63%	$3,729,794	$4,312,722	$215,636	$2,315,342
1999	14.53%	$4,097,086	$4,692,332	$234,617	$2,549,959
2000	-3.98%	$4,457,715	$4,280,300	$214,015	$2,763,974
2001	-7.64%	$4,066,285	$3,755,647	$187,782	$2,951,756
2002	-12.87%	$3,567,865	$3,108,825	$155,441	$3,107,197
2003	26.22%	$2,953,383	$3,727,734	$186,387	$3,293,584
2004	11.44%	$3,541,347	$3,946,317	$197,316	$3,490,900
2005	5.03%	$3,749,001	$3,937,729	$196,886	$3,687,786
2006	14.03%	$3,740,842	$4,265,775	$213,289	$3,901,075
2007	5.11%	$4,052,486	$4,259,721	$212,986	$4,114,061
2008	-25.13%	$4,046,735	$3,029,879	$151,494	$4,265,555
2009	17.65%	$2,878,385	$3,386,441	$169,322	$4,434,877
2010	12.81%	$3,217,119	$3,629,183	$181,459	$4,616,336
2011	-0.86%	$3,447,724	$3,418,177	$170,909	$4,787,245
2012	11.89%	$3,247,268	$3,633,450	$181,672	$4,968,918
2013	20.75%	$3,451,777	$4,168,130	$208,407	$5,177,324
2014	5.87%	$3,959,724	$4,192,039	$209,602	$5,386,926

WITHDRAWALS AT 5%

The preceding table illustrates the Growth Portfolio, assuming 1% expenses, with an annual withdrawal of 5%, rather than 4%.

The final portfolio value has fallen from $5,984,732 (with 4% withdrawals) to $4,192,039. See what the extra income does to portfolio values? Income in year 35 has fallen from $239,389 to $209,602. *Total income received is almost identical.*

If you want your portfolio income to grow over time, a 4% strategy works better than a 5% strategy. It is safer. It allows for more portfolio fluctuation. It gives you a better chance of having your assets and income keep pace with inflation.

PORTFOLIOS VERSUS INFLATION

Next, you will see two side-by-side tables. These tables illustrate the Growth Portfolio and Moderate Growth Portfolio. Each portfolio begins with $1 million in 1980. Each has 1% in expenses. Each withdraws 4% per year from the portfolio.

Both portfolios have outpaced 3% inflation. The growth portfolio outperformed the moderate growth portfolio, but not by much, especially when considering the extra risk. Remember the graph showing the volatility of the S&P 500 in Chapter 34? Stocks deliver a wild ride. You won't want to worry about your investments in retirement. They are supposed to be the "Golden Years," not the "Stressful Years."

A moderate mix of 50%-60% stocks, and 40%-50% bonds has historically proven to be a sound investment mix for retirement.

Growth W/4% Withdrawal
35 Years With 1% Expense Vs. Inflation

YEAR	Begin Value	Year-End Value	4% Withdraw	Portfolio At Inflation	Income Needed 3% Inflation	Pres Value Of Inc	Pres Value Of Port
1980	$1,000,000	$1,223,024	$48,921	$1,030,000	$40,000	122%	119%
1981	$1,174,103	$1,170,099	$46,804	$1,060,900	$41,200	114%	110%
1982	$1,123,295	$1,324,119	$52,965	$1,092,727	$42,436	125%	121%
1983	$1,271,154	$1,505,611	$60,224	$1,125,509	$43,709	138%	134%
1984	$1,445,387	$1,509,395	$60,376	$1,159,274	$45,020	134%	130%
1985	$1,449,019	$1,925,619	$77,025	$1,194,052	$46,371	166%	161%
1986	$1,848,594	$2,322,863	$92,915	$1,229,874	$47,762	195%	189%
1987	$2,229,949	$2,307,874	$92,315	$1,266,770	$49,195	188%	182%
1988	$2,215,559	$2,601,360	$104,054	$1,304,773	$50,671	205%	199%
1989	$2,497,305	$2,979,798	$119,192	$1,343,916	$52,191	228%	222%
1990	$2,860,606	$2,602,180	$104,087	$1,384,234	$53,757	194%	188%
1991	$2,498,092	$3,110,065	$124,403	$1,425,761	$55,369	225%	218%
1992	$2,985,662	$2,906,106	$116,244	$1,468,534	$57,030	204%	198%
1993	$2,789,862	$3,381,306	$135,252	$1,512,590	$58,741	230%	224%
1994	$3,246,054	$3,221,643	$128,866	$1,557,967	$60,504	213%	207%
1995	$3,092,778	$3,863,567	$154,543	$1,604,706	$62,319	248%	241%
1996	$3,709,024	$4,153,483	$166,139	$1,652,848	$64,188	259%	251%
1997	$3,987,344	$4,691,059	$187,642	$1,702,433	$66,114	284%	276%
1998	$4,503,417	$5,207,254	$208,290	$1,753,506	$68,097	306%	297%
1999	$4,998,963	$5,725,239	$229,010	$1,806,111	$70,140	327%	317%
2000	$5,496,230	$5,277,482	$211,099	$1,860,295	$72,244	292%	284%
2001	$5,066,383	$4,679,344	$187,174	$1,916,103	$74,412	252%	244%
2002	$4,492,170	$3,914,209	$156,568	$1,973,587	$76,644	204%	198%
2003	$3,757,641	$4,742,860	$189,714	$2,032,794	$78,943	240%	233%
2004	$4,553,146	$5,073,820	$202,953	$2,093,778	$81,312	250%	242%
2005	$4,870,867	$5,116,070	$204,643	$2,156,591	$83,751	244%	237%
2006	$4,911,428	$5,600,622	$224,025	$2,221,289	$86,264	260%	252%
2007	$5,376,597	$5,651,544	$226,062	$2,287,928	$88,852	254%	247%
2008	$5,425,482	$4,062,177	$162,487	$2,356,566	$91,517	178%	172%
2009	$3,899,690	$4,588,014	$183,521	$2,427,262	$94,263	195%	189%
2010	$4,404,494	$4,968,642	$198,746	$2,500,080	$97,090	205%	199%
2011	$4,769,896	$4,729,018	$189,161	$2,575,083	$100,003	189%	184%
2012	$4,539,857	$5,079,761	$203,190	$2,652,335	$103,003	197%	192%
2013	$4,876,570	$5,888,613	$235,545	$2,731,905	$106,093	222%	216%
2014	$5,653,069	$5,984,732	$239,389	$2,813,862	$109,276	219%	213%

Moderate Growth W/4% Withdrawal
35 Years With 1% Expense Vs. Inflation

YEAR	Begin Value	Year-End Value	4% Withdraw	Portfolio At Inflation	Income Needed 3% Inflation	Pres Value Of Inc	Pres Value Of Port
1980	$1,000,000	$1,186,301	$47,452	$1,030,000	$30,000	158%	115%
1981	$1,138,849	$1,158,740	$46,350	$1,060,900	$30,900	150%	109%
1982	$1,112,391	$1,317,564	$52,703	$1,092,727	$31,827	166%	121%
1983	$1,264,861	$1,463,335	$58,533	$1,125,509	$32,782	179%	130%
1984	$1,404,802	$1,485,670	$59,427	$1,159,274	$33,765	176%	128%
1985	$1,426,243	$1,839,900	$73,596	$1,194,052	$34,778	212%	154%
1986	$1,766,304	$2,168,892	$86,756	$1,229,874	$35,822	242%	176%
1987	$2,082,137	$2,139,116	$85,565	$1,266,770	$36,896	232%	169%
1988	$2,053,551	$2,361,133	$94,445	$1,304,773	$38,003	249%	181%
1989	$2,266,688	$2,677,014	$107,081	$1,343,916	$39,143	274%	199%
1990	$2,569,934	$2,424,283	$96,971	$1,384,234	$40,317	241%	175%
1991	$2,327,312	$2,825,090	$113,004	$1,425,761	$41,527	272%	198%
1992	$2,712,087	$2,694,507	$107,780	$1,468,534	$42,773	252%	183%
1993	$2,586,726	$3,046,652	$121,866	$1,512,590	$44,056	277%	201%
1994	$2,924,786	$2,892,039	$115,682	$1,557,967	$45,378	255%	186%
1995	$2,776,357	$3,409,506	$136,380	$1,604,706	$46,739	292%	212%
1996	$3,273,126	$3,610,121	$144,405	$1,652,848	$48,141	300%	218%
1997	$3,465,716	$4,012,961	$160,518	$1,702,433	$49,585	324%	236%
1998	$3,852,443	$4,413,296	$176,532	$1,753,506	$51,073	346%	252%
1999	$4,236,764	$4,707,534	$188,301	$1,806,111	$52,605	358%	261%
2000	$4,519,233	$4,462,297	$178,492	$1,860,295	$54,183	329%	240%
2001	$4,283,805	$4,050,187	$162,007	$1,916,103	$55,809	290%	211%
2002	$3,888,180	$3,537,268	$141,491	$1,973,587	$57,483	246%	179%
2003	$3,395,777	$4,096,363	$163,855	$2,032,794	$59,208	277%	202%
2004	$3,932,508	$4,298,885	$171,955	$2,093,778	$60,984	282%	205%
2005	$4,126,930	$4,305,718	$172,229	$2,156,591	$62,813	274%	200%
2006	$4,133,489	$4,612,236	$184,489	$2,221,289	$64,698	285%	208%
2007	$4,427,746	$4,663,935	$186,557	$2,287,928	$66,639	280%	204%
2008	$4,477,377	$3,658,996	$146,360	$2,356,566	$68,638	213%	155%
2009	$3,512,636	$3,964,507	$158,580	$2,427,262	$70,697	224%	163%
2010	$3,805,927	$4,215,942	$168,638	$2,500,080	$72,818	232%	169%
2011	$4,047,304	$4,079,393	$163,176	$2,575,083	$75,002	218%	158%
2012	$3,916,217	$4,290,923	$171,637	$2,652,335	$77,252	222%	162%
2013	$4,119,286	$4,762,607	$190,504	$2,731,905	$79,570	239%	174%
2014	$4,572,103	$4,834,368	$193,375	$2,813,862	$81,957	236%	172%

SEE THE INVESTMENT PATTERNS?

By now, you may have noticed that investments, just like people, have behavioral patterns. After all, companies are built by people. Markets are funded and controlled by people. Risk usually gets rewarded in the long run. But there are times when risk takers lose money. Over thirty-five years, the growth portfolio accumulated and paid out more money than the moderate growth portfolio. The moderate portfolio earned more than the capital preservation portfolio.

WHAT MAKE STOCKS GROW OVER TIME?

The "stock market" is a financial representation of the human condition. We seek to better our lives. We do so by providing services that have value to others. We are paid based upon the perceived "value" of our services. This value is affected by supply and demand.

If a service can be provided by many (despite its importance) it will usually have a lower value than a service that can be provided by only a few. There aren't many people that can consistently throw a baseball sixty feet six inches at a hundred miles an hour over the edge of a plate that is seventeen inches wide. There are many highly educated day care workers. One gets paid millions. The other doesn't. While some would argue that such incomes do not represent the relative importance of these professions to society, it doesn't matter. Society decides. Entertainers get paid because people pay to watch them. Specialists get paid because people need them. Professionals get paid because people hire them. Inventors and entrepreneurs get paid because people buy their products and services. Those that work around and for these people also get paid. The more relative value someone brings to others, the more society decides they earn.

An advanced economy becomes a smoothly working machine. Sometimes the machine breaks down, but it always gets fixed. The stock market grows with each person providing their piece to the societal fabric. When companies become successful, they raise capital to grow. As they grow, they hire people to deliver their service to society. Investors put their money to work by supporting and profiting from the products and services these companies create.

When an advanced economy is in place, like the United States, there are millions of businesses, all trying to deliver their value in the best manner possible. Each company seeks to outperform their competition. New products and services are crated. Advancements occur, every day.

The stock market becomes the measuring stick of the overall performance of the workers that support our economy.

STOCK MARKET VALUE

Value in the stock market comes from three main sources: earnings growth, expected earnings growth and current returns. Here is how it happens:

> 1. Productivity. As companies provide more goods and services with less, it drives productivity. Traditionally, productivity grows at about 2% per year. Productivity drives company earnings. http://www.nber.org/papers/w15834

> 2. Dividends. Dividends are a direct current return on investment. Since 1960, dividends for the S&P 500 Index have averaged about 3%. http://pages.stern.nyu.edu/~adamodar/New_Home_Page/datafile/spearn.htm

> 3. Inflation. As inflation grows, company earnings grow to match it. Since stocks trades on a P/E basis, inflation alone, without productivity growth, can move stock prices upward. We have already illustrated that the U.S. has experienced a long-term inflation rate of just over 3%. http://www.usinflationcalculator.com/inflation/consumer-price-index-and-annual-percent-changes-from-1913-to-2008/

Earnings growth is affected by productivity growth and inflation. Dividends usually grow as a function of earnings growth.

When you add productivity, dividends and inflation together you get a sum of 8%. This 8% provides the foundation for long-term growth in the stock market. For the first twenty years of our 35-year illustration, inflation was averaging close to 6%. Part of the strong stock performance was due to company earnings catching up to inflation.

Some will argue that today's average dividend yields are closer to 2% than 3%. Recent productivity growth has been lower than normal. Inflation is currently tamed. This may foretell a stagnant stock market for the next decade, maybe more. Then again, maybe not. If we look at the long-term graph for the stock market, it is up, way up. How it will perform in the short run? That is the big question, isn't it? Long-term averages provide the best estimation for a non-professional. And, as we all know, the professionals never agree.

MODEL PATTERN

Let's take a look at the 35-year patterns of the Growth Model and the Capital Preservation Model on the next page.

Notice anything?

Beginning in 1980, both models enjoyed outstanding historical performance. Both models more than tripled in value, plus they delivered an annual income of 4%. Outstanding.

THE MARKETS CHANGE

Then something happened. Twenty years into "retirement," things changed for the holders of both models. In 2000, the stock market fell. Technology stocks were decimated. Stocks continued to fall for the next couple of years. In 2003, everything turned around. Stocks soared. They fell hard again in 2009. By then, bond yields had become historically low.

Since that time, stocks have continued to yo yo. Bonds have remained anemic.

The capital preservation model hasn't grown at all during the past twenty years. The growth model has grown, but the values swing greatly.

If an investor retired in 1980 with either portfolio, most likely they would have been pleased.

The growth portfolio is worth nearly $6 million at the end of 2014. The capital preservation portfolio has doubled in value.

The capital preservation portfolio is worth one third of the growth portfolio. It has lost to inflation. But it is more stable and predictable for those who can't stomach the risk needed to achieve gain.

Asset Growth
Capital Preservation Model Vs. Growth Model
1% Expenses With 4% Withdrawal   1980-2014

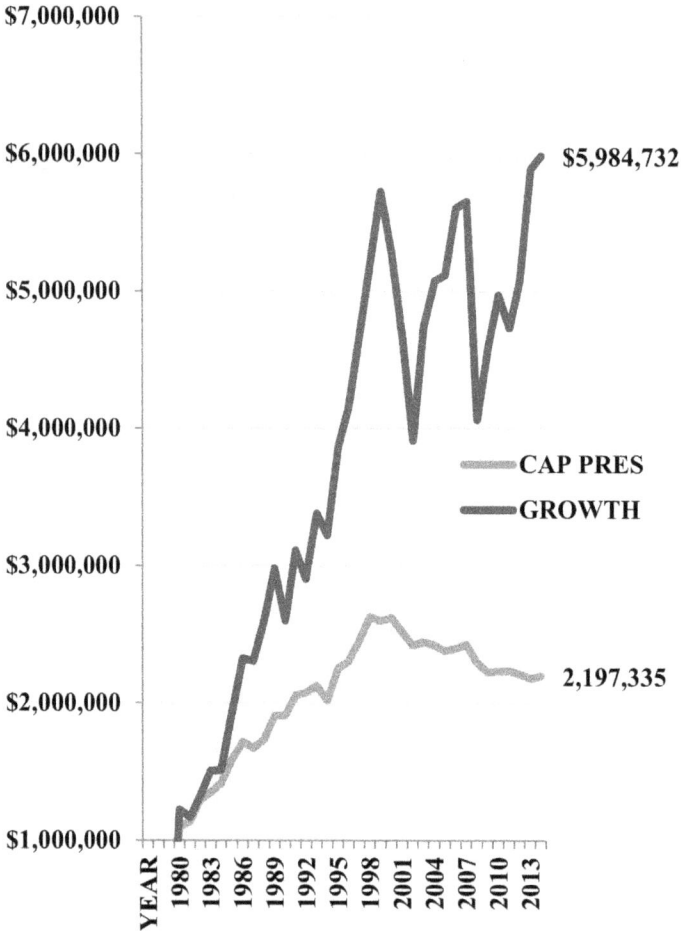

$5,984,732

CAP PRES
GROWTH

2,197,335

This page is intentionally blank, so that you can view the following chart beside its explanation. Learning about the stock market is confusing enough, without making you turn pages while you try to remember what you just saw.

The following table illustrates the same retirement history using the Moderate Growth Model.

We have already shown that this model outpaced 3% inflation over our 35-year retirement time horizon, while paying a 4% annual income.

The moderate growth model consists of 60% stocks and 40% bonds. This model delivered a more predictable retirement income. This book has shown how stocks and bonds can move in opposite directions. When stocks are down, the balance of bonds helps keep the portfolio from falling too much.

Look at the column entitled, "Mod Gro." This illustrates the year-by-year returns that were earned after a 1% expense. This portfolio lost money in only seven of thirty-five years. For twenty-eight out of thirty-five years, this portfolio had a positive return. The worst year was in 2008, during the mortgage crisis. The portfolio lost more than 18%. Then it delivered five consecutive years of positive returns. The 2008 loss was softened by positive bond returns. During the mortgage crisis, there was a temporary loss of confidence in our economic structure. Remember the $1 trillion bailout? When the government gets stressed, it spends money.

This book has stressed how investors must maintain their portfolio through the losing years. This shows why. If you had sold after 2008, you would have lost out on the big future gains.

Look to the final column, on the bottom right. This column shows the cumulative income that this portfolio would have generated over its 35-year history. The total income exceeds $4.6 million, all from a $1 million start. The total remaining portfolio (Year-End Value) now exceeds $4.5 million. Cumulative income is $1.7 million more than the capital preservation portfolio. The final value is about $2.6 million more. Does this make sense?

Moderate Growth Model W/4% Withdrawal
35 Years   With 1% Expense

YEAR	Mod Grow Portfolio	Begin Value	Year-End Value	4% Withdrawal	Cumulative Income
1980	18.63%	$1,000,000	$1,186,301	$47,452	$47,452
1981	1.75%	$1,138,849	$1,158,740	$46,350	$93,802
1982	18.44%	$1,112,391	$1,317,564	$52,703	$146,504
1983	15.69%	$1,264,861	$1,463,335	$58,533	$205,038
1984	5.76%	$1,404,802	$1,485,670	$59,427	$264,464
1985	29.00%	$1,426,243	$1,839,900	$73,596	$338,060
1986	22.79%	$1,766,304	$2,168,892	$86,756	$424,816
1987	2.74%	$2,082,137	$2,139,116	$85,565	$510,381
1988	14.98%	$2,053,551	$2,361,133	$94,445	$604,826
1989	18.10%	$2,266,688	$2,677,014	$107,081	$711,907
1990	-5.67%	$2,569,934	$2,424,283	$96,971	$808,878
1991	21.39%	$2,327,312	$2,825,090	$113,004	$921,882
1992	-0.65%	$2,712,087	$2,694,507	$107,780	$1,029,662
1993	17.78%	$2,586,726	$3,046,652	$121,866	$1,151,528
1994	-1.12%	$2,924,786	$2,892,039	$115,682	$1,267,209
1995	22.81%	$2,776,357	$3,409,506	$136,380	$1,403,590
1996	10.30%	$3,273,126	$3,610,121	$144,405	$1,547,995
1997	15.79%	$3,465,716	$4,012,961	$160,518	$1,708,513
1998	14.56%	$3,852,443	$4,413,296	$176,532	$1,885,045
1999	11.11%	$4,236,764	$4,707,534	$188,301	$2,073,346
2000	-1.26%	$4,519,233	$4,462,297	$178,492	$2,251,838
2001	-5.45%	$4,283,805	$4,050,187	$162,007	$2,413,846
2002	-9.03%	$3,888,180	$3,537,268	$141,491	$2,555,336
2003	20.63%	$3,395,777	$4,096,363	$163,855	$2,719,191
2004	9.32%	$3,932,508	$4,298,885	$171,955	$2,891,146
2005	4.33%	$4,126,930	$4,305,718	$172,229	$3,063,375
2006	11.58%	$4,133,489	$4,612,236	$184,489	$3,247,864
2007	5.33%	$4,427,746	$4,663,935	$186,557	$3,434,422
2008	-18.28%	$4,477,377	$3,658,996	$146,360	$3,580,782
2009	12.86%	$3,512,636	$3,964,507	$158,580	$3,739,362
2010	10.77%	$3,805,927	$4,215,942	$168,638	$3,908,000
2011	0.79%	$4,047,304	$4,079,393	$163,176	$4,071,175
2012	9.57%	$3,916,217	$4,290,923	$171,637	$4,242,812
2013	15.62%	$4,119,286	$4,762,607	$190,504	$4,433,316
2014	5.74%	$4,572,103	$4,834,368	$193,375	$4,626,691

The following chart compares the year-end values for the Capital Preservation Portfolio, the Moderate Growth Portfolio and the Growth Portfolio. Each mix is illustrated after an expense of 1%.

In the early years of our hypothetical retirement, the capital preservation portfolio continued to grow, even after paying an income of 4% per year. About fifteen years ago, this trend changed. Can you think of why? Bond yields fell. They were comparatively high in the 1980s and 1990s. For the past ten years bond rates have been lower. Can you think of why? The Federal Reserve lowered interest rates to stimulate an economy that won't fully respond. Developing countries, with low labor rates and little pollution controls, make inexpensive goods that we buy. This has kept U.S. inflation in check.

The Fed is trying to raise interest rates to normal levels, but it can't until the world economy strengthens.

Notice how the growth portfolio and the moderate growth portfolio tend to move in tandem? The growth portfolio has 75% stocks. The moderate growth portfolio has 60%. Stocks have more volatility than bonds, so the portfolios will change as stocks gain or lose money.

The moderate growth portfolio is less volatile than the growth portfolio. It has fewer stocks, but enough to keep pace with inflation over thirty-five years. What about the last fifteen, when stocks were unusually volatile? How did the portfolios perform then?

Growth Vs. Moderate Growth & Capital Preservation Models
1% Expenses With 4% Withdrawal   1980-2014

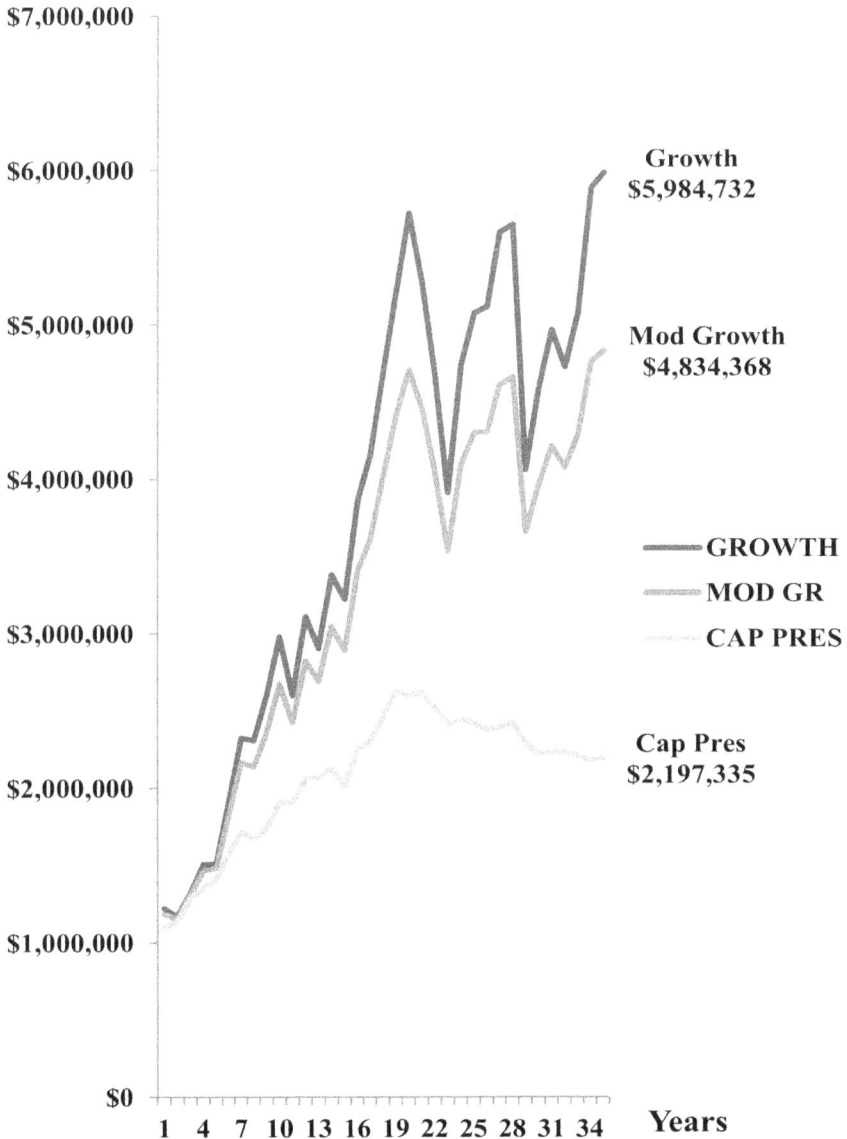

Growth
$5,984,732

Mod Growth
$4,834,368

GROWTH
MOD GR
CAP PRES

Cap Pres
$2,197,335

Years

TIMING IS EVERYTHING

The U.S. economy moves in cycles. Business profits expand. Then they slow down. Interest rates rise and fall.

Investors try to time the cycles. Emotions run hot and the markets react. Don't fall prey to chasing the latest hot fund or sector. If a fund makes the cover of Money Magazine, it may be time to steer clear and buy an asset with similar long-term growth that has been underperforming.

What if your retirement began just as the stock market was falling and bond yields were low?

Let's take a look. The following pages compare how our model portfolios behaved in the fifteen years beginning at the market top of 1999 through the end of 2014.

BAD TIMING

The following table shows the performance of the Capital Pres- ervation Model for fifteen years, beginning in 1999. This model is built from indexes to hold 20% stocks and 80% bonds. It has expenses of 1% and a 4% withdrawal.

The previous graph showed how this portfolio grew from 1980, but then leveled off after twenty years. Remember, if a portfolio doesn't grow, it losing purchasing power to inflation. The next table shows the numbers behind that graph.

There are a lot of figures here. But it shouldn't be hard to under- stand. The first column shows the **year**. The second column (Cap Pres 1% Fee) shows the **portfolio return** after 1% expenses. Col- umn three (Begin Value) shows the **portfolio value at the begin- ning** of the year. Column four (Year-end Value) shows the **value at the end** of the year, after earning the **return** shown in column two. The next column (4% W/D) shows a 4% **income taken** at the end of the year. The following column (Cum Inc) shows the **total cumulative income** received from the portfolio.

Capital Preservation With 1% Fee
4% Withdrawal   1999-2014

YEAR	Cap Pres 1% Fee	Begin Value	Year- End Value	4% W/D	Cum Inc	Portfolio At Inflation	Inc Need 3% Inf	Pres Val Of Inc	Pres Val Of Port
1999	2.96%	1,000,000	1,029,558	41,182	41,182	1,030,000	41,182	100%	100%
2000	5.07%	988,376	1,038,501	41,540	82,722	1,060,900	42,418	98%	98%
2001	0.14%	996,961	998,336	39,933	122,656	1,092,727	43,690	91%	91%
2002	-0.03%	958,403	958,120	38,325	160,981	1,125,509	45,001	85%	85%
2003	5.30%	919,795	968,533	38,741	199,722	1,159,274	46,351	84%	84%
2004	3.11%	929,791	958,703	38,348	238,070	1,194,052	47,742	80%	80%
2005	2.33%	920,355	941,819	37,673	275,743	1,229,874	49,174	77%	77%
2006	5.05%	904,146	949,802	37,992	313,735	1,266,770	50,649	75%	75%
2007	5.48%	911,810	961,788	38,472	352,206	1,304,773	52,169	74%	74%
2008	-1.49%	923,316	909,581	36,383	388,590	1,343,916	53,734	68%	68%
2009	0.92%	873,198	881,227	35,249	423,839	1,384,234	55,346	64%	64%
2010	4.57%	845,978	884,623	35,385	459,224	1,425,761	57,006	62%	62%
2011	4.25%	849,238	885,291	35,412	494,635	1,468,534	58,716	60%	60%
2012	3.09%	849,879	876,179	35,047	529,682	1,512,590	60,478	58%	58%
2013	2.73%	841,132	864,101	34,564	564,246	1,557,967	62,292	55%	55%
2014	4.95%	829,537	870,564	34,823	599,069	1,604,706	64,161	54%	54%

The last four columns of the previous table show how the portfolio value and income fared against a **3% inflation rate**. Remember how retirement income needs to grow to keep pace with inflation? The Portfolio At Inflation column shows what the portfolio would be worth with 3% growth. This is the growth we need from the portfolio to keep pace with our **inflation target**. The next column (Inc Need 3% Inf) shows the income we would need to maintain the **same living standard**. The final two columns show the relationship between the actual portfolio value and income to our inflation target.

If you look to the bottom of the table, you will see that the year-end portfolio value in 2014 is $870,564. To keep pace with 3% inflation, our portfolio should be worth $1,604,706. After fifteen years, the portfolio and income have the purchasing power of only **54%** of what we had when we started.

If possible, you do not want the inflation-adjusted value of your income to fall.

THE PRICE OF AGGRESSIVE INVESTING IN RETIREMENT

Throughout this book, it has been stressed that proper asset allocation is critical when investing in retirement. A balanced portfolio often works better than ones with too much or too little risk.

This book suggested that you withdraw no more than 4% from your retirement portfolio each year. What happens if you take more?

The next two tables compare the following:

- An aggressive retirement approach. This strategy uses the Growth Model with 5% annual withdrawals.

- A traditional retirement approach. This strategy uses the Moderate Growth Model with 4% annual withdrawals.

The two tables show annual income, year-end values and cumulative income from 1999-2014. The annual income and growth totals are compared to 3% inflation.

Look to the end of the column entitled "Cum Income," the cumulative income for each strategy. This is the total income received.

The aggressive portfolio (which is paying 5%) has yielded a total income of $749,700. The 4% portfolio has yielded a total of $647,109.

The aggressive portfolio delivered $102,591 more income.

Now, look to the columns titled "Year-End Value." The moderate portfolio is worth $1,141,052. The more aggressive portfolio is worth $1,023,176.

The moderate portfolio is worth $117,876 **more** than growth.

There was little gained by taking more risk. In 1999, the annual income differential between the two portfolios was nearly $13,000. By 2014, the income differential had narrowed to less than $6,000 per year. Lower risk is trending better than high risk.

Moderate Growth Model With 1% Expense
4% Withdrawal   1999-2014

YEAR	Mod Gr W/ Fee	Begin Value	Year End Value	4% W/D	Cum Inc	Port At Inf	Inc Need 3% Inf	Pres Val Of Inc	Pres Val Of Port
1999	11.11%	1,000,000	1,111,116	44,445	44,445	1,030,000	44,445	100%	108%
2000	-1.26%	1,066,671	1,053,232	42,129	86,574	1,060,900	45,778	92%	99%
2001	-5.45%	1,011,103	955,963	38,239	124,812	1,092,727	47,151	81%	87%
2002	-9.03%	917,724	834,899	33,396	158,208	1,125,509	48,566	69%	74%
2003	20.63%	801,503	966,861	38,674	196,883	1,159,274	50,023	77%	83%
2004	9.32%	928,187	1,014,663	40,587	237,469	1,194,052	51,523	79%	85%
2005	4.33%	974,076	1,016,275	40,651	278,120	1,229,874	53,069	77%	83%
2006	11.58%	975,624	1,088,622	43,545	321,665	1,266,770	54,661	80%	86%
2007	5.33%	1,045,077	1,100,825	44,033	365,698	1,304,773	56,301	78%	84%
2008	-18.28%	1,056,792	863,630	34,545	400,243	1,343,916	57,990	60%	64%
2009	12.86%	829,085	935,739	37,430	437,673	1,384,234	59,730	63%	68%
2010	10.77%	898,310	995,085	39,803	477,476	1,425,761	61,522	65%	70%
2011	0.79%	955,282	962,856	38,514	515,991	1,468,534	63,367	61%	66%
2012	9.57%	924,342	1,012,783	40,511	556,502	1,512,590	65,268	62%	67%
2013	15.62%	972,272	1,124,114	44,965	601,467	1,557,967	67,226	67%	72%
2014	5.74%	1,079,150	1,141,052	45,642	647,109	1,604,706	69,243	66%	71%

Growth Model With 1% Expense
5% Withdrawal   1999-2014

YR	Growth 1% Fee	Begin Value	Year-End Value	5% W/D	Cum Income	Port 3% Inf	Inc Need 3% Inf	Pres Val Of Inc	Pres Val Of Port
1999	14.53%	1,000,000	1,145,285	57,264	57,264	1,030,000	57,264	100%	111%
2000	-3.98%	1,088,021	1,044,718	52,236	109,500	1,060,900	58,982	89%	98%
2001	-7.64%	992,482	916,663	45,833	155,333	1,092,727	60,752	75%	84%
2002	-12.87%	870,830	758,789	37,939	193,273	1,125,509	62,574	61%	67%
2003	26.22%	720,850	909,850	45,493	238,765	1,159,274	64,451	71%	78%
2004	11.44%	864,358	963,201	48,160	286,925	1,194,052	66,385	73%	81%
2005	5.03%	915,041	961,105	48,055	334,981	1,229,874	68,377	70%	78%
2006	14.03%	913,050	1,041,173	52,059	387,039	1,266,770	70,428	74%	82%
2007	5.11%	989,114	1,039,695	51,985	439,024	1,304,773	72,541	72%	80%
2008	-25.13%	987,711	739,521	36,976	476,000	1,343,916	74,717	49%	55%
2009	17.65%	702,545	826,549	41,327	517,327	1,384,234	76,958	54%	60%
2010	12.81%	785,221	885,796	44,290	561,617	1,425,761	79,267	56%	62%
2011	-0.86%	841,506	834,295	41,715	603,332	1,468,534	81,645	51%	57%
2012	11.89%	792,580	886,838	44,342	647,674	1,512,590	84,095	53%	59%
2013	20.75%	842,496	1,017,340	50,867	698,541	1,557,967	86,617	59%	65%
2014	5.87%	966,473	1,023,176	51,159	749,700	1,604,706	89,216	57%	64%

Comparative Portfolios W/1% Expense (Except T-bills)
4% Withdrawal 1999-2014
Year-End Values

YEAR	GROWTH	MOD GR	CONS GR	CAP PRES	T-Bills
1999	$1,145,285	$1,111,116	$1,052,769	$1,029,558	$1,045,100
2000	$1,055,715	$1,053,232	$1,043,460	$1,038,501	$1,061,111
2001	$936,063	$955,963	$976,287	$998,336	$1,056,077
2002	$783,004	$834,899	$908,812	$958,120	$1,030,638
2003	$948,769	$966,861	$978,506	$968,533	$999,604
2004	$1,014,974	$1,014,663	$997,546	$958,703	$971,399
2005	$1,023,426	$1,016,275	$987,368	$941,819	$960,612
2006	$1,120,357	$1,088,622	$1,020,283	$949,802	$965,323
2007	$1,130,543	$1,100,825	$1,039,590	$961,788	$969,733
2008	$812,604	$863,630	$923,489	$909,581	$945,699
2009	$917,793	$935,739	$933,611	$881,227	$909,097
2010	$993,934	$995,085	$973,238	$884,623	$873,867
2011	$946,000	$962,856	$981,955	$885,291	$839,164
2012	$1,016,163	$1,012,783	$1,005,358	$876,179	$806,001
2013	$1,177,967	$1,124,114	$1,043,271	$864,101	$774,271
2014	$1,197,195	$1,141,052	$1,075,171	$870,564	$743,694

The previous table illustrates the comparative **year-end values of four model portfolios**, with 1% annual expenses, and 4% annual withdrawals taken from each asset class. These portfolios are compared to one of T-bills owned without expense. T-bills tend to mirror inflation. You can buy them direct from the U.S. Treasury.

These models were detailed in Chapter 37. For your convenience, they are summarized here:

- Capital Preservation: 20% Stocks, 30% Bonds, 50% T-bills

- Conservative Growth: 40% Stocks, 40% Bonds, 20% T-bills

- Moderate Growth: 60% Stocks, 25% Bonds, 15% T-bills

- Growth: 75% Stocks, 20% Bonds, 5% T-bills

- T-bills: 100% with no expenses

BAD TIMING

The period from 1999-2014 was a time of unusual volatility in the investment markets. Stock values grew in 1999, but fell for three consecutive years after that. Remember how taking money from a portfolio in decline can be hazardous to your retirement? This example shows how.

The capital preservation portfolio fell from $1 million to $870,564. This value is still more than unmanaged T-bills, which fell to $743,694. Paying high expenses on a low-yield bond portfolio can hurt your retirement. So can taking no risk at all.

The conservative growth, moderate growth and the growth portfolio performed according to risk. The growth portfolio has grown to nearly $1.2 million. The moderate growth portfolio is worth about $50,000 less. The conservative growth portfolio is worth about $65,000 less than the moderate portfolio.

All of the portfolios lost purchasing power against 3% inflation.

Comparative Portfolios
4% Withdrawal 1999-2014
Cumulative Income

YEAR	GROWTH	MOD GR	CONS GR	CAP PRES	T-Bills
1999	$45,811	$44,445	$42,111	$41,182	$41,804
2000	$88,040	$86,574	$83,849	$82,722	$84,248
2001	$125,483	$124,812	$122,901	$122,656	$126,492
2002	$156,803	$158,208	$159,253	$160,981	$167,717
2003	$194,753	$196,883	$198,393	$199,722	$207,701
2004	$235,352	$237,469	$238,295	$238,070	$246,557
2005	$276,289	$278,120	$277,790	$275,743	$284,982
2006	$321,104	$321,665	$318,601	$313,735	$323,595
2007	$366,325	$365,698	$360,185	$352,206	$362,384
2008	$398,830	$400,243	$397,124	$388,590	$400,212
2009	$435,541	$437,673	$434,469	$423,839	$436,576
2010	$475,299	$477,476	$473,398	$459,224	$471,530
2011	$513,139	$515,991	$512,677	$494,635	$505,097
2012	$553,785	$556,502	$552,891	$529,682	$537,337
2013	$600,904	$601,467	$594,622	$564,246	$568,308
2014	$648,792	$647,109	$637,628	$599,069	$598,056

CUMULATIVE INCOME

The preceding chart illustrates a 4% *income* withdrawn from the five portfolios.

T-bills delivered the least total income, despite no fees. The capital preservation portfolio yielded just slightly more. The growth, moderate growth, and the conservative growth accumulated total incomes were surprisingly similar.

The current yield on T-bills is about .5%. This destroys a portfolio that is removing 4% per year for income. If you look to the bottom of the previous table, you will see that the T-bill portfolio is losing about $30,000 per year.

T-bill source: **http://www.federalreserve.gov/releases/h15/current/**

SUMMARY

Hopefully, you are beginning to understand the balance between risk and reward. Remember, the reward from risk can *only* be earned if you hold the course through the bad years. If you sell when the markets fall, you won't get the benefit of the early, powerful upswings.

Taking too much income from a portfolio is risky. Making 4% withdrawals, with reasonable portfolio risk, has proven to be a sound long-term strategy.

You have seen how different stock and bond mixes behaved during the long-term. You have also learned how they can behave during challenging markets.

Nobody knows what the investment future holds. Hopefully, you have a better idea of which strategy works for you. The stock market will continue to represent the innate yearning of mankind to better itself financially. Such reward fills some of mankind's most fundamental needs. As long as we don't radically change, the stock market should continue to represent how people behave. If we prosper, the markets will prosper.

Comparative Portfolios W/1% Expense (Except T-bills)
4% Withdrawal 1999-2014
Year-End Values

YEAR	GROWTH	MOD GR	CONS GR	CAP PRES	T-Bills
1999	$1,145,285	$1,111,116	$1,052,769	$1,029,558	$1,045,100
2000	$1,055,715	$1,053,232	$1,043,460	$1,038,501	$1,061,111
2001	$936,063	$955,963	$976,287	$998,336	$1,056,077
2002	$783,004	$834,899	$908,812	$958,120	$1,030,638
2003	$948,769	$966,861	$978,506	$968,533	$999,604
2004	$1,014,974	$1,014,663	$997,546	$958,703	$971,399
2005	$1,023,426	$1,016,275	$987,368	$941,819	$960,612
2006	$1,120,357	$1,088,622	$1,020,283	$949,802	$965,323
2007	$1,130,543	$1,100,825	$1,039,590	$961,788	$969,733
2008	$812,604	$863,630	$923,489	$909,581	$945,699
2009	$917,793	$935,739	$933,611	$881,227	$909,097
2010	$993,934	$995,085	$973,238	$884,623	$873,867
2011	$946,000	$962,856	$981,955	$885,291	$839,164
2012	$1,016,163	$1,012,783	$1,005,358	$876,179	$806,001
2013	$1,177,967	$1,124,114	$1,043,271	$864,101	$774,271
2014	$1,197,195	$1,141,052	$1,075,171	$870,564	$743,694

COMPARATIVE VALUES - BAD YEARS

The preceding table repeats the year-end illustration of the four asset allocation models and the unmanaged portfolio of T-bills.

This is for a 15-year time frame when investments were unusually volatile. Let's take a closer look at how the models behaved.

The growth portfolio and the moderate growth portfolio are worth the most today. However, at the end of 2008, they were worth the least.

This table illustrates the volatility of growth assets. All of the portfolios began with $1 million.

In 2002, the growth portfolio fell to $783,004. It then rose to $1,130,543 before falling back down to $812,604. It appreciated again to nearly $1.2 million at the end of 2014.

The moderate growth portfolio didn't fall as far or rise as high as the growth model.

The conservative growth portfolio dipped to a low of $908,812. It was far more consistent during the gyrations of two large stock market drops, which included the "Great Recession."

The capital preservation portfolio has experienced a slow and steady loss since 2000. The T-bill portfolio has done the same, but at a faster pace.

The next page shows the same information in a line chart. Here, you can visualize the volatility and the reward of risk portfolios, as well as the slow fall of the risk-averse portfolios. Beside the 15-year chart, you will see the 35-year chart once again.

These pictures illustrate how differently the short-run and the long-run can affect your investments. The challenge is to manage your money for long-term return, without taking so much risk that you lose your money in the short-run.

Comparative Values 4% Withdrawals
1999 - 2014   With 1% Expense (Except for T-bills)

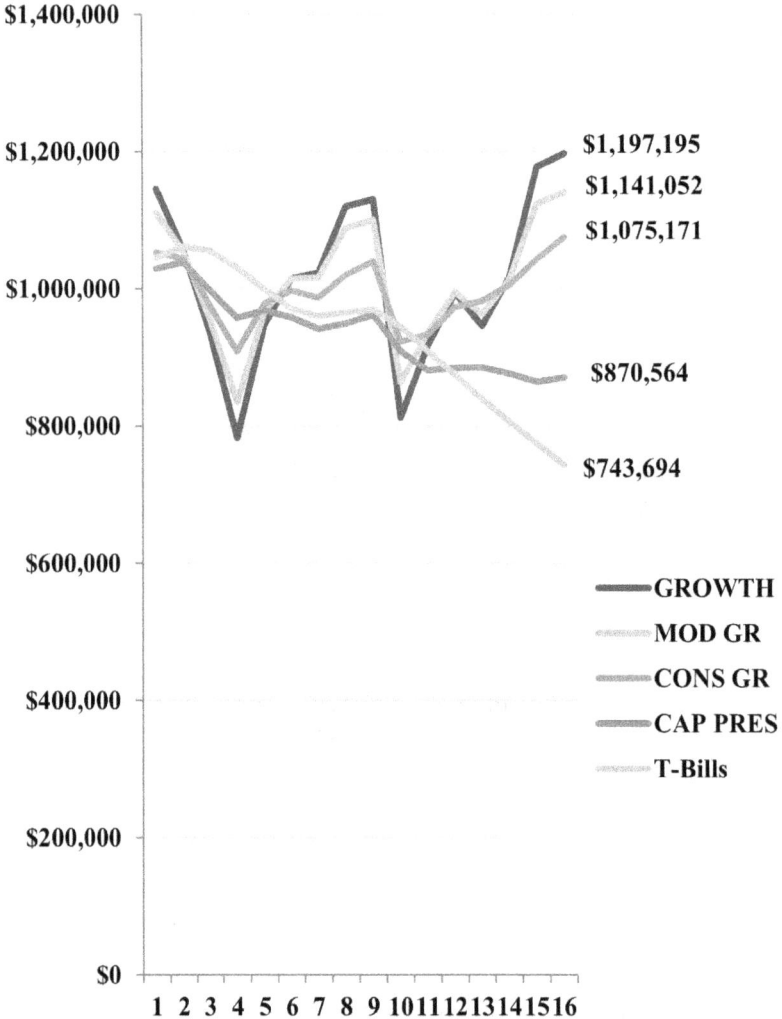

$1,197,195
$1,141,052
$1,075,171
$870,564
$743,694

GROWTH
MOD GR
CONS GR
CAP PRES
T-Bills

Asset Allocation Models: Year-End Value
1% Expenses With 4% Withdrawal   1980-2014

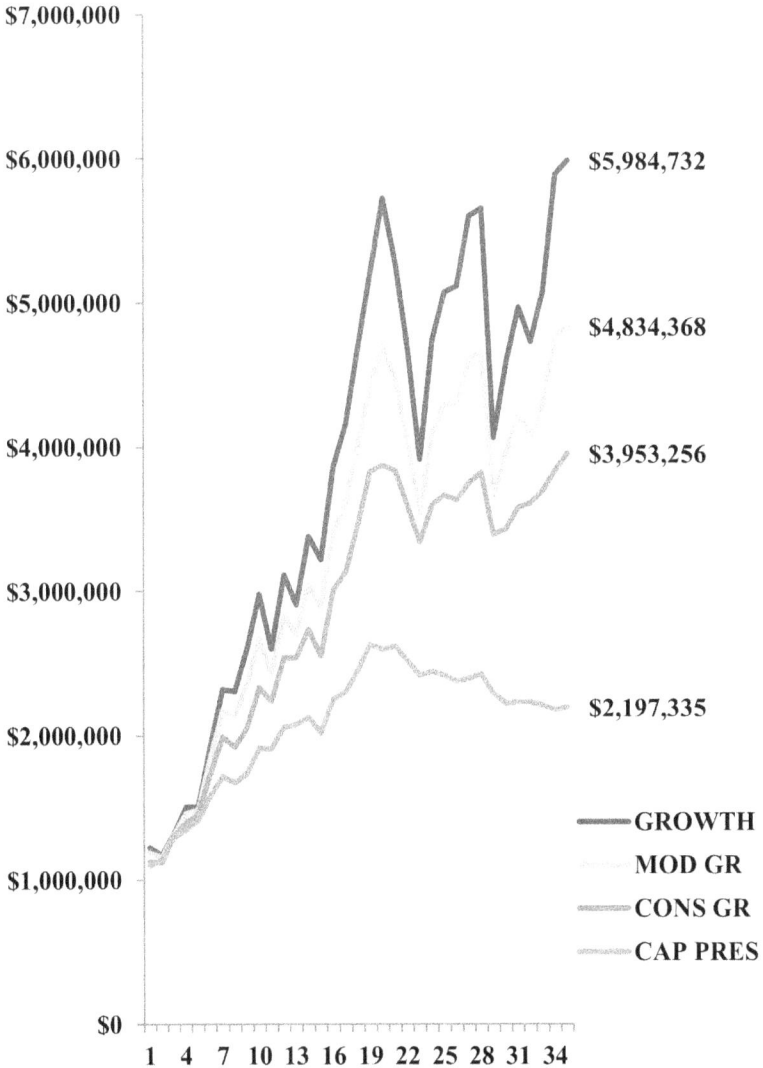

$5,984,732

$4,834,368

$3,953,256

$2,197,335

GROWTH
MOD GR
CONS GR
CAP PRES

The Cost of Waiting To Invest Age 25 - Investing $3,000 Per Year For 9 Years Only VS. Waiting 9 Years And Investing To Age 65

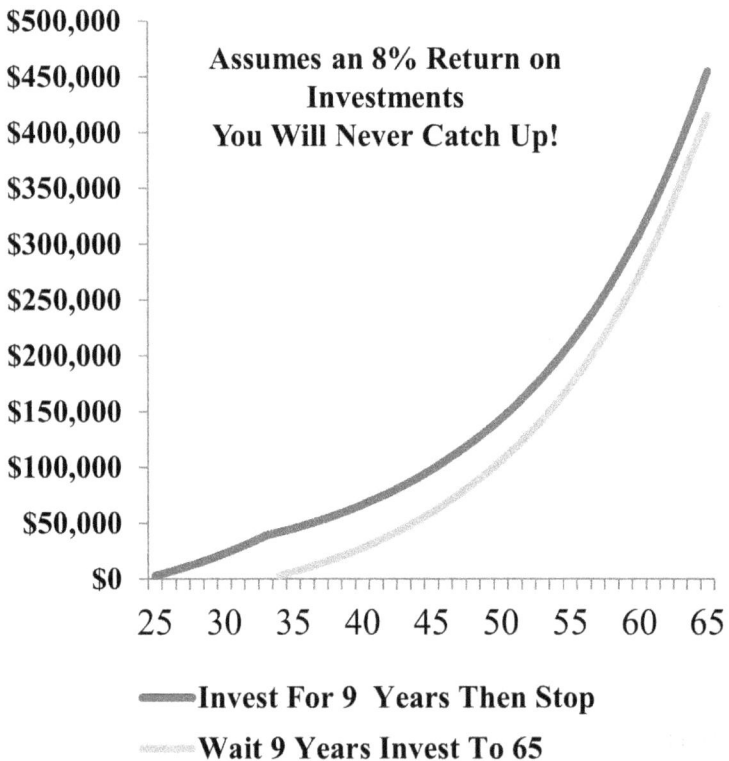

Assumes an 8% Return on Investments
You Will Never Catch Up!

━━━ Invest For 9 Years Then Stop

━━━ Wait 9 Years Invest To 65

Chapter Forty

R

The Cost Of Waiting To Invest

There is an opportunity cost to retirement investing. The longer you wait, the harder it is to achieve your goals.

This final chart illustrates the importance of investing as soon as you can.

*If, at age 25, you invest $3,000 per year for nine years only, and never invest again, you will have more money in retirement than if you wait nine years and invest $3,000 every year for the next 31 years! ***

When you invest early, your money earns compounded returns, which can grow substantially over time.

The road to a secure retirement is paved with positive choices. Everybody wants to save for retirement. People wait too long to begin. Prepare right now for retirement. You will like it more with extra funds in your portfolio.

Procrastination is the thief of your retirement security. Start investing today and never stop.

* Assumes a steady, 8% rate of return on investments.

$&¢

Chapter Forty-One

_____R_____

Summary

THIS BOOK'S GOALS

This book began with three primary goals.

- This book was designed to motivate people to plan for retirement. People must be motivated to save, because it involves sacrifice. Are you motivated?

- This book was written to educate, so people don't make the common mistakes that doom most retirement strategies. You are now educated.

- This book was designed to help you implement a plan. You now know how to plan.

This book explained the critical information that every investor should know. It showed you how to devise a retirement plan to fit your personal objectives. It demonstrated historical facts with charts and graphs and then used this information to help you personalize a retirement strategy. It used history to make recommendations. It repeated certain concepts over and over in different ways, with the hope that they become natural.

Now that you have slogged through four hundred pages of confusing investment speak, what does it all mean for you? How do you develop a retirement plan that will truly work as planned? This stuff can numb the mind.

SIMPLIFY

You have a decision to make. You can make things complicated. This book is complicated. Or, you can make things simple. This book is also quite simple.

- Here is all you really need to know.

KEY POINTS

LIKE BUYING A CAR

Planning for retirement is like buying a new car. You have a base model. Then you have options. A basic car will get you where you want to go. Options give you a more enjoyable journey.

While this book has explored a lot of things, there are only a few critical points that you need to understand and implement. A simple, basic plan can get you to your destination—financial independence.

Here is all you really need to know:

- The government has very large debts. These debts are growing every year. You must do everything you can to become self-sufficient. Plan for yourself.

- Social Security has no money set aside for your benefit. Social Security holds an IOU from the federal government. Benefits to retirees are paid by current workers. There are not enough workers to pay the promised benefits. If you plan on using Social Security to help fund your retirement, you should plan on less than the projected benefits.

- Most people should plan for at least 30 years of retirement.

- You will need to save between 10% and 20% of your income to achieve financial independence.

- You must invest your money for long term growth that will

outpace inflation.

- You must plan for inflation. Things will cost more when you retire. Costs will rise while you are retired.

- Qualified retirement plans, such as a 401(k), offer tax advantages that can help you accumulate more assets.

- Qualified plans have limits on how much you can save, and what type of investments can be offered.

- IRAs offer similar, but more limited tax benefits.

- You must overcome all excuses for not saving enough. If you increase the amount deducted from your paycheck, you will not miss it. Your lifestyle will naturally adjust. Have faith.

- You must choose an investment strategy.

- Your investment choices will usually consist of mutual funds, asset allocation models or index funds.

- Most investment choices will be mixes of stocks, bonds & cash.

- Stocks have the best long-term potential for gain. They also have the most short-term risk.

- Bonds have lower short-term risk but less potential for gain.

- With a time frame of twenty years or more, stocks have a greater chance of outpacing inflation than bonds. Therefore, when planning for retirement, stocks usually present the lowest risk.

- Investments are volatile. People are emotional. People sabotage a long-term plan by selling stocks when they have lost money. You must choose a long-term plan and stick to it.

- Over the long-run, common stocks have averaged about

10% per year.

● Over the long run, bonds have averaged about 5% per year.

● A portfolio of 80% stocks and 20% bonds might average 9% (80% stocks x 10% = **8%** return **plus** 20% bonds x 5% = 1% return). If you reduce this by 1% in annual expenses, you are left with 8%. This book's calculations use 7.5% with Factor 3, when doing hand calculations for The Number. Remember, you must accept the risk of stocks to achieve this return.

● You should plan on average, or below average, long-term returns. Examine your investment choices and see how they have performed against similar indexes. Do not chase the hottest fund choices. By the time you buy them, they may be ready to lose relative value. Look for steady funds that match or outpace the averages over the long run. Buy them over time. This creates dollar cost averaging.

● Morningstar and Lipper can help you analyze your investment choices.

● Expenses reduce investment returns. You must adjust your projected returns by expenses.

● Asset allocation reduces investment risk. Look for age-based or asset allocation models that have performed well against their target indexes. Use them.

● At retirement, make sure that your investment choices are appropriate. Risk is a friend when accumulating money for retirement. Too much risk becomes your enemy when retirement begins.

HERE'S YOUR PLAN

● Find your Number. This is your target, your retirement goal. Use Chapters 8 & 9 to help you do this. If you are enrolled in a 401(k) plan, ask someone to help you use its modeling software. Try the Yahoo Finance calculator. See if you can do your own calculations by hand using the Factor tables in this book.

• Your number will help you fine-tune your saving and investment strategy.

• Set aside *at least 10%* of your pay into a retirement plan. Use a 401(k) first. Then use IRAs and personal investments.

• Increase your investment percentage until you are saving *at least 15%* of your total pay. You may not think you can do this. But you can.

• If you have more than 20 years until retirement, you should invest to outpace inflation. This means considering a portfolio with at least 75% stocks. Probably more. Your portfolio should be diversified. It should have a blend with large, medium and small companies. Own both growth and value stocks. Look for an asset allocation model, or an age-based model with good, long-term performance and reasonable fees.

• Political and world financial crises will always occur. When they do, the stock and/or bond markets can fare poorly. You must stick to your plan. Make sure that your model regularly reallocates to your target percentages for each asset class.

• If you have between 10 and 20 years until retirement, you might begin to lower your risk. How much you adjust may depend upon how close you are to your number. The closer you are to your number, the more you might choose to preserve your gains.

• If you have less than 10 years to retire, you should start adjusting your portfolio toward your ultimate target mix.

• Over the long-run, a mix with 50%-60% stocks has proven to be a reasonable retirement investment strategy. With historical returns, a portfolio with 60% stocks might average around an 8% return. (60% stocks x 10% return = 6%. 40% bonds x

5% return = 2%). If you reduce this by a 1% expense, you are left with a 7% net return. This return should allow you to take 4% and have 3% growth left over to keep up with inflation. This book suggested using 5.5% with Yahoo Finance. Yahoo plans for your assets to be spent by the end of life expectancy. A lower return expectation gives you some asset protection.

• History says that you should maintain an investment mix with at least 50% stocks in retirement. This will give your portfolio a better chance of keeping up with inflation. 60% is the historical standard, and what you might see in a traditional balanced mutual fund.

• The more money you have, the less risk you can afford to take. Extra funds may also allow for more risk, to accumulate for your heirs.

• Compare your investments to appropriate index averages. Make sure that your fees and expenses are reasonable. Morningstar and Lipper can help you do this.

• Look for positive alpha.

• If your mix of funds has stocks and bonds, your beta should be significantly less than 1 when compared to the S&P 500 Index.

• Most mutual fund companies have free access to their fund information, even if you are not a client. Read brochures. Ask an advisor to help you run some long-term historical illustrations with different balanced mutual funds or mixes, and see how they behaved. There is a lot of free information to help you plan. With your new training, you will now have a better understanding of what you see.

• Independent websites, like Yahoo Finance, can also help you evaluate stocks and mutual funds. Type in a stock or fund name. You will see pages that include a Morningstar rating, style grid, expenses and performance data.

YOUR FINAL PLAN

Investing for retirement doesn't have to be hard.

Determine your Number. Your number becomes your portfolio goal at retirement. If this is too confusing, you can still get there.

Set aside as much as you can, with a target saving amount of at least 15% of your income.

Invest for long-term growth with a diversified portfolio. This portfolio should have at least 75% stocks.

Adjust your savings and investment strategy to achieve your number goal.

Make sure your fees are reasonable and competitive.

Compare your investments to relevant indexes. Look for positive alpha and beta below 1 for a diversified mix.

Don't chase performance. Stick to your accumulation plan.

Do not sell when the news gets bad, but do reallocate your portfolio to your target mix. This means holding, even buying stocks during a bad market.

As you approach retirement, reduce your portfolio risk, with no more than 60% stocks if you can. You will probably need at least 50% stocks.

Adjust your return expectations by using long-term averages, adjusted for expenses.

Plan to withdraw no more than 4% each year from your retirement portfolio.

That's all you really need to know to achieve financial independence. Go for it now. You can do it.